Albion Fellows Bacon

MIDWESTERN HISTORY AND CULTURE

General Editors
James H. Madison and Andrew R. L. Cayton

*Albion Fellows Bacon (ca. 1913) in her bedroom "office," where most
of her letters and speeches regarding housing reform were written.
The photograph on top of the desk is of her deceased daughter,
Margaret. Albion Fellows Bacon Collection,
Special Collections, Willard Library*

Albion Fellows Bacon

Indiana's Municipal Housekeeper

Robert G. Barrows (signature)

ROBERT G. BARROWS

INDIANA UNIVERSITY PRESS

Bloomington and Indianapolis

THIS BOOK WAS PUBLISHED WITH THE GENEROUS SPONSORSHIP OF

Barbara Evans Zimmer

This book is a publication of
Indiana University Press
601 North Morton Street
Bloomington, IN 47404-3797 USA
http://www.indiana.edu/~iupress
Telephone orders 800-842-6796
Fax orders 812-855-7931
Orders by e-mail iuporder@indiana.edu
© 2000 by Robert G. Barrows
All rights reserved

The paper used in this publication meets the minimum requirements of American National Standard for Information Sciences—Permanence of Paper for Printed Library Materials, ANSI Z39.48-1984.
Manufactured in the United States of America

Library of Congress Cataloging-in-Publication Data
Barrows, Robert G. (Robert Graham), date
Albion Fellows Bacon : Indiana's municipal housekeeper / Robert G. Barrows.
p.   cm. — (Midwestern history and culture)
Includes bibliographical references and index.
ISBN 0-253-33774-7 (cl)
1. Bacon, Albion Fellows, 1865– 2. Women social reformers—Indiana—Biography.
3. Authors, American—20th century—Biography. 4. Indiana—Social life and customs. 5. Indiana—Biography. I. Title. II. Series.

CT275.B144 B37 2000
303.48'4'092—dc21
[B]
                                                                00-025134

1   2   3   4   5   05   04   03   02   01   00

To my mother
and to the memory of my father

With thanks for nature *and* nurture

CONTENTS

ILLUSTRATIONS

ACKNOWLEDGMENTS

Many individuals and institutions contributed to the preparation of this book. Albion Fellows Bacon's descendants were of crucial importance. My largest debt is to the late Joy Bacon Witwer (Albion Bacon's youngest daughter), who opened her home to me, granted me two oral history interviews, and made available for reproduction and research use both manuscript materials prepared by her mother and family photographs. (She had previously donated other materials regarding her mother and her aunt, Annie Fellows Johnston, to the Willard Library in Evansville.) She could not have been more gracious and encouraging, and I deeply regret that I was unable to bring this project to fruition before her death. Joy's son, Scott Witwer, gave me a family copy of *Beauty for Ashes*, which I had never been able to locate outside a research library. Albion Bacon Dunagan (Albion Bacon's granddaughter) discovered in her father's possessions and made available for my use a manuscript reminiscence written by Bacon toward the end of her life. The late Hilary E. Bacon, Jr. (Albion Bacon's son) responded to a query very early in my research and offered an explanation for why some looked-for items (letters to Albion Bacon from Jacob Riis, for example) are apparently no longer extant. I very much appreciate the family's assistance and support.

During the course of my research I visited or corresponded with many libraries and archives. Some of them are large repositories, while others are quite modest institutions. Many of them (especially the publicly funded agencies) struggle with inadequate resources. The staffs of all were unfailingly helpful and knowledgeable, and their dedication to collecting, preserving, and making available the raw materials of history, often under trying conditions, merits our admiration. My thanks to the librarians and archivists at: Chautauqua Institution Library (Chautauqua, N.Y.), especially Alfreda L. Irwin; DePauw University Archives (Greencastle, Ind.), especially Wesley Wilson; Evansville–Vanderburgh County Public Library; Hoover Institution on War, Revolution and Peace Archives (Stanford, Calif.), especially Marilyn Kann; Indiana Historical Society Library (Indianapolis), especially Leigh Darbee; Indiana State Archives (Indianapolis); Indiana State Library (Indianapolis), especially John "Scotty" Selch and the late Marybelle Burch; Indiana University Archives (Bloomington); Indiana University Library (Bloomington); IUPUI University Library (Indianapolis); Indiana University School of Medicine Library (Indianapolis); Library of Congress, Manuscript Division (Washington); Lilly Library (Bloomington, Ind.); National Archives (Washington), especially Aloha P. South; Newberry Library (Chicago); Petoskey Public Library (Michigan); University of Southern Indiana, Special Collections Department (Evansville), especially Gina Walker; Willard Library (Evansville), especially Joan Elliott Parker, Lyn Martin, and Carol Bartlett.

Several past and present residents of the Evansville area are due recognition. Donald E. Baker, former head of the Willard Library (and later director of the public library in nearby Newburgh), provided encouragement, advice, and a few corrections. Joe Ballard at the Evansville–Vanderburgh County Area Plan Commission facilitated use of the early minutes of the Evansville City Plan Commission, and fought the bureaucracy on my behalf for a copy of Margaret Bacon's death certificate. Bill Bartelt provided access to the archival records and photographs of Trinity United Methodist Church. Darrel Bigham shared his extensive knowledge of Evansville, both in person and via his publications, and suggested helpful contacts. The late Joan C. Marchand, who was the historic preservation guru in Evansville's Department of Metropolitan Development, sent me information regarding the Bacons' house and Hilary Bacon's store. Kenneth P. McCutchan resolved an inconsistency regarding Albion Bacon's employment as a young woman. The late Margaret McLeish, who grew up on the same block where the Bacons lived and knew the Bacon children, shared her memories with me in an oral history interview. Sylvia Neff Weinzapfel made available the early records of the Evansville YWCA.

I am grateful to David Klaassen at the Social Welfare History Archives, University of Minnesota, for undertaking an ultimately fruitless search for Bacon materials in the collections there. Sarah McFall, assistant editor at the Atlantic Monthly Press, had better luck; she managed to track down correspondence dealing with Bacon's article "Consolation" as well as her book of the same name. The Indiana Federation of Clubs (specifically, then-Historian Vivien Freese) kindly granted permission to use the IFC records on deposit in the Indiana State Library.

James H. Madison and Thomas J. Schlereth, who were the general editors for the Indiana University Press series "Midwestern History and Culture" at the time this manuscript was submitted for consideration, both offered useful suggestions for improvement. I want to thank Jim Madison, in particular, for his support over the years of my scholarship and my career. Nancy Gabin read a draft of the final chapter and provided helpful advice; it's my own fault that I took only part of it.

I first proposed this project to Indiana University Press sponsoring editor Joan Catapano in the mid-1980s, when she surprised me by having *heard* of Albion Bacon. Joan then waited a long time; I appreciate her patience. Thanks also to Bobbi Diehl for her careful editing and to all the other pros at Indiana University Press who work the magic of turning manuscripts into books.

My colleagues in the history department at IUPUI offered encouraging words and, in some cases, literal votes of confidence. I am especially grateful to the department's two chairs during the past decade, William Schneider and Philip Scarpino, for facilitating my writing at some crucial points.

Emotional support of one's scholarship is desirable, but financial support is often essential. During the course of this project I have received assistance from several organizations, and it is a pleasure to be able to offer a public thank-you. The American Philosophical Society awarded me a grant from its Penrose Fund to study urban housing reform in the Midwest (a project which eventually morphed into this book). The Newberry Library awarded me a short-term resident fellowship to exploit its rich collection of state and local history materials. The Indiana Humanities Council (then known as the Indiana Committee for the Humanities) provided a 1988 summer fellowship that permitted me to spend several weeks in Evansville doing concentrated research. (Thanks, too, to Pamela J. Bennett, director of the Indiana Historical Bureau, for authorizing several weeks of unpaid leave that made it possible for me to accept the IHC award.) Finally, the IUPUI Office of Faculty Development granted me a Summer Research Fellowship in 1995.

Barbara Evans Zimmer made a generous gift to Indiana University Press to help support publication of this book. I applaud her interest in the history of Indiana women and I am grateful for her confidence in me and this project.

Portions of this book have previously appeared, in slightly different form, in the *Indiana Magazine of History* and *Mid-America*. I am grateful to the editors of those journals for permission to republish the material here.

The late Shirley S. McCord taught me much of what I know about Indiana history and most of what I know about historical editing. She volunteered to read the penultimate version of this manuscript while gravely ill, one measure of the depth of a friendship that I will always cherish.

I became interested in Albion Fellows Bacon and Leigh Darbee at about the same time, and in the years since there has been ample reason for the latter to begrudge the time I have devoted to the former. That she has not done so (at least not outwardly) is just one of the many reasons I'm glad we decided to build a "haven from a heartless world" together.

This book is dedicated to my parents, and anyone who knew my father or knows my mother knows why.

Historians of American urbanization once tended to focus on a few metropolitan giants to the exclusion of hundreds of second- and third-tier cities. While still granting the economic and cultural importance of the largest urban places, it is now apparent that smaller cities were also important in the overall process of urbanization. In 1900 a slightly larger number of the country's urban residents lived in cities smaller than 100,000 than in places of 100,000 or more. Although often overlooked, Dayton, Terre Haute, Peoria, and the like were as representative of the nation's urban experience as were the much more frequently examined New York, Philadelphia, and Chicago.

Such myopia has also affected the study of late nineteenth and early twentieth century reformers—especially women reformers. Few would dispute the profound impact of, for example, Jane Addams and her Hull-House colleagues on turn-of-the-century social welfare efforts. But the emphasis on Addams, Julia Lathrop, Grace and Edith Abbott, and a few other high-profile individuals has obscured the hard work and valuable contributions of scores of "second-tier" reformers whose lives and careers have been too little examined and whose accomplishments are seldom acknowledged in general histories. This book is a step toward redressing the balance.

Albion Fellows Bacon (named for her deceased father) was born in Evansville, Indiana, in 1865, the same year that the Civil War ended and Abraham Lincoln was assassinated. She died, also in Evansville, in 1933, the same year that Franklin Roosevelt was inaugurated and the New Deal began. Her life thus spanned an epoch that witnessed, in the words of one historian, "the shaping of modern America."[1] It was a time when social and cultural transformations occurred at all levels: national, state, local, familial, individual. It was a time of change, especially for American women, and Albion Bacon's life reflects both new possibilities and lingering limitations.

Although she was born in Evansville and returned to the city to attend high school, Bacon spent most of her youth in the rural hamlet of McCutchanville several miles to the north. Besides her mother, two sisters, and extended family, the principal influences of her early years were the local school and the nearby Methodist church. The lessons that she learned from those individuals and institutions, as well as her delight in open spaces and keen observations of the natural world, profoundly affected the course of her adult life.

Intelligent and disciplined enough to graduate from high school as salutatorian in just two years, Bacon very much wanted to go on to college. Her widowed mother could not afford the expense, however, so Albion taught herself shorthand and accepted a position as private secretary to her great-uncle, a prominent Evansville attorney. She continued with this work, as well as serving as a court stenographer, until her marriage in 1888 to Hilary Bacon, a local merchant. The couple, both of whom had been boarding with relatives, set up housekeeping in the same well-to-do suburban neighborhood where they were already living. Following the custom of the day for middle-class women, Bacon quit gainful employment when she married. She gave birth to daughters in 1889 and 1892, followed by boy/girl twins in 1901, and seemed to settle into a comfortable domesticity complemented by what she herself called "a pleasant social round." It was, she concluded some years later, a "sheltered life," but a life with which she seemed outwardly content during the late 1880s and early 1890s.

Beginning shortly after the birth of her second child, Bacon experienced a prolonged bout of ill health that was diagnosed with the catch-all term "nervous prostration." There *were* physical manifestations of the disease, most notably extreme fatigue, and Gilded Age physicians routinely blamed the syndrome (especially in the case of women patients) on excessive mental stimulation and prescribed extended periods of bed rest. This study suggests that, at least for Bacon, the cause was not *over*stimulation but rather the *absence* of appropriate outlets for her intelligence and creativity. What she needed, in short, was activity that forced her (or allowed her) to move beyond the "sheltered life" of self and family. She eventually found such activity, as did many other women during the early twentieth century, in myriad voluntary associations and social welfare campaigns. Bacon serves as an example of historian Anne Scott's observation that "able, ambitious women gravitated" to such organizations and endeavors because it was in such settings that they could "create impressive careers"—"careers from which the income was psychic rather than material."[2]

Reared in a rural environment and a Victorian atmosphere, Bacon was, like many turn-of-the-century Americans, troubled by some of the pernicious effects of late nineteenth century industrialization and urbanization. So, again, like many of her contemporaries during the first decades of the twentieth century, she sought to improve conditions that she perceived to be both physically unhealthy and morally unwholesome. She contrasted her idyllic childhood in McCutchanville with the experiences of impoverished children in congested cities, and longed to do something to ameliorate the condition of the latter. She took very seriously Christian, and especially Methodist, mandates for social service, writing in 1915 that her involvement in reform activities had "grown from an act of religious consecration."[3] And she became, in time, Indiana's preeminent "municipal housekeeper," a Progressive-era term for women who applied their (supposedly inherent) domestic skills to social problems plaguing their communities. Bacon's efforts in this regard began modestly, locally, and with a maternal motivation: her first excursion into civic work was to seek an improved playground at her daughters' school. But her activities gradually expanded to encompass citywide and then statewide initiatives. Indeed, as a result of books and articles she published, lectures she gave, service she rendered on the boards of national organizations, and her participation in a Pan American Congress and a presidential conference, her influence came to extend well beyond the Hoosier state.

When Bacon is mentioned, always briefly, in histories of Indiana, she is described as a "housing reformer." Certainly she did rise to prominence because of, and is best known for, her work on behalf of tenement reform and improved housing conditions. After service as a "friendly visitor" for the Associated Charities of Evansville, leadership of the Evansville Flower Mission, and presiding over a Working Girls' Association, she came to the conclusion that alleviating poor housing conditions was essential if other social welfare efforts were to have any chance of success. She began by having tenement regulations added to a proposed building ordinance for Evansville. When that ordinance stalled, she decided that a statewide approach would be more fruitful. Between 1909 and 1917 she attended every session of the Indiana General Assembly to lobby on behalf of housing reform. In three of those sessions (1909, 1913, 1917) she came away with meaningful legislation. At the beginning she ran virtually a one-woman crusade, but quickly attracted others to the cause and helped to coordinate their efforts. The

Indiana Federation of Clubs (the state affiliate of the General Federation of Women's Clubs), which Bacon persuaded to adopt as its slogan "The Homes of Indiana," was particularly important in extending the lobbying effort throughout the state.

Merely describing Bacon as a "housing reformer," however, is to ignore several other areas of activity and accomplishment. As an obituary observed, "her interests were amazing in their catholicity."[4] She played a particularly important role with regard to improving the lives of Indiana's children. During World War I she headed a child welfare committee (closely allied with the federal Children's Bureau) that was part of the State Council of Defense. Among other things, Bacon oversaw a drive to assess the physical development and well-being of preschool children, an effort that detected correctable health problems in hundreds, perhaps thousands, of cases. Then when the conflict ended in 1918, she helped transform her small piece of the state's wartime bureaucracy into a private organization, the Indiana Child Welfare Association.

The next year the state's lawmakers created a five-member study commission charged with examining child welfare in Indiana, making recommendations for improvements, and drafting possible legislation. Bacon was appointed to this commission, was an exceedingly active member of it, and used her contacts in the Children's Bureau to good effect in crafting proposed new standards for the state. The 1921 General Assembly enacted several measures based on the commission's recommendations. First, the legislators revamped the state's system of juvenile probation. Among other things, they created the position of state juvenile probation officer, along with an Advisory Juvenile Committee to guide Indiana's juvenile probation operation. Bacon was appointed to this committee, elected president of it by her fellow members, and served in the position from 1921 until her death. Second, and probably the most important result of the work done by Bacon and the other commissioners, was passage of a law that codified and revised previous legislation regarding school attendance and the employment of minors. This statute strengthened the state's minimum educational requirements and limitations on child labor, and brought Indiana much closer to recommended national standards.

While working on behalf of such statewide initiatives as housing reform and child welfare, Bacon remained very active in efforts for social and cultural betterment in her hometown and county. She served as either president or board member (sometimes both) of the Vanderburgh County Tuberculosis Association, the Public Health Nursing Association, the Vanderburgh Child Welfare Association, the Family Welfare Association, and the Southwestern Indiana Historical Society. Perhaps most prominently, she became involved with the sometimes contentious issues of city planning and zoning. In 1921 Mayor Benjamin Bosse appointed her to the newly created Evansville City Plan Commission, and her colleagues unanimously selected her as the commission's first president. She continued to serve on the Plan Commission for the rest of her life, and was either president or vice-president throughout the 1920s. Thus, she had a central role in establishing the agency as an accepted and important part of municipal government. She was especially influential in lobbying for the city's first zoning ordinance, which was passed in 1925. And, once again, what began as a local interest led to state-level activity and visibility. In both 1924 and 1925 she was elected vice-president of the Indiana Conference on City Planning; when the group met in Evansville during the latter year a local newspaper observed that Bacon was considered to be one of the best known leaders in the state's city planning movement.[5]

Along with her social welfare pursuits, Bacon also found time to write. She had begun writing poetry as a schoolgirl, coauthored a volume of verse with her sister Annie, and except for the period of her illness in the 1890s generally had some sort of literary project underway. Much of what she wrote during her adult years was an outgrowth of her social reform efforts, particularly the housing work. Her articles appeared in local and specialized publications such as the *Indiana Bulletin of Charities and Correction* and *Illinois Health News,* but also in national journals like *The American City* and the reform-minded *Survey.* The most significant of her housing-related publications was a book, *Beauty for Ashes* (1914), that detailed her passage from "sheltered life" to "municipal housekeeper." She also prepared articles and booklets that proclaimed her religious faith, as well as publishing one volume of children's stories. In addition, she authored several pageants, including Evansville's state centennial pageant in 1916 and a 1923 *Program for Citizenship Day* prepared for the General Federation of Women's Clubs.

One subject that Bacon did not write about, at least publicly, was women's suffrage. Although she was active on behalf of numerous social reforms during the early twentieth century, precisely the time when women's agitation for the ballot reached high tide, she was never an active participant in the suffrage crusade. She did not oppose votes for women, as did some of her female contemporaries, but neither was suffrage at the top of her priority list. Her public support of the cause came late, about 1915, and was based largely on the belief that women's votes would advance the social welfare reforms that were closer to her heart. A generation ago such a position would have earned Bacon the label "social feminist," a description that has since been criticized for being so all-encompassing that it renders the "feminist" portion of the phrase meaningless. The present study argues that although Bacon was a lukewarm proponent of women's suffrage the reality of her participation in public affairs had (to borrow a term from historian Nancy Cott) a "feminist aspect" that, even if unintentionally, advanced the cause of women's political equality and provided a role model for future generations.[6]

"Moderation was the hallmark of Indiana's progressive reform," writes a leading student of the state's history, and in many ways Bacon's de facto career supports that contention.[7] There was not much original in the social welfare initiatives she championed and nothing really radical in the methods she used in an effort to secure the reforms she sought. She worked within the strictures of the political system of the day, and she came to rely on the organization and mobilization of voluntary associations to spread information and apply political pressure when necessary. If her willingness to grant the state increased regulatory authority in order to combat social ills did not meet with universal approbation, she nonetheless garnered significant support for that position even in "conservatively progressive" Indiana. And while municipal housekeeping brought many women into the public arena for the first time, the movement's rhetoric stressed that they were merely exporting traditional domestic activities from the home to the larger community.

Bacon was unusual, however, in the range of her reform interests, the zeal she brought to them, and the doggedness with which she pursued her goals. Moreover, while she eventually came to rely on the aid of women's voluntary associations, she began her first statewide crusade without such organizational support. Although reluctantly at first, she accepted positions and responsibilities that were highly visible at local, state, and even national levels. Also unusual was the fact that she combined what she once called her "frenzied philanthropy" with prolific authorship in a variety of genres. She did not accomplish all that she wished, either personally or in the realm of public policy; she probably overemphasized environmental causes for social pathologies; and she was not immune to the prejudices of her time and place. Still, few Hoosiers of her era worked so hard to improve life for so many, expended so much personal time and energy to ensure for all "beauty for ashes." She was, indeed, Indiana's municipal housekeeper.

Albion Fellows Bacon

One

The Sheltered Life

In the laconic style of the day the *Evansville Daily Journal* of March 4, 1865, reported the sad, unexpected news: "Died on Thursday, March 2d, Rev. Albion Fellows, aged thirty-eight years." The paper advised that the funeral was scheduled for the next day at the Locust Street Methodist Episcopal Church, the congregation the deceased had served for the past few years. Two days later the *Journal* noted that the "peculiarly solemn and impressive" service had been attended by a "vast assemblage." The death of a relatively young man was no novelty in 1865, of course, given the carnage that the nation had endured during four years of civil war. Still, Evansville's residents probably felt particular sympathy for Fellows's widow, Mary, who was left with two young children and was pregnant with another. When this third child arrived several weeks later, Mary honored the memory of her late husband by naming her new daughter after him. Thus, in just over a month, Indiana's "Pocket City" witnessed the burial of one Albion Fellows and the birth of another.[1]

The Reverend Albion Fellows had been born near Sandwich, Carroll County, New Hampshire, in 1827. His family's American roots went deep, to the Great Migration of the 1630s when forebear William Fellows emigrated from England to Ipswich, Massachusetts. When he was seven, Fellows's family resettled in the vicinity of Dixon, Illinois, in the northwestern corner of that state. In the late 1840s he attended Rock River Seminary in nearby Mt. Morris and, eventually, moved on to Indiana Asbury (later DePauw) University, in Greencastle. There he

followed a theological course, tutored younger students, and was graduated and ordained in 1854. That year or the next (the sources disagree)
he married Mary Erskine, a native of McCutchanville, Indiana, a small
village in Vanderburgh County eight miles north of Evansville. Mary
had just completed a two-year course of study at the Greencastle Female
Collegiate Seminary.[2]

Most of Mary Erskine's life prior to her marriage had been spent in
the small, tightly knit community of McCutchanville, and her father
and two brothers lived there still. Mary's father, John Erskine, had been
born in County Antrim, Ireland, in 1797, emigrated with his family, and
settled in McCutchanville in 1820, just four years after the Hoosier
state had been admitted to the Union. Five years later John wed Harriett
Igleheart, whose parents (Levi and Anne Eleanor Taylor Igleheart) had
"left Maryland because for conscience's sake they had freed their slaves
and then found it impossible to continue the old régime without them."
They moved to Kentucky in 1815 and then in 1823 to a farm in Warrick
County, Indiana, about seven miles east of McCutchanville. John
Erskine and Harriett Igleheart's union produced eight children; Mary,
born in 1828, was the second child and the first daughter.[3]

Mary Erskine's childhood and youth were typical of pioneer life in
frontier Indiana. At a very early age she was given responsibility for care
of younger siblings; later she carded wool, spun yarn, helped make soap
and candles, and endured the deprivations resulting from (for example)
the once-a-year delivery of sugar up the rivers from New Orleans. Religious services were held at her grandfather Levi's house, the largest in
the village, "and then only a few times a year when an itinerant minister came that way." Schooling was equally problematic since it "did not
last more than eight or ten weeks then, and most of her studying had
to be done at home between tasks." Her brother Joseph, two years her
senior, planted the seeds of desire for a more thoroughgoing education,
promising that when she was eighteen the two of them would go off
to college. But during the summer of her eighteenth year (1846), her
mother died in an epidemic. "She had carried the load of eldest sister in
a family of nine," one of her daughters wrote years later; "now she must
be mother as well, with the youngest just a baby." Then Joseph, too, "was
swept out of her life by a sudden swift illness." The hope of further
education was put away for a time, as there was "only work and more
work, the meeting of a mother's problems with a girl's inexperience."[4]

By the early 1850s, however, the old dreams rekindled, not only for
herself but for her younger brothers and sisters as well. Thus, in the fall
of 1852, Mary and three siblings traveled to Greencastle, rented rooms,

and began their studies, the two brothers "going boldly up the college steps" while the sisters were "slipping timidly in by the door of the Ladies' Seminary." So successful was the arrangement that they returned the following fall with another sister and two cousins. This year, however, was marred by an outbreak of typhoid that claimed the life of one of the cousins and required a lengthy convalescence by one sister. These difficulties meant that Mary's second year at the college was "irregular and disappointing." Still, she had made the most of her opportunity and fulfilled a long-time dream. And she had met Albion Fellows.[5]

After his ordination the Reverend Fellows joined the North-West Indiana Conference of the Methodist Episcopal Church and he and Mary embarked upon the peripatetic life of a Methodist minister. They spent a year or two following their marriage first at Valparaiso (Porter County) and then at Westville (La Porte County). By 1857, when their daughter Lura was born, Fellows was a professor of Greek at the denomination's Fort Wayne College.[6] (A family genealogy records Lura's birthplace as McCutchanville, suggesting that Mary may have returned temporarily to her childhood home to be with relatives during the late stages of her pregnancy.) Following his transfer to the Indiana Conference in the southern part of the state, Fellows pastored during 1859–1860 in Boonville, the seat of Warrick County. In the latter year a census enumerator listed him as a Methodist minister with modest holdings of real and personal property ($600 and $300, respectively). After brief stays (1860–1862) in Patoka (Gibson County) and Mt. Vernon (Posey County), the family moved to Evansville, the largest city in southwestern Indiana and, with 11,500 residents as of 1860, the third largest city in the state. The Evansville directory for 1863 reported that Rev. Albion Fellows lived at 66 South Second Street; while it did not list him as the pastor of any of the Methodist congregations recorded in the "church directory," the volume did give his occupation as "presiding elder." The year 1863 also saw the addition of another daughter to the family; like her older sister, Anna (generally known as Annie) was born at McCutchanville.[7]

Two years later Fellows's residence had not changed, but his status had; he was now identified as the pastor of the Locust Street Methodist Episcopal Church and, the directory observed, of a "new church now building" at the corner of Third and Chestnut. This impressive edifice —Trinity Methodist—was completed in 1866. A booklet produced for the church's centennial celebration observed that "the work of building the new church and advancing the Cause in Evansville overtaxed the

Trinity Methodist Episcopal Church shortly after its completion in 1866.
Evansville and Its Men of Mark (1873), courtesy Bill Bartelt and
Trinity United Methodist Church

strength of Rev. Albion Fellows," leading to his premature death. Oral tradition in the family indicates that he became soaked and chilled while returning on horseback from a rural church and subsequently contracted a fatal case of pneumonia. Whatever the case—and the two stories are not mutually exclusive—Mary Fellows was left to carry on.[8]

Albion's drawing of her childhood home in McCutchanville.
Courtesy Joy Bacon Witwer

Following her husband's death, and the birth of his namesake daughter, Mary moved the family to McCutchanville, locating in a house on her father's farm. After a stay of two or three years, they returned to Evansville; the city directories of the late 1860s and early 1870s list a "Mrs. Mary E. Fellows, widow" who lived first on Gum Street and then on the northeast corner of Second and Chestnut. The enumerator responsible for Evansville's second ward in the 1870 census recorded Mary as the head of a household that included her three daughters as well as schoolteacher Anna Erskine, her younger sister. In spite of (or, possibly, because of) Reverend Fellows's death, the family had increased its wealth during the Civil War decade; Mary reported $5,000 of real property and $600 worth of personal property.[9]

Annie later recalled that after a few years in the city her mother "decided to locate permanently in the country, and built a house within a stone's throw of the old homestead" in McCutchanville. Two of Mary's brothers, James and Levi, were neighbors on what became known as Erskine Lane. "Here . . . on a ridge of hills," as Albion described it over forty years later, "the families dwelt in a little community of their own, like a highland clan upon its own peaks." Her reference to a highland clan was apt, since many of the original settlers, like her Erskine forebears, were of Scotch-Irish descent. In spite of its physical proximity to Evansville, "on the calendar it was a whole generation back from it." McCutchanville had no streets and no stores, and its post office was in a private home where mail was delivered weekly. "It was," Albion recalled, "simply a scattered settlement having two foci, the church and the school house. Its laws were the Ten Commandments, the Golden Rule, and the customs of the fathers."[10]

Growing up in this essentially rural setting—"scarcely a hamlet, since it had not even a store"—profoundly influenced Albion's sensibilities and, at least in part, the pattern of her adult life. In her late forties she still described her youth in McCutchanville in rapturous terms. Moving from the city had been, she wrote, "like waking from a grey dream into a realm of colour and light." In part this had to do with her almost mystical appreciation of the natural world. She "wandered in a maze of delight," she remembered, and thought the area "a wonderland, with Heaven among its hills and fairyland in its hollows." Her youngest daughter recalled that, even in her mother's late adult years, McCutchanville remained "pure poetry." Albion herself, well after she had become known as an urban-oriented reformer, reflected that she had managed to retain a "vision of those wind-swept, sun-crowned hills, and the feeling of those great free spaces." It was this memory, she acknowledged, "that makes our cities choke me."[11]

During her childhood, community activities revolved around the church and the school. The earliest settlers represented a variety of Protestant persuasions, especially Presbyterian. Eventually, however, most residents of the area "came within the folds of Methodism," perhaps because that denomination's circuit riders proselytized the pioneer community more frequently than the clergy of other faiths. The hamlet's first church, dedicated in 1848, was initially considered a "union" structure since a bequest that aided its construction stipulated that it "be free to all Christian denominations." The fact that it was a Methodist minister who dedicated the house of worship, however, suggests the de facto denominational leanings of the congregation from its earliest years.[12]

This frame structure, standing in a grove of locusts and cedars, was still in use when the Fellows family returned to McCutchanville in the early 1870s. Given their Methodist heritage and the proximity of the building to their new house (it was just at the end of Erskine Lane), it is not surprising that this became the church of Albion's youth.[13] Looking back as an adult, she described herself as a "quite devout" child who "lived in a religious atmosphere." The Fellows and Erskine families "went to church whenever its doors were open, to 'preaching,' class meeting, prayer meeting, Sunday school, revivals." Impressed by the revivals, she "supposed I had to repent, and was worried because I did not know anything to repent of." Relieved when a "sensible minister advised us children to simply follow Christ," she joined the church at age eleven. She reminisced fondly about her experiences there, referring in a poem titled "The Old Church" to "That sweet, bright calm, my childhood's Sabbath day." Yet she was able, in this same work, to present a realistic, child's-eye perspective of the church and her attendance there:

> Its straight, uncushioned seats, how hard they seemed!
> What penance-doing form they always wore
> To little heads that could not reach the text,
> And little feet that could not reach the floor.
> . . . .
> With half-shut eyes, across the pulpit bent,
> The preacher droned in soothing tones about
> Some theme, that like the narrow windows high,
> Took in the sky, but left terrestrials out.[14]

"All of our elders were devout," she wrote, "and with the narrow views of the times." It was in this physical setting and intellectual milieu, where she was told "that every evil thing I saw or heard would leave a stain upon my soul," that she embraced a religion, as she later put it, of "personal righteousness rather than social service." She would, "whenever evil occasion required," adopt a hear-no-evil, see-no-evil attitude, "thinking hard all the time of a rose or an icicle." It is one measure of the tremendous changes that took place in her life, and in the world around her in the early twentieth century, that by 1914 she could describe these attitudes of her youth and young adulthood as "the ideal religion of that age and the relic of this."[15]

The McCutchanville school, the other major institution in young Albion's life, stood not far beyond the church—an easy walk from the Fellows's house. The building in use when the family first located in the hamlet was a modest frame structure erected in 1852 and described by Annie in her memoirs as "a very primitive affair." Shortly thereafter work began on a new, two-story brick schoolhouse, which opened in 1874 or 1875. This building had two classrooms on the ground floor and an upstairs auditorium ("the hall") that served for several decades as a meeting place for community activities.[16]

Albion had little to say in later years regarding the caliber of instruction afforded by this simple country school. She recalled that during her first two or three years she was "so paralyzed by fear of my teachers . . . that I think I learned *nothing*." Later, however, with gentler instructors, she overcame her fears and "learned easily." She remembered that her sense of wonder at the natural world followed her through the schoolhouse door. In her first years "arithmetic was as occult as Hindu numbers, and the parsing of the older grammar classes seemed to me some weird incantation, though the verses they parsed became a part of my very fibre." Annie, too, provided a brief glimpse at the curriculum; she remembered never being bored since she could listen to the "big scholars' recitations" whenever she tired of her own work: "Many an incident in history and many an extract from Webster's speeches or from Shakespeare's plays were learned simply by listening to the higher classes recite." In spite of the paucity of evidence, it seems fair to conclude—especially given the quantity, quality, and diversity of their adult writing—that the Fellows sisters' elementary education provided a firm foundation for their future accomplishments.[17]

While the church and the school were vitally important influences, Albion's childhood experiences in McCutchanville were not confined to those institutions. When they moved to the country she and Annie had six cousins in the immediate vicinity, a number that grew in subsequent years. (Because her sister Lura was eight or nine years older, left for college shortly after the family's move to McCutchanville, and then married, she was not as dominant a figure in Albion's youth as might otherwise have been the case, although she wrote in later years of her childhood "reverence and admiration" for her eldest sibling.) The cousins shared "every kind of adventure," including riding a hay fork in the barn "so high that it would have been instant death had the rope slipped or our hold given way." The sisters also enjoyed taking whatever part they could in seasonal farm activities; sorghum-, cider-, and hay-making all had their special charms, and "from sheep-shearing time until wheat-threshing was over in the autumn, there was always something of interest to watch."[18]

Mary Fellows was a dominating presence in the girls' lives. Albion recalled "no influence so practical" and "none so inspiring" as her mother, and one of Mary's grandchildren remembered her as being "very, very strict" and a person of enormous self-discipline. Widowed, of modest means, relying on relatives for various kinds of assistance, she "spent her life in a passion of self-sacrifice, ministering to all who were in trouble." "In *very* tender years," Albion wrote late in her life, "I remember needing and getting a great many punishments. But I came to a place where I realized it gave my mother distress, and yielded to her will, no matter what it entailed." She also reminisced that being in her mother's presence engendered "a quickened sense of responsibility" and a feeling that one must "amount to something."[19]

In retrospect, Albion also acknowledged the influence of her peer group on her development. She recalled "how much more the playground taught than the school room, the playmates than the teacher!" Indeed, she credited "the equal rights of that playground . . . and the exercise to the full of every girl's abilities" with preparing her to function effectively, as an adult, in situations and institutions dominated by men. Writing at the height of the early twentieth century agitation for women's suffrage she observed that "years before the wave of feminism had swept over the country, little streams were hastening down to swell the great river, from other springs as obscure as this country school."[20]

In other ways, as well, the girls' education continued beyond the walls of the schoolhouse. Mary Fellows had sacrificed in order to attend Indiana Asbury, and she clearly cherished learning. Her household, consequently, was one where books were present, prized, and read. Verse attracted both Albion and Annie, and they often recited long poems while engaged in household chores. They read Lura's collection of poetry, and also found much of interest in their father's theological library: Foxe's *Book of Martyrs*, Aesop's fables, *Pilgrim's Progress*. ("'Lives of Great Men,'" Albion later observed, "are like hasheesh to an imaginative child.") And there were various children's magazines over the years—*The Children's Hour*, *St. Nicholas*, *Youth's Companion*. When these were exhausted Annie remembered that they "were forced to turn to the periodicals of our elders": *The American Agriculturist*, *Harper's Weekly*, *The Christian Advocate*.[21]

With such voracious, even precocious, reading habits, it is not surprising that the sisters also tried their hand at writing. Albion recalled years later how "amidst our work Annie scribbled stories and I verses with illustrations." When she was fourteen, and Annie two years older, a periodical called *Gems of Poetry* came to hand. In addition to selections from, as Annie put it, "all the old poets," it devoted space to "some brand new ones who had not yet arrived." Thus encouraged, the girls both submitted verses to this publication. They were thrilled when,

*Albion (left) and Annie Fellows (ca. 1880). Albion Fellows
Bacon Collection, Special Collections, Willard Library*

with no advance notice, Albion's "Rain" and Annie's "The Harvest"
appeared some time later. "The intoxication of actually seeing our
verses in print," Annie recalled, "sent us about with our heads in the
stars for days." But although they "scribbled continually," they did not
attempt to publish anything again for several years. They did, however,
continue to hone their writing skills, both in the classroom and at "The
Literary," a local society that met in the public hall on the second floor
of the schoolhouse.[22]

Only a few fragments remain of Albion's written work during her
early teenage years. The most significant of these are contained in a
ledger she apparently used as a school copybook in 1879. Inscribed
"Allie M. Fellows, McCutchanville," much of the ledger is filled with
information seemingly copied from different sources—facts and figures
about European countries, for example, or the dates the states ratified

the U.S. Constitution. Interspersed with this material, however, are numerous poems, a few apparently copied but most concluding with the notations "By Allie" or "Allie M. F."[23]

The content of these verses reflects, besides her literary bent, Albion's concern even as an adolescent with both nature and things spiritual. The blending of these interests runs throughout her early titles. In "Sunshine," for example, she contrasts the ephemeral rays of the sun with the radiance of a positive personality; while the former can become obscured, the latter always shines through.

> The clear, blue sky of the summer,
> Is changed for clouds of grey,
> That hide from the frozen landscape,
> The sun of the wintery day.
> . . . .
> But even the thickest clouds cannot hide,
> The smile of a heart that's good,
> It brightens the home of the blighted soul,
> It cheers the heart that's sad.

Similarly, her otherworldly preoccupations are manifested by such poems as "Paradise," an unoriginal description of "the beautiful Realm of Immortal Souls":

> There cruel Winter never comes,
> And Pleasure never flies,
> For all is Joy, and Peace and Love,
> In that far off Paradise.

She also blends the natural and supernatural in "Afloat," which a marginal notation indicates was written in April 1879:

> As the crimson leaves in autumn,
> Float adown the silver stream,
> Whirling, rushing, quivering, pausing,
> Like the shadows in a dream.
>
> So, upon life's boundless ocean,
> We are left, each to his fate,
> Never will the tide be quiet,
> Nor the rushing waves abate.
>
> Now the billows sweep above us,
> Now a high wave lifts the boat,

But till on the shores of heaven,
We will always be afloat.

After reading these and other of Albion's contemporaneous verses, it is obvious that her youthful style left room for improvement. Still, it is hard not to be impressed with these attempts of a fourteen-year-old schoolgirl to deal in a serious way with difficult and profound themes and concepts.

The final item in her copybook is a poem titled, appropriately, "The Last Day." Written about (and possibly during) her last day in elementary school, it presages literary abilities and emotional depths that were to become more pronounced in later years.

Our days at school are almost past,
And this, the brightest, is the last,
The last of all those hours so bright,
Illumined with sweet wisdom's light.

But still the sun rolls on the same,
Its burning orb of living flame,
Though those who loved its cheery light,
Are parted from each other's sight.

The brook still ripples o'er the stone,
Heedless of what Old Time has done,
Though those that wandered by its side,
Will soon be scattered far and wide,
While in the hearts of us alone,
Will live the thoughts of all that's gone.

❖

As the decade of the 1870s gave way to the 1880s, the Fellows family underwent several changes. Lura married George P. Heilman, son of a prominent Evansville family, and moved to the city. Annie, at age 17, began teaching at the McCutchanville school. And Albion, following completion of elementary school, took art lessons in Evansville. "It was," Annie later remembered, "a year of change for all of us." The next year was, for her, even more of a departure; she attended the University of Iowa during the 1881–1882 academic year, staying with the family of a paternal uncle who was on the faculty at the Iowa City school. Also in 1881, Mary moved the family back to Evansville once again, living first on Gum Street and then on Chandler Avenue. Albion entered the city high school that fall, taking the "German" course (as opposed to the "Latin" or "Business" curriculum), and completed the requirements for graduation in two years. "I could not afford to take longer," she recalled forty-five years later, "as I had to earn my living soon." Annie, a year of formal teacher training behind her, began work in the Evansville public schools in 1882 and taught for the next three years.[24]

This was, it seems, a period of intense and highly focused intellectual effort for Albion. Reminiscing in her early sixties she described as "wonderful" her course of study and her teachers, and claimed that her "intellectual awakening" took place during these two years: "I wanted, not just to lead, but to learn. To know—to know! I realized it was only a beginning, a foundation, but I felt I could go on studying all my life." She also recalled, with a note of chagrin, that during high school she had "learned nothing but books." She subsequently realized that during her travels to and from school she "learned nothing of the town or the people who lived in it, for theorems and conjugations were written in the air, in front of me." Her focus on her classes, to the exclusion of the city around her, at least paid academic dividends: she was salutatorian of her class.[25]

The 1883 graduates numbered forty, the largest group ever, composed of seven men and thirty-three women. (The *Evansville Daily Journal* referred to the "natural and numerical priority" of the "young ladies.") As was the custom, a class song—words and music by Albion M. Fellows—was prepared for the ceremony and printed in the newspaper. It bore more than a faint resemblance to Allie's thoughts on "The Last Day" of elementary school at McCutchanville. The first stanza gives the flavor:

> The fateful years that quickly pass,
>> And bear us in their flight,
> Have crowned with joy the happy life
>> That we must leave tonight.
>
> Too soon the chime will mark the time
>> When we must say "good bye,"
> One path we have together trod
>> Now each his own must try.[26]

Following tradition, each student prepared a brief graduation essay. Since, in the words of the *Journal,* "it would not do to let all the essays be read," fourteen were selected for presentation during the graduation ceremony. Albion's salutatorian address, an appreciation of children's literature, was titled simply "Mother Goose." She observed at the outset that she brought "no laurels to wreathe the brow of a Homer or Dante," and that the writing of the historical Elizabeth Goose "sent forth no grand, inspiring anthem to awaken to higher purpose the hearts of men." But she promptly asserted that Mother Goose had done "what greater geniuses could not do": made "the heart of childhood merry with your simpl[e] melodies, which still ring a sweet accompaniment to the memory of our early joys." A brief sketch of Elizabeth Goose's life followed and then, with her youthful metaphorical excess, the claim that: "Like the ancient geese, whose cackling aroused Rome to a sense of danger, this Mother Goose aroused the world to a sense of the necessity of literature for children." The essay concluded with a plea that posterity not "pluck a leaf from her laurel crown because baby hands placed it upon her brow."[27]

❖

Both of Albion's parents, as well as both of her sisters, had completed some collegiate instruction, and she was anxious to do the same. She was particularly interested in continuing her study of art. The family's financial resources had been stretched to the limit, however, and as her daughter explained: "came the third girl, that was just one too many, so mother didn't get to college." Albion herself wrote in the 1920s that "a girl never longed for college more than I did," and she remembered it as "a crushing fate that I could not go ahead."[28]

Instead, she accepted an offer from her great-uncle, Judge Asa Iglehart, to be his private secretary. She taught herself shorthand in six weeks and joined her uncle "to write out his letters and briefs at dictation, to handle his law books, even to report special cases in court." Her professional skills developed rapidly, and a few years later a trade publication described her as "a most efficient court stenographer" who possessed "to a rare degree rapidity of mental and manual action." She claimed, in retrospect, that this experience was more valuable than college courses would have been. "It was," she came to believe, "the making of me. It gave me a balance, a discipline, a schooling, I could have had nowhere else." Besides becoming knowledgeable about business correspondence and legal records and phraseology, she learned "to go without fright into public buildings, to keep my own counsel, and to avoid feminine flutterings." Often the only woman in a courtroom, she also learned, as she put it, to "'see men as trees walking,' with perfect forgetfulness of them and of myself." This ability would serve her well in later years when her public activities took her to such male preserves as commercial clubs and the state legislature.[29]

When they resettled in Evansville in 1881, Mary, Annie, and Albion apparently moved in with Lura and her husband, George Heilman. Albion continued this arrangement for a year or so after her graduation from high school, a period when the entire family was located at 311 Chandler Avenue in one of the city's most desirable residential neighborhoods. But by 1885, now a nineteen- or twenty-year-old working woman, she began to take some tentative steps toward greater independence. In that year she left the home of her immediate family and began boarding at her Uncle Asa Iglehart's house on adjacent Upper Second Street. She continued this living arrangement for the next two or three years.[30]

The details of her life during this period are sketchy. She was obviously busy at work, even reporting trials in nearby counties. She had affiliated with Trinity Methodist Church after moving to the city—the church her father had under construction at the time of his death—and was a regular and active congregant. Church records indicate that she was involved with the Young Ladies Foreign Missionary Society in the mid-1880s, including stints as the group's treasurer and on its literary committee.[31]

And she continued to write. While still in high school she and Annie had formed the Crambo Club with two sisters living across the street who also had literary aspirations. (Crambo is a word game in which one player gives a word or line of verse to be matched in rhyme by other players.) "It was," Annie remembered, "good practice in versification." The four also wrote a novel "by Alma," a name that their initials spelled, each member writing a chapter in turn. The effort was somewhat hindered, Annie allowed, "by our all shying away from the chapter containing the love scenes."[32]

After graduation, Albion later recalled, she "wrote lots of verses in my uncle's office and published some. Got a little notice." These poems, signed sometimes with her full name and sometimes simply "Albion," appeared in a wide range of periodical publications—newspapers in both Evansville and Indianapolis, the *Saturday Call*, the *DePauw Monthly*, and *Frank Leslie's Illustrated Newspaper*, among others. Her subjects varied from nature studies ("Pansies") to poetic obituaries ("Remeny—Drowned September, 1887"). She penned one of her longer verses—"Reunion of the Blue and Gray"—in 1887 for a gathering of Union and Confederate veterans in Evansville, and then recited this paean to reconciliation at the opening exercises. Her work could also be light-hearted, however, and she even won a prize from a trade journal for a poem describing the "wondrous magic things" done by the deft fingers of a proficient typist.[33]

It was during these years that Albion met her future husband, Hilary Bacon. The specific details of their introduction and courtship are not known; she wrote virtually nothing about them in her few auto-biographical pieces, merely noting at one point that her plans to pursue artistic training were put aside because of "a charming man who beckoned." She had, according to one of her daughters, several beaus, including a lawyer who wanted to marry her. Bacon won out, however, perhaps in part because Mary Fellows was very much in favor of the match and brought her influence to bear on her daughter's decision.[34]

Hilary Edwin Bacon was born November 6, 1851, in Roaring Springs, Trigg County, Kentucky. His father, Charles Ashby Bacon, emigrated to Kentucky from Virginia in 1832, first establishing a store and later turning to tobacco farming. Charles's first wife died in 1840, leaving three sons. His second wife, Margaret Gibson, also bore three sons, of whom Hilary was the youngest. Reared on the family farm (or, as his youngest daughter referred to it, "the plantation"), the youth helped out in the fields during the Civil War after his older brothers had gone to military service and the family's slaves had been emancipated. Rising before dawn to pick tobacco worms off the plants by hand, he would return home wringing wet from dew and increasingly anxious to move from the plantation.[35]

Convinced "that he was not made to order for farm life," at the age of thirteen or fourteen he began clerking in a Roaring Springs store at a salary of $25 per year. When the owner moved the store back to its original location in Hopkinsville, Kentucky, sixteen or seventeen miles away, Bacon moved with it. His salary steadily increased, and he boarded in the proprietor's home for a time. When the owner decided to dispose of the dry goods department in which Hilary was employed, he resolved to relocate to an area with greater commercial possibilities. Thus, in 1873 he moved some 80 miles due north to Evansville.[36]

One of Hilary's half-brothers, Charles Parks Bacon, also moved to Evansville in 1873. An 1861 graduate of the University of Pennsylvania medical school, he decided to relocate his practice from Cadiz, the county seat of Trigg County, to a larger urban area. As a "man of means and affairs" (the description in a late nineteenth century biographical sketch), he no doubt was able to ease Hilary's transition to this new setting. Indeed, Hilary boarded for over a decade in his brother's household at 921 Upper Second.[37]

Hilary arrived in Evansville with $20 or $25 in his pockets and promptly accepted a position as a clerk with the Hudspeth Dry Goods Company. After several years' experience in various department stores about town, he and three other clerks (Andrew Keck, Henry F. Miller, William McClain) established their own dry goods firm—Keck, Miller, & Company—in the late 1870s. Family assistance may well have helped finance this venture. One source notes that Hilary invested $450 of his own money, "carefully saved from his meager earnings," and that "a friend backed him to the extent of $3,000." This "friend" may well have been Emma Mayes Bacon, Charles Bacon's wife. Hilary's youngest daughter remembered that the family tradition was that Aunt Emma "loaned him . . . a couple of thousand dollars, and he set himself up in business."[38]

The store prospered from the first, at least in part because of an enormous amount of sweat equity invested by the owners. "Due to the scarcity of capital," one source notes, the four partners "did practically all the work in the store themselves." During its first year the enterprise doubled its capital, and over the next several years two of the founders sold out their interests. By 1887 the firm was styled Keck & Bacon, doing business at 207 Main Street, a situation that would continue for the next decade.[39]

As we have seen, Albion Fellows began boarding in the mid-1880s with her Uncle Asa at 1003 Upper Second Street. Hilary Bacon was living with his brother Charles, whose home was at 921 Upper Second. Residing so near one another, it is not surprising that the two should soon have met or been introduced. Hilary, then 34 and well-established in the dry goods business, apparently was smitten. According to their daughter Joy, "father said he saw that girl, mother, with her braids hanging down her back and said 'that's the girl I'm going to marry.'" Albion may initially have been less certain—recall that she apparently had several other beaus and at least one proposal—but by late 1887 or early 1888 the couple announced their engagement. At virtually the same time Annie became engaged to William L. Johnston, a widowed druggist with three children, and the sisters planned a double wedding for the fall of 1888. "But first," Annie recorded, "we had to carry out another plan which we had considered since we were very small. That was to go abroad together."[40]

Hilary Edwin Bacon (ca. 1888).
Courtesy Joy Bacon Witwer

The "Grand Tour" began on May 21, 1888. Accompanied by their fiancés, the sisters traveled first to Vincennes, changed trains, and rode on to Cincinnati. There Hilary and Will bade them farewell, and they proceeded by rail to New York City. After a stay of a few days, visiting acquaintances and shopping, they embarked on the *Umbria*. A novice at water travel, Albion apparently became seasick at the start of the journey. Her diary of the trip describes the first night and day on board as "nightmarish" and refers to her illness, obliquely, as "that awful fugitive fleeting breakfast in my berth." But thereafter, she reported, "I was not much sick, & the strong stiff wind was such a tonic."[41]

Aside from transitory physical complaints, Albion seems to have relished her shipboard experiences. She enjoyed walking on the deck—

"with effort towards the bow, and half blown back towards the stern"— and recounted with obvious satisfaction "the times in the music room —singing for all of them but most of all for myself." She also performed at a shipboard concert to benefit an orphanage, noting that she "was announced as *Mr.* but the *mis*-take was corrected." Although she made several male friends during the passage (one of whom she and Annie would visit later in the trip), she had a more difficult time getting to know the women passengers: "Most of the ladies on board were wrapped up & practically lifeless, or else, absorbed by some man or men."[42]

The *Umbria* docked at Queenstown, on the southern coast of Ireland, early on the morning of June 2. As the sun rose, Albion reflected on the appropriateness of the nickname "Emerald Isle." The land "rose against the sky," she wrote, "fresh with all tints of green, still veiled in the thinnest mist, that seemed less to obscure than to make visionary and mirage-like." They located their guide and the other members of their traveling party (years later Annie would refer to this journey, with a hint of disparagement, as "the usual trip that tourists take"), breakfasted and took a nap, and traveled by rail to Cork. It was here, in the Imperial Hotel, that Albion began her diary of the trip.[43]

For the next twelve days they traveled throughout Ireland: to the ruins of Blarney Castle (where, for unstated reasons, they did *not* kiss the Blarney Stone), to Glengariff and the Bantry Bay area in southwestern County Cork, to Killarney, to Dublin and Londonderry, and finally to Belfast. Her diary entries for these days are usually prosaic descriptions of natural wonders (the "wild and rugged" Kerry Mountains, for example) or the numerous castles and churches they visited. Occasionally, however, her prose mirrored the beauty that surrounded her, as when she wrote of a mist-shrouded mountain road where "The cloud caught us up in its skirt, & washed our faces roughly, like a scolding nurse."[44]

Sometimes, too, the diary became a record of such personal thoughts that she wrote them only in code. On visiting one area of unusual rock formations, she sat in the "wishing chair" and made three wishes. These were, she wrote, "the wishes of my lifetime, since it really began." The precise meaning of that portentous phrase is unclear, however, since her next sentence is written in some form of personal shorthand. Another journal entry seems, in retrospect, prophetic. While on the road from Bantry to Glengariff the party passed a number of rude, thatched cottages. Albion described these as "very small & wretched looking to me, though the inmates doubtless have more or less comfort." Her interest in the quality of residential structures would grow in later years, and her concern with the welfare of the inhabitants would deepen markedly.[45]

On June 14 they boarded a ship for an overnight journey across the North Channel of the Irish Sea and up the Firth of Clyde to Glasgow, Scotland. Here they contacted a Mr. Clement, whom they had met on board the *Umbria* during their Atlantic crossing, and he gave them a personal tour of the city and its environs. The next day they traveled to Edinburgh, visiting Stirling and Loch Lomond along the way. Their two days in Edinburgh were highlighted by attendance at Sunday services at St. George's Church and visits to Edinburgh Castle, St. Margaret's Chapel, and Holyrood Palace.[46]

They left the Scottish capital on the 20th, en route to London. They stopped along the way at Abbotsford, the country estate of Sir Walter Scott, and visited the famous abbey nearby ("a grand old pile, full of grace and beauty"). At Abbotsford itself they toured Scott's study and library; the former, Albion recorded, contained "the desk at which he wrote & his writing chair, in which of course I sat." This was an appropriate conclusion to the sisters' stay in Ireland and Scotland since, as Annie later wrote, they saw everything in those two countries "through the glamour of song and story" familiar to them because of their Scotch-Irish heritage.[47]

The five-day stay in London was a whirlwind of sightseeing and shopping. Albion's description of their first day as "delightful . . . but too hurried" seems accurate, since they managed to spend time at the Tower, Westminster Abbey, St. Paul's Cathedral, and the National Gallery of Art. The next day they visited the Crystal Palace and the British Museum ("Saw old dug up things from Egypt & every other old historic place"), followed on day three by a trip to the Zoological Gardens and a carriage ride through Hyde Park. "Am I tired?" she wrote in her diary one night. "Oh, not at all, only a little weary. 'I 'gin to be weary of this flesh.'" She and Annie had strength enough, however, to spend all of one morning shopping at Peter Robinson's, whom she described as the "big merchant of London—one of them." Here, with the assistance of a woman from Baltimore who was part of their tour group, they selected and ordered their wedding gowns. The cost, dutifully noted in Albion's diary, was £8-4s-0d.[48]

The party left London on the evening of June 25, crossed the North Sea overnight, and arrived in Holland at 10:00 the next morning. They spent several days touring in the Low Countries: Rotterdam, Amsterdam, The Hague, Antwerp, Brussels. By the Fourth of July they were in Heidelberg, and the constant and rapid travel was beginning to take its toll. Albion began her diary entry that night with the confession that "I have had the hardest time to remember what we did after we left Brussels—it seems so long ago." She eventually recalled that they had taken a train from Brussels to Cologne, then transferred to a steamer for a trip up the Rhine. The castle at Heidelberg was, she felt, "the grandest ruin we have yet explored." From there they went to Baden-Baden, in the heart of the Black Forest, and continued on into Switzerland.[49]

At this point Albion and Annie left their tour group for a visit with American cousins who were living in Switzerland. The three Page brothers, located "in the shadow of the Rigi on Lake Cham between Zurich and Lucerne," were "rearing their families as good Americans, with American tutors and governesses. They even sent over to America for peanuts and maple syrup." The sisters had intended to stay for a week but, Annie remembered years later, "they kept us on one pretext and another for a month." Needless to say, they had time to see a great deal of Switzerland: Lucerne, Lake Zug, Zurich, the Rigi, Interlaken. Albion's poetic inclinations were stimulated by the mountain scenery, and her diary entry for July 24 concluded with this quatrain:

> I found it on a mountain side,
> A wee forget-me-not, so high
> It seemed its dainty lips had brushed
> The tender azure of the sky.[50]

Rejoining their tour group, they traveled from Interlaken to Berne and then by train to Paris, arriving August 10 or 11. Albion recorded that she had "never [been] more weary than when I got home" from a day of shopping at the Bon Marché and other Parisian stores. Since her diary ends at this point (or, more accurately, since the pages that would have covered the remainder of the trip are missing), the details of their subsequent itinerary are not known. They did return to London for the final fittings of their wedding gowns, and it seems likely that they sailed from England on their return voyage. The entire trip took about three months, perhaps a bit longer. While it seems apparent from her journal that Albion enjoyed the tour, there was also an "absence makes the heart grow fonder" aspect to the experience. She wrote, some years later, that the trip had two results: "I loved my own 'rocks and rills' better (after a foreign Fourth of July) and I had become more than ever anxious to study art."[51]

Albion Fellows at the time of her marriage (1888). Albion Fellows Bacon Collection, Special Collections, Willard Library

First, however, there was the matter of a wedding, which took place on the evening of October 11, 1888. The *Evansville Daily Journal* accorded the event considerable space, observing that "It is quite an unusual thing to witness double marriages, which fact, with the prominence and standing of the parties, made the affair doubly interesting." Trinity Methodist "was jammed," the paper reported, "and many were compelled to secure standing positions." Albion and Annie looked "charming in white China silk, heavily embroidered and without train." Hilary, Will, and the ushers "were attired in the regulation black." The introduction and closing of the ceremony were performed jointly for both couples, but they repeated their vows individually. "The parties," the *Journal* observed, "are well known in Evansville and will receive the warm congratulations of many friends."[52]

Albion and Hilary began housekeeping at 1025 Upper Second

Street, just doors away from the relatives with whom they had been boarding. It was, as she described it, "a pretty home in a pretty part of the town." Initially reluctant to settle permanently in the city, she quickly adjusted to their suburban setting "where the houses were far apart, and every one had his own individual air to breathe." And she apparently settled comfortably into her new life, as well. Although she had been self-supporting for several years, and engaged in interesting and challenging work, as a middle-class, married woman in the late nineteenth century she was expected to give up gainful employment. But, she recalled, "my husband, my housekeeping, flowers, music, reading, my friends, and a pleasant social round, filled up the hours." She resumed her study of art, and took cooking lessons. With "so many happy and pleasant things" in her new life, "what room was there for anything else?" It was, as she later termed it herself, a "sheltered life." But it was not to last.[53]

Two

The Clutch of the Thorns

"For the first few years after marriage," wrote historian Roy Lubove, "Mrs. Bacon's horizon did not extend much beyond the spacious, roomy house nestled at the edge of town. She led the pleasant existence of the middle-class housewife at the *fin de siecle*." Bacon's own description of her life during these years seems, at first reading, to support Lubove's observation. "All my friends lived on pretty streets," she later recalled. "All the houses were roomy and comfortable. All the lawns were large, with many trees and flowers. . . . I didn't miss the country as much as I had expected, and decided that the town had many advantages, especially as every one [so she then thought] had city water and sewerage."[1]

Since all her friends lived on "pretty streets," and her shopping was done "in the best business blocks," she did not have to see much of the rest of the town. "When we drove," she remembered, "we never went through the factory district where the working men's cottages were, but chose the boulevards, along the [Ohio] river or the parks, or took the country roads." Once during a drive along the river with a "maiden lady who was interested in mission classes and factory people," her companion remarked that, for some people, the world was less beautiful than the lovely panorama spread out before them. Taken aback, and deciding that her acquaintance must have been "embittered by disappointment," Bacon resolved that she "was not going to be soured," and that she would "exclude every ugly or blighting thing from my life." This seemingly exclusive focus on her own family, home, and neighborhood was reinforced with the birth of two daughters—Margaret Gibson in September 1889, and Albion Mary in January 1892—after which, she later wrote, "all else became secondary."[2]

Yet if Bacon was leading a pleasant, middle-class existence in the early 1890s, and if her social consciousness, by her own admission, was not well developed, it is perhaps too much to claim, with Lubove, that her horizons did not extend beyond her domestic role. The support for this contention, if somewhat indirect, is still compelling. It begins with a simple, seemingly prosaic fact: In the early 1890s, sometime after the birth of her second child, Albion Fellows Bacon became ill.

This was not a brief, transitory illness; some of the symptoms lasted for years. But in spite of its immediate effect on her life and its import for her future activities, she said very little about it in her autobiographical writings. Indeed, her youngest daughter (born in 1901) claimed in an interview to be totally unaware of this incident in her mother's life. It is necessary, therefore, to quote Bacon's one brief description of the episode in full.

> There was one long while that I could not hold them [her daughters] in my arms. The house was hushed and darkened, and the servants went about with noiseless steps. For months I was very ill. Then, for nearly a year, I dragged about, white and thin as "snaw [snow] wreaths in the thaw," weary, listless, indifferent, with no special interest in anything but my family.

> For hours I would sit idly, not making an effort even to read, content to rest my cheek upon a golden head. It seemed as if the wheels of life had suddenly stopped, and I had no ambition to set them running again. I never went to look down the White Road, for I had a feeling that there was a great wall across it. Nervous prostration does that. It was two years before I took any interest in people, two more before the shadow of the eclipse had wholly moved off my world. It was eight years at least before all my energy and enthusiasm and joy of living returned.[3]

The diagnosis that Bacon apparently received—nervous prostration—is significant. This is another name for "nervous exhaustion" or "neurasthenia," a malady that became, if not an epidemic, certainly commonplace among middle- and upper-class urban Americans during the late nineteenth and early twentieth centuries. Some called it the "American disease," and it afflicted among others such well-known men and women as William and Alice James, Charlotte Perkins Gilman, Jane Addams, Theodore Dreiser, James Whitcomb Riley, and Edith Wharton. Characterized by "excessive fatigue from slight exertion," sufferers "complained of fatigue so pronounced that they could arise only with extreme difficulty and could not attend to their usual affairs"—a description that mirrors Bacon's recounting of her affliction. Although neurasthenia has no equivalent in modern medicine, between 1869 (when neurologist George M. Beard coined the term) and the 1920s it was, according to one of its foremost students, "used to characterize practically every nonspecific emotional disorder short of outright insanity, from simple stress to severe neuroses."[4]

Beard, who popularized the complaint, argued in his *American Nervousness* (1881) that modern industrial society had placed unprecedented demands on individuals. Middle-class, urban "brain workers" were especially susceptible to exhausting their stock of "nerve force." Women, whose constitutions were presumed to be more delicate, were also considered prone to the syndrome. Margaret Cleaves, one of the few women physicians to write about neurasthenia, observed that "In no country or time has there been so much would-be mental activity among women as here and now." It was the ambitions and strivings of "those women occupying the higher social plane, women of intelligence, education and culture" that were the "predisposing or exciting causes of neurasthenia."[5]

Turn-of-the-century physicians, while generally agreeing on neurasthenia's symptoms, achieved no consensus on the most efficacious remedies. One response to the assertion that the cause of nervous prostration was too much mental activity was to eliminate or at least reduce perceived mental overstimulation. At its most extreme this took the form of the famous Weir Mitchell Rest Cure. In this regimen, prescribed almost exclusively for women, patients were ordered to bed for a month or more, were allowed no visitors, and were prohibited from reading or writing.[6] In spite of its evident paternalism, the rest cure became increasingly popular during the Gilded Age. Its most noteworthy failure was probably Charlotte Perkins Gilman, who tried the treatment briefly, rejected it utterly, and then drew on the experience in her renowned short story "The Yellow Wallpaper," in which the female narrator slowly goes mad during her enforced isolation.[7] While there is no evidence that Bacon was subjected to the rest cure in its most extreme form, her own description of her condition makes it clear that her social interactions were greatly limited for quite some time.

Medical historian F. G. Gosling observes that another group of physicians "held ideas consistent with middle-class morality . . . [and] used the image of nervous invalidism to speak out against the emergence of the 'new woman.'" While they did not necessarily agree with

Mitchell and others that women should be isolated to avoid nervous exhaustion, they did suggest that deviations from "woman's proper sphere" as wife/mother/homemaker frequently led to problems. In the words of historian John Haller, Jr., these physicians argued that "the neurasthenic disorders of the urban woman were the product of her wanderings outside domesticity." Too much education, or an attempt to take up a professional career, would only prove injurious since women's "sensitive organizations" were "more easily injured by [the professions] than are the tougher organizations of men."[8]

By the end of the nineteenth century, a third group of physicians was beginning to explain neurasthenia in a way that more nearly comports with current understanding of the syndrome. As Gosling observes, by the 1890s it was accepted "that many of the physical symptoms of nervous patients were imaginary or psychosomatic, and that mental manifestations, particularly depression, were most crucial to diagnosis." Mental symptoms, and especially depression, became "the chief signs by which physicians recognized the American disease." There were doubtless patients diagnosed as neurasthenic who did, in fact, have trouble adjusting to and coping with the pressures and frenetic pace of Gilded Age urban life. But there were countless others who, as Gosling puts it, "suffered not from overexcitement but from grief, depression, anxiety, and the overwhelming tedium of their lives."[9]

Depression, or tedium, or both, may help to explain Albion Bacon's mysterious illness. (Depression here means *clinical* depression, not the temporary feelings of sadness or dejection that periodically afflict almost everyone.) Recall that Bacon's symptoms appeared at some point following the birth of her second child. One possibility is that what Bacon's physician called nervous prostration would today be diagnosed as postpartum depression. A second possibility, for which the evidence is even more inferential, is that Bacon was responding, perhaps subconsciously, to a certain "tedium" in her life, to a desire for more challenges than her outwardly comfortable domestic routine provided. In his thought-provoking *American Nervousness, 1903*, Tom Lutz shrewdly observes that neurasthenia could be caused "by indecision about one's life work or by idleness. . . . In either case, the disease was related to changing notions of work."[10]

If Bacon was, in fact, in a quandary over what her life's work should be, she had considerable company. This was a problem that plagued many young, well-educated women toward the end of the nineteenth century. In the 1870s and 1880s, writes historian Allen Davis, "young women of the upper and middle classes were often afflicted by nervous prostration and periodic breakdowns from overwork. . . . Almost all of the first generation of college women seemed to have suffered from poor health and nervous prostration." Many of these women graduates "had a difficult time finding a suitable career, or even a feeling that they were needed."[11]

One of the best-known case studies in this regard is Jane Addams, co-founder and moving spirit behind Chicago's famous Hull-House settlement. Following her graduation from Rockford College in 1881, Addams returned home and, in the words of her biographer, "suddenly became ill and despondent." This condition persisted, off and on, for seven or eight years, during which time she tried both the Mitchell rest cure and the supposedly recuperative effects of extended European sojourns. Addams later referred to the "sense of maladjustment" she felt during these years, and described her graduation as an entry into "that trying land between vague hope and definite attainment." It was not until 1888 that, in company with Ellen Starr, she formulated the "creative solution" that ultimately became Hull-House.[12]

A few years later, in a paper discussing the then new settlement house movement, Addams clearly called on her own experience when she described "a fast-growing number of cultivated young people who have no recognized outlet for their active faculties" and whose "uselessness hangs about them heavily."[13] This was, in effect, a self-diagnosis of the physical and psychological trials she had faced during the 1880s, and it was one with which an increasing number of physicians agreed. By the early twentieth century Dr. H. J. Hall could suggest, in an article entitled "The Systematic Use of Work as a Remedy in Neurasthenia and Allied Conditions," that neurasthenic women were best served not by a rest cure but by "bringing about a gradual progress [in] the conditions of a normal life, a life of pleasant and progressive occupation, as different as possible from the previous life and resulting in self-forgetfulness."[14] It was a prescription with which Addams concurred. In an oft-cited chapter concerning "filial relations" in her *Democracy and Social Ethics* she observed that many an educated woman was "longing that some demand be made upon her powers." If the psychological strain of her situation led to physical problems the solution was not "to be put to bed and fed on milk" but rather "simple, health-giving activity, which, involving the use of all her faculties, shall be a response to all the claims which she so keenly feels."[15]

There is no definitive contemporary evidence that in the early 1890s Albion Bacon felt that "uselessness hung about her heavily." But, with the exception of the fact that she had not attended college, her situation and symptoms seem to parallel those of women such as Addams and Gilman. She was well read, high school–educated, and intelligent (salutatorian, recall, of her high school class). She was artistically creative, with serious interests in writing, art, and music. She had worked prior to her marriage, holding a responsible position in a male-dominated and respected profession. And she had made the "grand tour" of Europe. There is ample reason to question, in short, Lubove's claim that Bacon's horizon, even in the early years of her marriage, was limited strictly to her home and family.

True, she wrote in 1913 that there were "many happy and pleasant things in [her] new life," and she asked rhetorically "what room was there for anything else?" But in an autobiographical essay prepared for her children in the mid-1920s, she recalled that she "never gave up hoping to have a chance to study art & really learn the technique until after my marriage." She observed, as well, that

> As I grew older I had the natural ambition that goes with writing and other creative work. I wanted it to be "good," to be recognized by my peers. I wanted to be one of the goodly fellowship of authors, not to stand outside looking in. I couldn't *bear* to stand outside looking in.

She admitted, too, that she had "not only a passion for excelling but for *leading*. After I had a taste of it in High School," she remembered, " . . . it was intolerable to me that anyone should 'beat' me or go ahead of me."[16]

Externally, it may have appeared that Bacon led the "pleasant existence of the middle-class housewife." Internally, it seems likely that she felt (in Addams's words) a "sense of maladjustment," and that her neurasthenic symptoms reflected not overwork or too much mental stimulation but rather dreams abandoned and the *absence* of appropriate challenges, stimulation, and creative activity. Ultimately, the lack of definitive, unambiguous evidence makes the precise nature and cause of Bacon's extended illness in the 1890s speculative. But one of Lutz's generalizations about the syndrome may, in this case, come close to the mark: "many women at the turn of the century did not feel able to approach their husbands directly about their desire to pursue a career or other interests, and for them the indirection of neurasthenia was a great help."[17]

Bacon's recovery, as she herself described it, was a gradual process that took several years. It is impossible at this remove, with fragmentary evidence, to disentangle cause and effect, but her strength and renewed interest in life seem to have returned about 1896 and coincided with two notable events. First, the family moved into a comfortable, commodious new house they had built at 1221 Upper First Street (1121 First in today's numbering system). This structure, just a few blocks from their former residence on Second Street, would be Albion and Hilary's home for the remainder of their lives.[18]

At the same time Albion and her sister Annie were putting the finishing touches on a co-authored book. This collection of poems, titled *Songs Ysame* (pronounced Is-a-may), was published in 1897. Though they are usually undated, it appears that most of Albion's contributions to the volume were written prior to her illness, many prior to her marriage. There are, for example, reflections on "Grandfather," "The Old Church," and "The Old-Time Pedagogue" that harken back to her McCutchanville days. And one poem, "An Alpine Valley," was written in Cham, Switzerland, during the sisters' European trip in 1888. "Motherhood," however, was apparently written after the birth of her second daughter in 1892, since it refers to "two dear heads of bronze and amber, . . . two who cling, and kiss, and clamber."[19]

If, as hypothesized earlier, Bacon's illness was indeed a psychosomatic response to frustrated ambition, her final few poems in *Songs Ysame* suggest that she may have begun to accept—or at least adjust to—less lofty goals. "At Last" begins by asking:

> What will you give me, O World, O World!
> If I run the race and win?

The poet's answer, several lines later, is clearly no paean to blind ambition:

> Ashes to ashes, dust to dust,
> Fame will fade and crowns will rust.

The theme is even more explicit in "A Resolve," which argues that unless one has the ability and circumstances to make a unique contribution—as a writer, artist, or composer, perhaps?—then there is nothing to be gained by self-flagellation or remorse over what is not meant to be:

The fields of thought are plowed so deep,
So carefully are tilled,
That all the granaries of the world
With plenteous store are filled.
Unless I deeper plow or sow,
What sheaf, then, can I bring?
So like the black-bird in the field,
I'll eat the wheat and sing.[20]

And, as the dark clouds of her nervous prostration began to dissipate, she did start to "sing" again, to participate in family, church, and community life. "A Dante club, a Browning circle, even a psychology class, in turn became tempting," she later wrote. "When at last the paints and brushes were brought out, it showed a complete restoration, and the whole family posed in various attitudes of joy." Although she was a member of Trinity Methodist, she did not participate in any of the special interest groups within the church during the early- and mid-1890s. Then, in 1896–1897, she joined the Woman's Foreign Missionary Society, a membership she retained throughout her life. A few years later she became involved in the Ladies and Pastors Union (later the Ladies Aid Society). And a "Calendar of Evansville 1898," illustrated with city scenes, included four poems apiece by Albion and Annie.[21]

This renewed activity did not, however, include involvement in local social welfare and civic reform efforts. When a committee from the Evansville charities organization came calling to solicit her participation, she responded that she and Hilary were happy to contribute financially. But, she told them, "I don't know anything about that kind of work, and I think it is better for those more experienced to do it." Similar explanations met her friends who tried to interest her in civic improvement. When asked to assist with a vice problem—presumably prostitution—she later recalled being "too indignant to make any excuses." Her continued attempt to "exclude every ugly or blighting thing" from her life extended even to modern fiction and newspapers:

> If, after carefully choosing a book, the turning of a page disclosed an unexpected "problem" or ugly suggestion, I threw it from me in disgust, as I would a fine peach with a worm in it. As to newspapers, I read the poetry first, skimmed the head lines, and skipped the politics, turning under the crimes and accidents.[22]

The blinders Bacon was wearing (her own later description of herself) began to be removed toward the end of the 1890s. The proximate cause of this awakening was not a suddenly invigorated social conscience but rather a narrow, personal concern for the welfare of her children. On a visit to daughter Albion's school to inquire about a classmate who had been annoying the youngster, she saw as she left the building that the grounds were covered with cinders and broken rock, and that a pile of decaying garbage from an adjacent grocery lay next to the school yard. Why, she wondered, with so much vacant land around the school, couldn't there be a proper playground? That afternoon ("with a new gleam in my eye and a new determination in my step") she discussed the matter with leaders of the Civic Improvement Association whose children went to the same school.

A few days later she joined a delegation that visited the city attorney's office to determine whether the city had clear title to a tract of land that could—and, they argued, should—be used for a playground. In recounting the event some years later Bacon remembered that she "had expected to remain in the background, but, with some surprise and confusion" found herself "taking a hand in the argument. It was like a plunge through ice into freezing water. But—the ice was broken, and I was initiated into civic work!" Although resolution of the matter took some time, and Bacon was not able to join in the continuing and ultimately successful effort, she had taken a first, halting step toward a life of public activism.[23]

The next step was also prompted by concern for her children. Both daughters came down with scarlet fever, apparently contracted from classmates. When she had visited the school Bacon had observed, in addition to the tidy, well-scrubbed children of her friends, unkempt and poorly clothed youngsters from the city's working-class neighborhoods, some of whose complexions "had a greyish hue that might come off and might not." Now she learned that some of these children had attended school while covered with red spots and afflicted with sores. One child, herself with a persistent cough, had been absent to attend the funeral of her mother, who had died of tuberculosis. Stunned by these revelations, Bacon called her friends to announce that she was now prepared to serve on the sanitation committee of the Civic Improvement Association. In retrospect, she admitted that she had no idea what the poorer children's homes were like or what needed to be done. But, as she put it, "'sanitation' had a remedial sound, and something was wrong, and I wanted to take hold somewhere."[24]

Take hold she did, if none too firmly at first; she later described her early work on the sanitation committee as giving her "a pleasant sense of light responsibility." But, gradually, she began to educate herself, and her evolving interest was marked by subtle changes in behavior. Formerly, when passing an alley, she had turned away rather than confront disagreeable sights and smells. Now she stopped, looked, sniffed the air, observed the presence of children playing. Instead of searching first for poetry in magazines and newspapers, she now sought articles on sanitation and began to take note of local politics. To the belles lettres on her reading list she added works such as *How the Other Half Lives* (1890), Jacob Riis's vivid description of tenement life in late nineteenth century New York City. After completing this volume, as well as several other works by Riis, she found her mind becoming "a saturated solution of slums."[25]

She had not, however, actually visited the kinds of homes about which she had begun reading. The opportunity arose when she met Caroline Rein, general secretary of the Associated Charities of Evansville, to whom she exclaimed: "I want to know where to find some poor families, so I can visit them in their homes. Won't you take me to see some of them?" Rein, who had plans to organize a Friendly Visitors Circle and knew a likely (if naive) prospect when she saw one, readily agreed, acceding to Bacon's desire that they go as soon as possible.[26]

Evansville, like most American urban areas, had been profoundly affected by the linked phenomena of in-migration and industrialization during the late nineteenth century. One student of the city's history has noted that "the three decades after midcentury witnessed the transformation of Evansville from a small commercial settlement of 3,325 residents into a diverse manufacturing city of nearly 30,000." Twenty years later, at the turn of the century, a population of 59,000 made it the second largest city in Indiana. The new arrivals, most of whom came from either the rural tri-state region (southern Indiana, southern Illinois, western Kentucky) or from Europe (especially Germany), were "attracted by the opportunities for employment afforded by river and rail transportation, public and domestic service, and manufacturing establishments." The latter included flour, grist, and lumber mills, furniture manufacturing, and tobacco processing. (Swans Down cake flour and Fendrich cigars became nationally known "name brands.") By 1880 over 3,000 men, women, and sometimes children were employed in Evansville's shops and factories. Twenty years later some 14,000 residents worked in manufacturing, many of them in low-skill, poorly paid positions, and their tenuous economic circumstances were often reflected in their dwellings.[27]

As they rode the streetcar across town to the factory district the next day, and as she observed block after block of shabby, nondescript

Old St. Mary's tenement in Evansville. Bacon, Beauty for Ashes;
photograph courtesy Indiana Historical Society, C8155

houses, Bacon asked Rein a question that she often, in later years, had
to answer for others: "We haven't any slums in Evansville, have we? Not
the real sure enough ones, with those terrible conditions that Jacob Riis
writes about in New York?" Rein, who had dealt with some of the less
pleasant consequences of the community's growth and transformation,
assured her that, yes, the city had some very bad conditions, "real slums,
I think." Indeed, except for the extreme congestion, all of the problems
of the nation's largest city were present, in lesser degree, in Evansville.
If Bacon had doubts, they were dispelled when the pair arrived at their
destination—"Old St. Mary's," one of the largest tenements in the
city.[28]

    This former hospital, in a park-like setting that sloped down to the
Ohio River, belied its stately appearance and scenic location. Its three
stories sheltered dozens of families, each in a single room. Bacon remembered Riis's description of the one-room slum in New York as the
worst of all, and saw nothing to make her question that evaluation. As

Rein made her rounds, with Bacon in tow, the latter tried to be nonchalant, "to seem not to be looking at anything, yet seeing all." What she saw stunned her. Her youth in McCutchanville, her adult years living on fashionable First and Second streets, even her recent nonfiction reading—none of it had prepared her for the coarseness and squalor, the disorder, the lack of privacy, the noise and dirt of this teeming tenement. "Not one line or spot of beauty was there," she wrote some years later when describing the scene, "in all that mass of hopeless ugliness."[29]

Her visits at Old St. Mary's completed, Rein announced that they had another stop to make "if you can stand it," and Bacon silently nodded her assent. At this second dwelling, built flush with the pavement and virtually on the ground, she recalled that "the same general impressions rushed out to meet me, the mean, shabby ugliness of the place, the overwhelming number of women and children, who boiled over out of every window and door, even onto the pavement, in a most surprising way." The children were all unwashed; the back yard was littered with garbage and trash; and in a damp, downstairs room, where a boy was ill with tuberculosis, a portion of the floor had rotted through to reveal the wet earth immediately below.

Responding to Bacon's query about why the residents didn't clean and repair the property, Rein explained the harsh realities. Not only could the tenants not afford paint and wallpaper, or tools and lumber, most of them lacked the skills to use them if they did have them. Cleanliness was difficult when water, supplied by a single cistern, was always scarce. And the landlord had refused to make improvements that, under existing law, he could not be forced to make. So Bacon's wish—to visit with the poor in their homes—had been fulfilled. And she returned to her own home and family, she later wrote, "with bowed head and lagging feet, seeing before me all the time those awful rooms, those babies of the slums."[30]

One hesitates to make too much of Bacon's emotional, retrospective description of this outing. Yet it seems clear that it was a significant, even a transforming experience. In a book published in 1914, some fifteen years after the fact, she wrote of that day that "sights and smells rose and assaulted me, choked and gashed me, and the scars remain yet. . . . I had never dreamed that people lived like that *in our city*." She came to see as symbolic a minor, momentary incident that occurred as she left Old St. Mary's: the branch of an overgrown rose bush snagged her dress and briefly detained her. Haunted by what she had seen, her memories of the excursion became "the clutch of the thorns" from which she could not disentangle herself.[31]

Moved by a newfound desire to help, Bacon accepted assignment as a "Friendly Visitor" to the poor, asking only that Rein accompany her at the beginning to ensure that she made no mistakes. Obviously aware that her latest recruit had been overwhelmed by the tenements, Rein assigned her "a higher class family, in a single house." The household consisted of a German-born woman, her ill son, and a grandson. Bacon began her first visit by admiring a beautiful bedquilt, thereby encouraging the woman to show off other pieces of handwork. With rapport thus established, subsequent visits were easier and Bacon took over the case by herself. As Rein explained, "she needs just a friend to look after her a bit, for there is no one she can turn to in that neighborhood." The Associated Charities supplied practical needs when such were found to be necessary. Friendly Visitors, however, were enjoined from providing financial assistance and instructed to "never take anything you would not take to your own friends—only books, delicacies, flowers, and such things. Alms are forbidden to Friendly Visitors," Rein explained. "It spoils the effect of the work."[32]

Bacon found this stricture difficult to accept at first. It seemed "hard-hearted" to visit the needy and ignore financial realities, even when charitable groups were giving aid. But gradually, as she and the other women of the Friendly Visitors Circle exchanged case histories, she became aware of the complexity of the problems they faced and accepted the proposition that "the poor suffer for other things, much more than for money." Joining a public-policy debate that continues even now, she later quoted Rein approvingly: "'To give material help is so often like giving a narcotic to help ease the pain, when what is needed is a tonic or a surgical operation.'"[33]

Bacon continued her work with the Friendly Visitors Circle for several years, learning something of the causes and effects of urban poverty both from her personal contact with a variety of clients and from the tales her compatriots shared at their monthly meetings. These experiences, she recounted, "upset my notions about classes, and made clear to me the necessity of dealing with individuals." She admitted candidly how much she and her friends in the circle did not know, how often they had to rely simply on their "mother-nurse experience." But she remembered with evident pride the group's successes as they "untangled domestic knots, helped the poor mothers plan and contrive, taught sanitation when possible, and gave instruction about baby food and nursing in general."[34]

Some cases proved insoluble. Landlord-tenant disputes, which often focused on dangerous or unsanitary conditions, were frequently intractable and were seldom resolved satisfactorily. Other cases simply did not come to the circle's attention. Bacon observed that Evansville's African-American population rarely applied for charity (her simplistic explanation was that "they look well after their own people, in sickness or want") and thus did not often come within the purview of the Associated Charities. One result, she conceded some years after, was that she and her colleagues "did not realise until later how uniformly miserable and unsanitary were their dwellings."[35]

Other cases beyond the ability of Bacon and her women friends were those where there were "unmanageable men or boys in the family, who set our work at naught, and kept the family in extremities." After arranging for a gentleman to intercede in one such case, she organized a men's circle of Friendly Visitors composed of sixteen men (including her husband Hilary) "prominent in church and civic work." This circle met at the Bacons' house with the conscious goal that their children would "grow up with the idea of using the home for social service." The men, Bacon observed, approached their cases in a more straightforward and businesslike manner than did the women's circle; "they were not squeamish, as we were, about calling things by their right names." Nor did they heed Rein's admonition at their organizational meeting to "go simply as a friend and neighbour." Every single man took alms, some offered employment, and one man moved his client family into another house so that the husband would no longer have to pass a multitude of saloons on his way home from work. The periodic meetings of this group to recount their activities left Bacon energized. "No other evenings, merely social," she wrote, "left such a sense of satisfaction."[36]

Indeed, she found so much satisfaction in the work that she began to proselytize her friends and acquaintances to become involved. Besides the salutary effects on the "clients," she declared, the effort was worthwhile because of the "effect upon the spiritual health that came from this good exercise." She thought, at first, that service as a Friendly Visitor was the perfect solution for the "unemployed church member." Surely anyone could visit the poor and bring a measure of comfort; it required only "earnestness, good sense, and politeness." Upon further reflection, however, she decided that not all church members had the requisite tact to succeed as visitors in the city's slums, tenements, and hovels, and that such volunteers might do more harm than good. She concluded, in a well-turned phrase, that "it would be a sin to exploit the poor to save the souls of the well-to-do."[37]

❖

Bacon's work as a Friendly Visitor gradually led her to become involved in other local social welfare activities. At about the turn of the century she joined several women in the creation of a Visiting Nurse's Circle. This group both supervised and financially supported a nurse whose responsibility was to visit the sick poor in their homes and provide basic health care. The circle met monthly (and continued to meet for many years) in the homes of the sponsors "to hear the nurse's report and to discuss the best care of the patients." The members also took turns making visits with the nurse, and Bacon later observed that these sojourns "opened my eyes to many things that even friendly visiting had failed to teach me."[38]

Their patients were found in "un-looked-for places": in sheds and stables, over saloons and warehouses, downtown and on the fringe of town. The illnesses Bacon observed as she made her rounds with the nurse were of all kinds: tuberculosis, pneumonia, rheumatism, typhoid, dysentery. Many of these afflictions were, of course, related to environmental conditions in and around patients' dwellings. Uncovered cisterns were a particular problem, and Bacon's descriptions of some that she examined retain the power to nauseate even today. These visits impressed her with the amount of preventable illness in Evansville and the fact that so much misery "was entirely unnecessary and could have been so easily remedied by repairs and better sanitation."[39]

Though she had become increasingly involved in charitable enterprises, Bacon devoted only a few hours per week to these activities. "It was all done," she noted, "when the children were in school, and would not need me." And for two years in the early twentieth century, her involvement in such endeavors virtually ceased. In 1901 she gave birth to twins—Hilary, Jr. and Joy. With two older daughters, two infants, and two nurses, she recounted, her "hands were full, without hunting up more cares in the slums."[40]

In 1903, however, as her domestic situation once again settled into a regular pattern, she founded and became the leader of the Evansville Flower Mission. The purpose of having the men's circle of the Friendly Visitors meet in the Bacon home—to inculcate the children with a sense of social responsibility—apparently had had an effect. Eleven-year-old Albion approached her mother to announce that she and two girlfriends wanted to have a club. While they weren't quite sure what *kind* of club to form, they wanted "to do something for the poor." Various possibilities were considered and rejected before Bacon suggested a flower mission to raise flowers and deliver them to sick people. The girls accepted the plan, and worked on it with enthusiasm, but practical considerations intervened; the immediate neighborhood did not furnish enough cases, and Bacon was (at least at first) unwilling to have the children make deliveries in the slums. The result was that the girls prepared bouquets and Bacon delivered them as she resumed her Friendly Visitor and Nurse's Circle activities. The flowers were "so gratefully received, and so pathetically enjoyed," far beyond her expectations, that she set about to organize a program for the whole city.[41]

Rein heartily approved of the scheme, the Visiting Nurse's Circle agreed to help, and Bacon hosted a flower tea to explain the plan and recruit members. A committee structure resulted in which some were delegated to get flowers, some to distribute them, and others secured the carriages needed for delivery. Once a week loads of blossoms arrived, some donated by florists but most hand cut from the gardens of upper- and middle-class homes. Under the trees, on the Bacons' lawn, the flowers were spread out, sorted, and tied into individual bunches. Then Flower Mission members, working in pairs, loaded their fragrant gifts into the donated carriages and delivered them to homes of the city's sick and poor.

Lydia Metz, the Visiting Nurse, provided a list of individuals and families where the illness was not contagious. Bacon herself made the deliveries to some dwellings where she felt conditions were too extreme for her adolescent and young women volunteers. And she continued to involve her children in the project. Margaret and Albion helped sort the flowers and took turns assisting with their delivery. Bacon sometimes took the twins, as well, recalling later: "they always sat at a safe distance, outside, unless, at some clean and safe place, where there was no contagion, I took them to the door, to speak to our friends." Later, when they were old enough to carry small baskets, Hilary and Joy accompanied her on visits to hospital wards.[42]

It was Bacon's intent that delivery of the flowers should also provide the occasion for a brief "friendly visit," and this expectation was frequently fulfilled. The flowers, they found, solved the often awkward problem of initiating a conversation, since "hearts and doors flew open at the sight of the blossoms." The response, it seems, startled even Bacon, who was touched by the emotional reaction to this small kindness, this little bit of beauty. "The response to our confidence in the poor was their confidence in us," she wrote. "Our friendship won their friendship. But the simple act of taking flowers, being an acknowledgment of their higher nature, woke into bloom their finer and sweeter qualities."

She was struck by the "delicate expressions of appreciation, from those naturally rough and uncouth of speech." And she became frustrated when some skeptics suggested that food, not flowers, was what the poor needed, responding that "rarely did any one starve for want of food in our city, but many starved for friendship and beauty." She later reminisced that "there was nothing, in any form of charity work, that gave me the satisfaction the Flower Mission did."[43]

Bacon also became involved in efforts to improve the lot of Evansville's "working girls." Contrary to what the term might suggest, many of these were not adolescents but rather young and even middle-aged women. The industrial growth of the late nineteenth century had created numerous new factory positions, especially in textile and cigar manufacturing, and farm girls and women from southwestern Indiana and nearby Kentucky counties migrated to the city in search of employment, independence, and urban amenities. What they often found was low pay, poor working conditions, terrible housing, and little opportunity for socializing or, as Bacon and her middle-class cohorts would have put it, "wholesome recreation." Concern with the "vice question"—sexual promiscuity and, potentially, prostitution—clearly was one motivation of those who founded and ran what became known as the Working Girls' Association. As Bacon euphemistically put it, the girls who gave them the most anxiety were those "who had sisters or friends who walked obliquely." As she heard stories of girls seduced and abandoned ("ruined"), and of white slavery, she decided that in addition to her other activities she "wanted to do something for the girls in the world around me, outside of the slums, to keep them from being drawn into those dreadful traps."[44]

She began by consulting with the president and probation officer of the Board of Children's Guardians, who educated her about conditions faced by the city's young people, young women in particular. She put her newly acquired knowledge to use as a member of the program committee of a Home Missionary Society that had recently been organized at Trinity Methodist. There was a division of opinion in the society about whether their efforts should focus on Evansville or not. Bacon used her position to ensure consideration of local conditions. "So we took up," she later recalled, "a study of the needs and conditions of our city, from every social standpoint, including schools, asylums, jails and slums." Outside speakers such as the police matron, the YMCA secretary, and staff from the Board of Children's Guardians addressed the missionary society meetings, describing some of the situations they encountered in their work. These were tales, Bacon related, "the like of which our women had never heard in all their sweet pure lives." But, she continued, "they were made of good Methodist stuff, and to know their duty was to do it. Not a word of persuasion was needed to make them take up a work for girls, in our city."[45]

The group began by opening a room as a temporary shelter for women or girls who might be stranded or new to the city but without family or friends—a sort of Travelers Aid operation. Notices posted in railroad and interurban cars and stations advertised the shelter and gave directions to it. Then Eleanor Foster, assistant secretary of the Associated Charities and also a member of the Home Missionary Society at Trinity Methodist, suggested the need for a "shelter" for the city's working girls—a "comfortable, cosy place" where the young women could spend their noon hour relaxing in a pleasant atmosphere instead of eating a cold lunch in the factories "in the midst of the muss of their work." The missionary society thereupon detailed Foster, Bacon, and a church deaconess to serve as an investigating committee to survey the shops and factories and see what was needed and feasible.[46]

This was Bacon's first visit to industrial worksites and, as on her first visit to the slums, she was shocked by what she saw. When, previously, she "had driven past these huge buildings, and had heard the roar of the machinery" she thought "only of the moving bands and the buzzing wheels." Now, inside, "where ranks of girls stood, with machine-like motions," she realized "that human lives were woven on those looms, or wound among those wheels." Timing their visits for the noon hour, the group confirmed Foster's previous observations; although many of the girls went home for lunch, some—including those who worked in cigar factories and laundries—simply spread their lunch on benches and work tables. Others journeyed to nearby saloon dining rooms, or subsisted on what we would today call "junk food" purchased at a confectioner's shop.[47]

Bacon and her cohorts discovered that, as she put it, "infinitely more tact was needed to approach the girls than had been needed for Friendly Visiting." These young women were independent and had not solicited assistance; there was no assurance that they would accept what could easily be perceived as middle-class meddling. Many, indeed, were indifferent to the plan, but enough expressed interest and promised to patronize such a facility that the investigating committee recommended proceeding. Trinity's Home Missionary Society then called a mass meeting and "gave the enterprise to the churches and clubs of the city,

Bungalow at the Working Girls' Association summer camp. Bacon, Beauty
for Ashes; *photograph courtesy Indiana Historical Society,* C8157

drawing the committees of [the] permanent organisation from them
all." By unanimous agreement, Foster was made manager of the club-
rooms of the newly christened Working Girls' Association (WGA).[48]

The group secured space in the business district sufficient for a dining room, kitchen, rest and reading room, and lavatory. Girls "poured
in" for the warm and inexpensive noon meals (furnished, Bacon later
boasted, at an average cost of 11 cents "before meat and potatoes went
so high"). At night the dining room became a simple gymnasium for
exercise classes, and different committees also organized singing, cooking, and sewing instruction. Eventually, the association acquired a
house near Main Street and rented bedrooms to as many girls as could
be accommodated. And, in time, a summer camp was fashioned near
the edge of town at the end of a trolley line. For a 5 cent fare the girls
could journey directly to and from work, spending the evening and
night at the camp's two bungalows.[49]

The Working Girls' Association continued to operate along these
lines for several years. The constant need to raise funds, however, gradu-

ally began to wear on Bacon and the other WGA directors. It was, she recalled, "the one irksome task in connection with our work," and she and her colleagues "came to a place where we would have broken rock in preference to asking another dollar." Happily, at about the same time that continued financial support for the WGA was becoming problematic, the Young Women's Christian Association (YWCA) began to consider the establishment of a branch in Evansville.[50]

Although the "Y" had a broader mission and aimed at a larger pool of potential members than the Working Girls' Association, the existence of the latter provided a foundation upon which to build the former. Thus, as Bacon described it, the WGA "re-organised, opening up into the larger work." She and several other WGA leaders actively involved themselves in the new organization. At the very first meeting of the YWCA's board of directors in March 1911, Bacon was named a member of the "provisional executive committee"; a month later the nominating committee recommended her as a vice-president (which, apparently, was tantamount to appointment). At the April meeting she also summarized the work of the WGA, stressing the focus that the group had placed on the city's working girls. The newly appointed secretary of the "Y," Roberta Stahr, assured the WGA members that "those classes of girls should have special attention." This was not mere lip service. An "Industrial and Extension Committee" was created and its report for June 1913 refers to meetings held at the Fendrich cigar factory and White Swan laundry. In addition, several girls employed at the Evansville Cigar Company ate their lunch at the "Y's" facilities. Former WGA clients also benefitted from the YWCA's broader focus, national reputation, and fund-raising capabilities. Three years after the "Y" began operations Bacon could write happily that the former WGA patrons "now . . . have a fine gymnasium, a swimming pool, and a bigger dormitory."[51]

Bacon's involvement with the Working Girls' Association proved to be an important step in her gradual evolution into an activist social reformer. When the first president of the WGA was unable to continue in the position, Bacon was persuaded to take her place. "The enterprise couldn't have been more on my heart," she later observed, "but the official position placed it more upon my shoulders. . . . It was the making of me." Assuming responsibility for an organization and having the obligation and authority to make decisions for the enterprise developed new abilities. "These things strengthen one's fibre wonderfully," she wrote. "I've seen it often, in the case of other women, who, all untried, were put at the head of some organisation."[52]

She disliked public speaking and recalled that the "hardest duty" of her position was giving talks about the WGA to clubs and societies, though "the ordeal became less severe each time." She found it a pleasant duty, however, to write pieces for the newspapers in order to attract public notice to the association's endeavors. She quickly achieved a fine working relationship with the local press, recalling that they even used cartoons she drew to spotlight the WGA's goals and needs.[53]

By about 1906, therefore, Bacon was no longer leading, at least not exclusively, "the pleasant existence of the middle-class housewife." Her family, to be sure, was still the principal focus of her life. She was by no means a professional social worker (an occupation that, in fact, was only then emerging), or a professional anything else. Her excursions into the realms of social welfare were unpaid, volunteer efforts accomplished principally through the mechanisms of women's voluntary associations. In this she was little different from the countless other women of the era, especially those with strong religious orientations, who carried on the work of benevolence throughout the country.

But she had, it seems, come to feel more than the "pleasant sense of light responsibility" that attended her appointment to a sanitation committee several years earlier. Her reading of Riis, and her subsequent work with a variety of benevolent groups, had made her, if not a professional, at least a very well informed amateur with an eye for relationships and connections.

> This experience with working girls [she later wrote] furnished the connecting link in the social study that I had begun with Friendly Visiting. Putting bit with bit, it was like matching the parts of a puzzle picture. It gave us the girl on the street, in the factory, in our association rooms, in her home.[54]

And it was the home—or, more properly, the *house*—that Bacon began to see as the place where most social problems converged, and to which she would increasingly devote her attention and energies.

Three

Ambassador of the Poor

As the first years of the twentieth century wore on, Bacon's involvement with social welfare initiatives in her home town continued to expand. She later recalled how "year after year the demands upon me grew heavier, as church work, charity work and civic work made irresistible appeals." To one of her sisters she described her increasingly hectic routine as "a case of frenzied philanthropy."[1]

A new organization with which she became associated at this point served to broaden and deepen her knowledge of social welfare issues, as well as to introduce her to experts from outside Evansville. Caroline Rein, who as general secretary of the city's Associated Charities had taken Bacon on her first visit to the slums, had left for another position, and Marcus C. Fagg had replaced her. Fagg began what became known as the Monday Night Club, a group of about twenty-five men and women, including some government officials, who represented different civic and philanthropic organizations in the city. As had the men's circle of Friendly Visitors, the club frequently met in the Bacons' home.[2]

Among its other activities, the Monday Night Club sponsored a series of lectures. As chair of the "lecture course committee," Bacon was called upon to "fill every post from advance agent to property man." She made business arrangements with the speakers, secured the lecture hall, handled publicity, and often entertained the speakers while they were in town. More important than this experience organizing local arrangements, however, was the opportunity to meet, listen to, and learn from experts in the social welfare arena. Many of the speakers were leaders in

the Indiana Conference of Charities and Correction; their presentations, Bacon later recalled, were a "new school for me."[3]

The Monday Night Club also established a housing committee, in
which Bacon immediately became active. The housing conditions endured by the city's poor had haunted her ever since her first excursions
with Rein, and she had gradually become convinced that improvements
were a necessity, a *sine qua non*. She came to believe that the many
charitable activities with which she had been involved did no more
than *alleviate* wretched conditions—they were palliatives, but not cures.
Thus, the various strands of philanthropic work in which she had
participated coalesced into one principal area of concern.

> From every quarter there was borne in upon me the definite convic-
> tion that I could do more for child welfare and for civic welfare, more
> to fight tuberculosis and typhoid, more to prevent vice and to pro-
> mote social purity, by bettering the *homes* of our city than by all the
> varied lines of effort that had engrossed me. I began to notice how the
> threads of the social problems, the civic problems and even the
> business problems of a city are all tangled up with the housing prob-
> lem, and to realise that *housing reform is fundamental*.[4]

Bacon's increasing involvement with social welfare activities during the first years of the century, and her evolving focus on housing as an
area of special interest and concern, reflected the temper of the times.
Reform efforts of many kinds, proposed by reformers of many stripes,
were an important part of the public agenda during the Progressive era.
"Never before," observe two historians of the phenomenon, "had the
people of the United States engaged in so many diverse movements for
the improvement of their political system, economy, and communities."
Their goals and remedies were varied (and sometimes contradictory),
but progressives "made the first comprehensive efforts to grapple with
the ills of a modern urban-industrial society" and to "intervene in
economic and social affairs in order to control natural forces and impose
a measure of order upon them."[5]

Indiana participated in these initiatives. The seeds of progressive
reform had been planted during the last decade of the nineteenth
century when the General Assembly had, in the words of a state historian, "created an important body of political reform measures, albeit of
a relatively moderate nature." Indeed, a close student of Progressive era
politics in Indiana argues that although the state "shared in the reform
wave that submerged America nationally in the years 1900–16," the
roots of those developments "lay deeper in time and reflected . . . the

distinct native context in which they grew." Although the impulse ebbed during the earliest years of the twentieth century, the decade before World War I witnessed the enactment of notable reform measures. These included bills to regulate trusts, railroads, and private banks; a corrupt practices act; a public utilities commission; and a system of workmen's compensation.[6]

It is not surprising that, in an age of reform, housing conditions should have become a subject of concern. The "housing question" was a subject much discussed in the late nineteenth and early twentieth centuries, and extensive literature on the topic was already available by 1900. Of particular concern was housing for those variously described as the "poor," the "working classes," or the "laboring classes."[7]

Housing reform in America had its genesis in New York City, the subject being "forced upon the attention of the city" by the "overcrowding incident to its being the initial port of entry for foreign immigration."[8] Agitation for some form of regulation began in the 1840s, and the nation's first tenement law was enacted for New York City in 1867. Concern with this problem grew as urbanization continued apace during the last third of the nineteenth century. Historian Roy Lubove observes that while not every city had a tenement problem, "nearly all had slums inherited from the free-wheeling expansion" of the era. Publication in 1890 of *How the Other Half Lives*, Jacob Riis's classic examination of tenement life, further focused attention on deficiencies in urban housing. (This book, as noted earlier, was one of the first things Bacon read after she joined the sanitation committee of the Civic Improvement Association.) The late nineteenth century movement culminated with passage of the New York State Tenement House Law of 1901. Similar legislation was enacted shortly thereafter in New Jersey (1904), Connecticut (1905), and Wisconsin (1907).[9]

Although she was increasingly interested in the subject, it was not immediately apparent to Bacon by what mechanism or by whom such reforms might be effected in Evansville. As she later recalled, "it certainly did not occur to me that I should have a hand in it." But upon learning from the newspapers that a building ordinance was to be presented to the city council for consideration, she realized that the bill could be a vehicle for tenement house regulation. When she approached Mayor John Boehne to inquire if the ordinance might include language regulating tenements, he assured her that he would see to it that such provisions, modeled after those used in other cities, were introduced. There was just one catch: the mayor asked Bacon to prepare the proposed sections.[10]

Surprised by the request, but accepting the challenge, she wrote to New York, Chicago, and smaller cities requesting copies of the regulations in effect at those places. She was stunned to discover, when the return mail brought her unexpectedly "bulky packages," how large and complex tenement laws could be—a whole book, in some cases. And she was, initially, disappointed to discover the highly technical nature of such regulations, reading some of them aloud to her husband and children with a sense of confusion and frustration. While she hoped "to give the poor some comforts, some conveniences," she found nothing that would "make the wretched old houses look any better or more homelike." But as she dug deeper and began to understand the meaning and effects of the convoluted legal language, she became more encouraged. "After all," she wrote, "I found that tenement laws require light and air, fire protection, water, drainage, sewerage, repairs, prevention of dampness, prevention of overcrowding and all those unsanitary conditions that caused us so much trouble in our tenements." She very quickly realized that although there were many things a tenement law could not do to improve conditions, "those things a law could do were the most vital of all."[11]

Bacon set about the task of extracting from the materials she had solicited the appropriate sections to fit the Evansville situation. The housing committee of the Monday Night Club advised her to "make it simple" and "not too long." It was difficult, she soon discovered, to adhere to such guidelines; a "simple housing law" was a contradiction in terms. Adjusting space requirements proved particularly troublesome, since a change in one dimension of a room or an interior court altered everything else, and she spent hours exploring the variations. It was tedious work, but also energizing. In a letter to her sister Annie, in which she mentioned that she had been helping draft a tenement reform ordinance, she observed: "I have put in days of study . . . and am certainly as steeped in information about these things as if I had taken a term at a University. And I never enjoyed anything more." She believed the end product, if passed by the council, would be "the finest thing ever done in the city for the poor."[12]

When she completed her task the housing committee reviewed it and suggested minor modifications. Then a lawyer who served on the committee put the draft in proper legal form and Bacon took it to the mayor. She described it later as a "comprehensive little bill, though more than the 'few sections' I was to prepare, and less than the larger cities had." It was added to the building ordinance, which the council eventually took up and then promptly pigeonholed. The bill lay for

*Albion Fellows Bacon (1907). Albion Fellows Bacon Collection,
Special Collections, Willard Library*

many months, in Bacon's words, "gathering dust and anathemas." Only later, when some of the men from the housing committee introduced them quietly as a separate ordinance, were tenement regulations for the city adopted and put into effect. By then Bacon, while still involved in a wide range of social welfare initiatives in Evansville, had begun to broaden the scope of her activities.[13]

❖

The origin of a crusade for statewide housing reform in Indiana can be dated with some precision. In October 1907, the Indiana Conference of Charities and Correction met in Evansville. Bacon was one of the participants and had agreed to deliver a paper at the meeting describing "The Homes of the Poor" in her native city. By the time of the conference, at least in part because of the reception accorded her proposed regulations for Evansville's tenements, she had become convinced that local action was not the most promising way to proceed. Accordingly, she "took every opportunity to discuss the need of a state housing law with leading members of the conference." Most of her conferees supported the idea and Bacon's course was soon set: "I determined to get all the necessary information, and the advice of housing experts, then to compile different housing laws, and find some organisation that would secure the passage of a state law."[14]

Bacon's efforts to assemble information regarding the "housing question," begun during her work on the proposed Evansville ordinance, continued during the winter of 1907–1908. Then in May of the latter year, she attended the National Conference of Charities and Correction in Richmond, Virginia, and participated in a roundtable discussion on housing. Here she met several leaders prominent in national reform efforts and came away with many new ideas and a list of housing materials to read. Here, too, she met Charles S. Grout, director of the Charity Organization Society (COS) in Indianapolis. Grout informed her that the Indianapolis COS was conducting a survey of housing conditions in the capital city and that the Indianapolis Commercial Club, which was assisting with the investigation, was "'looking about for a suitable housing ordinance.'" He advised her to "'get in touch with them and interest them in the movement for a state law.'"[15]

Back in Evansville, Bacon "rushed off letters hither and yon, for laws and books and pamphlets." Two of her correspondents were Jacob Riis and Lawrence Veiller, the latter the author of the New York tenement law of 1901 and the nation's acknowledged expert in housing reform. Both men provided useful advice, and early in the summer of 1908 Bacon set about crafting a state tenement law. With the draft completed and subjected to scrutiny for correct legal form, she double-checked the state statutes to make sure there was not already some obscure legislation on the subject. Satisfied "that Indiana would have nothing to say if her tenements were built fifty stories high, without a single window in one of them," she set about the task of assembling proof that the bill she had drafted was in fact needed.[16]

The remainder of Bacon's summer and early fall was taken up by extensive correspondence. First of all, she needed to obtain reliable information concerning housing conditions in cities other than Evansville and Indianapolis. To this end she sent a questionnaire to all the charities secretaries in the state. The replies convinced her that "all the larger cities, most of the towns, and many of the villages contained slums." Secondly, "realising that housing reform was a new thought in our state, and that the responsibility of the landlord was an unpopular as well as an unfamiliar doctrine," she began a campaign of education. "The endless part of my task," she later remembered, "was the personal letters that simply had to be written. . . . Click, click, click, click, click, went the typewriter, from June [1908] till January [1909], all day from morning till twilight, with stops only for household cares or for the children." As she put it in a magazine article the following year, "making laws and concocting soups and salads are widely different fields of action, and it took months for one pair of hands to write all those letters, being all hyphenated with domestic dashes."[17]

In October Bacon attended her second Indiana Conference of Charities and Correction, held at South Bend. Again she was on the program, this time with a paper discussing "The Housing Problem of Indiana." She also took along her draft of a tenement house bill, which the conference voted to approve. Equally important was the message conveyed by Grout, who also attended the South Bend meeting: "'The educational committee of the [Indianapolis] Commercial Club invites you to meet them at luncheon, as you return home, to discuss your housing bill.'"[18]

The Indianapolis Commercial Club, forerunner of the city's Chamber of Commerce, had been founded in 1890 for the purpose of promoting the "commercial and manufacturing interests and the general welfare" of the city.[19] The club's directors were an early target in Bacon's educational campaign and in her search for "some organisation that would secure the passage of a state law." She had written them early in June 1908, and her letter was referred to the club's committee on education. That body spent the next few months surveying housing conditions in the capital city and considering Bacon's proposed legislation. At a meeting of the committee in late September two club members (one of whom was Grout) were requested "to secure what information they could from Mrs. Albion Fellows Bacon, and, if they considered it advisable, to invite her to be present at a meeting of the Educational

Committee at some future date." Two weeks later, and just a few days prior to the conference in South Bend, a five-member subcommittee (again including Grout) was appointed "to examine and report upon the draft for a bill entitled the 'Housing Act,' and also to confer with Mrs. Albion Fellows Bacon, of Evansville, on her visit to the city next week."[20]

The meeting took place on October 22, 1908. Grout had told Bacon privately that her letter to the club "had won by being practical and business-like." Fearful of spoiling that impression, she later remembered "checking myself in a description of the conditions of the poor, for fear I should verge on sentiment." The luncheon and meeting lasted three hours, and at the conclusion the committee expressed general satisfaction with the bill but asked if Bacon would go over it, word by word, with a subcommittee. She readily agreed, and a second three-hour meeting took place that evening. The subcommittee was chaired by Arthur W. Dunn (head of the Department of History and Civics at Shortridge High School in Indianapolis) and included Grout, Dr. John N. Hurty (secretary of the State Board of Health), and State Senator Linton A. Cox (R–Marion County). Dunn's subsequent report noted that Bacon's draft was "approved in all its general features" by the subcommittee and then "recommended to the Board of Directors of the Commercial Club for their endorsement." The club's board of directors approved the subcommittee's report on November 17 and went on record "as favoring a housing bill."[21]

Bacon had thus succeeded in finding an organization to sponsor the bill. Her part in the effort was over—or so she thought. At the conclusion of the evening meeting on October 22 she advised the committee with "unconcealed delight" that since they had approved the measure "let it be the Commercial Club bill, and let me leave it in your hands to be put through the legislature. . . . Leave me entirely out of it. All I want is to have the bill passed." The committee members conferred briefly and then informed the startled Bacon that the bill would stand a better chance of passage if it were "presented by some individual who is known to be working for the cause of humanity," rather than as a Commercial Club measure. "We will do all we can to push it," they told her, "and we will stand back of you and do whatever you want done, but you will have to be the leader. . . . You will have to come to the legislature."[22]

Bacon had never anticipated direct involvement in the legislative process and was taken aback by the committee's demand. "I saw myself," she remembered a few years later, "with horror, a married woman with a 'career.' I saw my family, whom I had never left except for a few days, suffering for my care; . . . my husband, with a southern man's ideas of such things, his indulgence already strained. I saw my friends, disgusted at such publicity. I saw enemies, frowns,—brickbats!" She remonstrated that she had never seen a legislature in action, did not know what to do, and wanted no honor for herself. The committee members stood firm, however, and after a few moments' reflection Bacon agreed to their request. She "took the leap," she recalled, "with the desperate deliberation of a suicide who jumps into the icy water."[23]

❖

The tenement bill (a more exact term than "housing bill," since it proposed to regulate only multi-family residences, not all houses) was introduced in both chambers of the General Assembly on January 13, 1909, and assigned to the health committee of each house.[24] In Evansville Bacon received the "dread summons" and hurried north by train, fearful of "doing the wrong thing, that would wreck the whole business." A joint meeting of the House and Senate health committees had been arranged for the evening of January 19, and Bacon was the principal speaker. Though hardly a novice at public address by this time, her fear of "doing the wrong thing" was not alleviated by the circumstances of this legislative hearing: some in her audience were "haggard and sleepy from a late caucus of the night before" while others came and went "with a slight confusion in the room." She later wrote: "I had thought to speak with some of the fire that burned within me, but my sentences seemed to me as if just taken out of an ice box." This self-assessment was clearly too modest. The next day a reporter from her hometown described her hour-long presentation as "eloquent," and an Indianapolis journalist noted that she "impressed the committee members as an advocate thoroughly conversant with the tenement-house question in Indiana."[25]

Bacon was followed by Dunn, who served as spokesman for a contingent from the Indianapolis Commercial Club. Dr. Eugene Buehler, secretary of the Indianapolis Board of Health, also testified, telling of the "futile attempts to compel landlords to remedy evils in rooms and houses kept for lodging purposes." As the hearing concluded, Bacon recalled, "every one woke up, and, to my surprise, the meeting ended in enthusiasm, and we were given the assurance that both committees would report favourably on the bill."[26]

Two days later Bacon had an opportunity to sway more than just a legislative committee: she was accorded the rare privilege of addressing a joint session of the General Assembly. Describing her investigations of the homes of the poor, she "asked the Representatives if they would not make these homes fit for human beings to live in." The *Indianapolis Star* reported that she "made her argument in a convincing way, pointing out to the members that it was a problem that came home to all of them." With the heartfelt environmental determinism so common among Progressive-era social reformers, she argued that "tenement houses . . . produced disease and criminals and forced young girls into the streets because of the fact that they could not entertain at home. These unfortunates were elbow companions with the children of the members [of the General Assembly] and others in the same class of life."[27]

While her address to the joint session ensured that virtually every legislator had his consciousness raised on the issue of tenement reform, the less ceremonial lobbying efforts engaged in by Bacon and her supporters probably had more telling effect. Before leaving Evansville for the capital she had secured photographs of some of the Pocket City's worst tenements, mounted them on cards, and added "sketches and suggestive titles" on the margins. They made "a very striking set of posters," Bacon thought, and she hung them on a line in the corridor of the State House.[28] Her "entire days were spent at the state house" button-holing members, explaining the bill to them, and showing her photographic display. When the legislators were busy, she talked with their wives. But she took care, as she put it, "to avoid sentimentality, and to stick to the practical issues, in a practical way, having ready all the business arguments in favour of the law."[29]

Although Bacon possessed the technical expertise to explain the complex bill and was quickly understood to be an "ambassador of the poor" with no personal stake in the tenement bill, she had no background in legislative maneuvering. She needed help, she knew it, and she freely acknowledged such assistance in her memoirs. Besides the sponsors of the bill, Republican Ezra Mattingly in the Senate and Democrat Homer L. McGinnis in the House, she leaned heavily on the abilities and encouragement of Senator Cox, Representative J. Delbert Foor (D–Vigo County), and their wives. Foor, who was a physician, and Cox were on the health committees of their respective chambers and supported the bill both in committee and on the floor. Republican Senator William R. Wood, who was president pro tem in 1909, and Representative Jesse Eschbach, Republican minority leader in the House, were both recruited to the cause.[30]

The Indianapolis Commercial Club, of course, worked energeti-

*"Cheese Hill" tenement in Evansville. Bacon, Beauty for Ashes;
photograph courtesy Indiana Historical Society, C8147*

cally for passage. In early March the club's legislative committee reported to the directors that "the active interest we have been taking in
the . . . 'Housing Bill' is having effect." Also working behind the scenes
was the secretary of the State Board of Health, Dr. Hurty. Bacon had
originally contacted him during her letter writing campaign the previous summer (Hurty was also a member of the Indianapolis Commercial
Club), and the two continued to correspond as the legislative session
approached. Hurty was an old hand at dealing with the General Assembly (he had held his position since 1896) and made a number of practical suggestions. In addition, he arranged to convey an article by Bacon
explaining the background and necessity of the proposed law to an
agent of the American Press Association, which distributed typeset
copies to member newspapers throughout the state. And during the
Assembly session, when Hurty wrote letters detailing the measures
"bearing upon the public health and morals of the people . . . in which

the State Board of Health is deeply interested," he never failed to mention the tenement bill.[31]

Following the joint meeting of the House and Senate health committees and Bacon's address to the joint session, the two bills began to wend their separate ways through the legislative process. The Senate bill (S.B. 51), when taken up for final action in early February, was amended to apply only to cities of 50,000 or more population. Senator Franklin Kistler (D–Cass and Pulaski counties), who offered the amendment, argued that smaller cities should not be asked to meet the requirements of the statute. "He said," reported the *Indianapolis News*, "that the matter was an experiment, and if the larger cities wanted a law of the kind, he would help them get it, but he stood opposed to any move to saddle the bill on the smaller cities of the State." Senators Cox and Mattingly opposed the Kistler amendment, the latter arguing that the bill should be passed as it stood since it was intended to protect "poor people all over the State who were forced to live in tenement houses." The amendment was approved by a vote of 30–18, however, and the bill then went on to final passage by a margin of 37–6.[32]

In the lower chamber, H.B. 3 was read a second time on January 26 and brought up as a special order of business on January 29. At this point several amendments were offered, and the bill, with all pending amendments, was recommitted to the health committee. It surfaced again before the full House on February 4, when it was considered section by section as amended in committee. The *News* reported that Bacon "trembled for the fate of her bill and flitted from member to member, as opposition showed itself. As action advanced and section by section the amendments were adopted unanimously, her spirits rose." On February 8 the committee report, with all pending amendments, was adopted and ordered engrossed, and one week later the bill came up for final consideration. Representative Charles Gauss, a Democrat from Marion County, made the only speech in opposition to the measure, reportedly arguing that "if the people of the state kept on being 'so nice' they would cease to live for lack of microbes to disturb them, an argument built upon the theory that a reasonable number of fleas is good for a dog." A sufficient number of House members were apparently "nice" enough since the bill was approved by a vote of 62–27.[33]

The House bill was introduced in the Senate the next day and the health committee quickly reported it out with a "do pass" recommendation. Although passed by the House and endorsed by the relevant Senate committee, passage was by no means assured: as time went on opposition became more organized. Hurty had commented in a letter written at the end of January that "this good bill has met with rough sledding, and I do not know why, unless it is because some *interests* are opposed to it." Such "interests" were not hard to identify, as Hurty surely knew, and an Evansville reporter put the case more baldly: "A real estate and landlord's lobby has fought the bill from the start."[34]

Bacon quickly discovered the same thing. She had gone home during a brief lull in the proceedings and upon returning to the capital "found that enemies had been busy. Letters had been pouring in, and a horde of landlords had come in my absence . . . stirring up opposition and sowing doubts." She later recounted, without naming names, that some of the strongest opposition to the bill "came from men, in both houses, who owned tenements, or whose brothers, cousins or clients owned them." Many of the opponents, she noted, "did not even plead the common cause of landlords. It was, 'My house.' 'It will cost *me*.'" There was also opposition from some concerned with the specter of government "paternalism" and from what Bacon described as "little towns, that were not willing to yield even so much space on their building lots as New York City gives!"[35]

At this crucial juncture the bill received "lobbying" assistance from an unexpected source—William Jennings Bryan. The "Great Commoner," a three-time Democratic presidential nominee, visited Indianapolis on February 26, and it was arranged that he should address the legislature. Seizing the opportunity, Bacon wangled a brief interview with Bryan, quickly explained the situation, and asked if housing reform could be included among the topics of his speech. Bryan's reply was noncommittal. In the course of his address to a joint session of the General Assembly, however, he indeed found time to "call attention to laws that are being made necessary for the better homes of the poor" and to warn the legislators that if they ignored the issue "growing sentiment will find some way of filling this hall with people who will respond to this demand of a higher intelligence and of an awakened conscience."[36]

The day following Bryan's address the Senate took up H.B. 3 for final consideration. This turned out to be a virtual replay of Senate action on S.B. 51 three weeks earlier. Senator Kistler began the proceedings by moving an amendment that would make the bill applicable only in cities with a population of 59,000 or more (that is, Indianapolis and Evansville). Mattingly once again objected, arguing that "the small cities and towns are just as filthy and congested" as the state's two largest cities. But Senator Edgar Kling (R–Howard and Miami counties), referring to the bill as an experiment, suggested that the scope of the measure could be expanded during the next legislative session if such action then seemed warranted. In the end the Kistler amendment passed 29–13.[37]

Then, in a bit of legislative sleight of hand, Democratic Senator Samuel Royse of Clay and Vigo counties moved to amend the House bill by deleting everything after the first section and substituting the language of S.B. 51 as it had passed the Senate on February 4. This maneuver was promptly accepted, and, so amended, the bill was ready for a final vote. The outcome remained in doubt until the last moments. When the roll was called, there was a deadlock: 25 "aye," 20 "no," with 26 needed for a constitutional majority. Just as the doorkeepers were about to be instructed to locate absent members, Senator Robert Proctor (D-Elkhart) announced that, to expedite matters, he would change his "no" to an "aye." Two days later the House concurred in the Senate amendments, and on March 3 Governor Thomas Riley Marshall signed the measure.[38]

"LAW FRAMED BY MRS. BACON NOW ON BOOKS" read the *Evansville Press* headline the next day. "Philanthropists and social workers," the paper reported, "believe that the moral effect of Mrs. Bacon's work will be very great, as it will be the first time in any western state, that the state has assumed the right to regulate housing conditions as a matter of public health and safety." During the General Assembly session, in fact, social welfare advocates in several other states, including Michigan and Minnesota, had written for copies of the bill. Bacon's draft, observed another Evansville newspaper, had "attained a wide celebrity."[39]

In early February, when her proposed law was facing a raft of amendments in both houses of the legislature, Bacon was heard to remark: "Better a half loaf than none." In 1909 that is precisely what she got. The law applied only to tenement, lodging, and apartment houses, not to all residential dwellings; many minor, technical features of the original proposal were stricken out; and enforcement of the law was left to local health boards instead of the State Board of Health. Finally, and most disappointingly, the law affected only the state's two largest cities. But it was a beginning—and the expectation was that a future General Assembly would broaden the law's applicability. "It is not intended," Bacon reportedly said following the law's approval, "to be all that would be desired to secure good housing but only the first step to prevent bad housing."[40]

As she prepared for the journey home, packing as souvenirs some worn and marked copies of her bill, Bacon was approached by a holdover senator (one who would serve two years hence) who expressed

The Albion Apartments. Robert G. Barrows

hope that she would return for the next session. "Oh, thank you," she later remembered saying, "but I'm through now, and I never expect to come again.[41]

Upon her return to Evansville, Bacon spent some time during the spring and summer of 1909 working to create the office of building inspector in her home town. Her efforts on behalf of tenement reform were recognized locally when an Evansville industrialist and philanthropist, A. C. Rosencranz, announced in July that he planned to name his proposed model apartment block the Albion Apartments in her honor. Bacon "expressed delight" when informed of this accolade.[42] Then late that fall, in stark contrast to the many gratifying events that had taken place during the year, she and her family suffered from the shock and sorrow occasioned by the sudden death, at age 20, of her eldest daughter.

*Margaret Gibson Bacon (b. 1889), the Bacons' eldest daughter, who died
unexpectedly at age 20. Courtesy Joy Bacon Witwer*

Margaret Gibson Bacon had been born in September 1889, the year
following her parents' marriage. She attended Evansville public schools
and, as we have seen, assisted her mother with the Flower Mission work.
Following graduation from high school "with honor" in 1907, she spent
a year at Mt. Vernon Seminary, a finishing school in Washington, D.C.
She seems to have been an especially intelligent and vivacious young
woman. Her sister Joy remembered her as "beautiful and popular and
smart, and absolute perfection in everything." An Evansville newspaper eulogized her as a "social favorite" with a "vivid personality and
brilliant mind." In mid-November 1909, she traveled to El Paso, Texas,

to serve as a bridesmaid for one of her friends from the seminary. On the eve of the wedding she was suddenly stricken with a previously undiagnosed (and probably congenital) heart ailment and died within hours.[43]

For some months thereafter Bacon was unable to continue with outside activities. But as winter gave way to spring she "began to feel a craving for work, employment, something to force my mind to new channels." At first this need was met by work with the various Evansville charitable organizations with which she was associated. Housing reform was never far from her mind, however, and she and Hilary hosted Jacob Riis when he visited the city in January 1910 and lectured at Trinity Methodist on "The Battle with the Slums." Soon thereafter Bacon found herself faced with "a challenge to all my powers" as the 1909 law came under attack from various quarters.[44]

The measure's constitutionality had been questioned almost immediately. A test case filed in Marion County concerned a "very handsome" Indianapolis flat "that failed to conform to the law in some slight particular." The case dragged on for some time, but eventually the legality of the statute was upheld. A potentially more serious challenge came from various real estate men and architects in Evansville and Indianapolis who had discovered what they perceived to be negative implications (especially financial) for themselves in the tenement law. As early as July 1909 they had approached the Civic Improvement Commission (an arm of the Indianapolis Commercial Club) with their concerns, and that body had appointed a tenement house committee "to investigate the merits of this law in all particulars."[45]

The committee pursued its investigations over the course of the next year, culminating with a meeting of the full Civic Improvement Commission in June 1910. William K. Eldridge, an architect and member of the tenement house committee, read a lengthy paper criticizing the law. He was at pains to point out that he was not "attacking the principle upon which [the tenement law] is founded or the motives of those who framed it." Indeed, he maintained that reputable architects, property owners, and real estate dealers "feel in hearty sympathy with the objects and aims of the law, and would aid in its enforcement *if properly drawn.*" Following Eldridge's presentation the commission moved to appoint a committee (in effect, to reappoint the tenement house committee) "for the purpose of studying the law with a view to protecting it in all its features which eventually would be regarded as right."[46]

Bacon, who was no doubt kept apprised of these developments by her friends in Indianapolis, naturally felt that the 1909 law was properly drawn and that any changes should be for the purpose of broadening and strengthening the measure. Thus, she thought "the authors of the proposed bill should have demonstrated to them just what the effect of every change would be." She concluded that "there was no one in the United States who could do that with such authority and conclusiveness as could Mr. Lawrence Veiller."[47]

Veiller, as noted previously, had authored the New York State Tenement House Law of 1901; he was also instrumental in founding the National Housing Association (which he was then serving as secretary) and had years of experience shepherding legislation through the New York Assembly. He had just published two important books on housing reform when he responded to Bacon's plea for assistance. Veiller arrived in Indianapolis in early September 1910 and, as Bacon put it, the Commercial Club "decreed a banquet, in Mr. Veiller's honour, and mine," to which were invited both the friends of housing reform and "the framers of the proposed dangerous bill, so that we might cement our purposes with patés and coffee, and friendly discussion."[48]

The banquet was an impressive affair. The entire membership of the Civic Improvement Commission was present, as well as eight of the Commercial Club's directors. Among the many guests were veterans of the 1909 campaign (Cox, Hurty, Grout); the Indianapolis building inspector, Thomas Winterrowd; the secretary of the Indianapolis Board of Health, Dr. Charles S. Woods; and several architects, including Eldridge. Following a brief talk by Bacon, in which she summarized the struggle for the 1909 law, Veiller made the principal address and discussed the "symptoms, causes, and remedies" of bad housing. Then Eldridge and another architect "set forth what they termed the defects in the present law, showing where in their opinion the law should be strengthened." At Veiller's suggestion a committee of five was appointed (Cox, Grout, Eldridge, Winterrowd, Thomas A. White) to meet with him and Bacon the next day "to discuss the law fully and make suggestions for changes that will be for the betterment of all." The meeting adjourned following a "rising vote of thanks" to Bacon and Veiller.[49]

Bacon described the following day's meeting, attended by several architects and builders as well as herself, Veiller, and the tenement house committee, as an "extended session" at which the participants "mowed, reaped, shocked, threshed, ground, sifted, baked, masticated and digested every grain of the proposed bill." At the conclusion of the discussion Veiller "gathered up the views of the company, and took them back to New York, to reduce the chaos to order."[50]

There matters stood until early January 1911 when Veiller returned to Indianapolis with the draft of a proposed new law. Cox, who chaired the Civic Improvement Commission's tenement committee, called together all those who had an interest in the bill. Those responding included lawyers, doctors, real estate men, bankers, charity workers, and representatives of the Indianapolis and state architects' associations. The meetings lasted for several days as Veiller patiently explained each section and drew diagrams to show what the results would be if certain dimensions were changed or certain restrictions were modified. In a speech the next year Bacon described the experience as "the most continuous and exhausting mental strain I ever went through." Finally, however, "no one could ask any more questions, and we all shook hands and promised to work together for the bill we had agreed upon, and Mr. Veiller returned to New York."[51]

And Bacon, her prediction at the end of the 1909 session notwithstanding, reluctantly returned to the General Assembly. She feared that a reprise of her 1909 efforts "would give me the savour of a professional lobbyist, or a 'crank.'" Even sixteen years later the things that she remembered of her forays to the legislature were "the exhausting work, the anxiety, the milling crowds, the apathy to be overcome, the heartsick times of suspense." But she could not resist the opportunity to try for her goal of a statewide law. Moreover, those architects who had joined the movement for Hoosier housing reform expected her to help "remedy the shortcomings of the law of 1909 which had been caused by hasty amendments." Finally, she had reasonable expectations of success, telling the *Evansville Journal-News* that she did not know "a single force that will operate against my bill except selfish wealth."[52]

Although she hoped to have the bill introduced quickly, "some of the parties to it began to haggle over little points," and the measure (H.B. 578) was not dropped into the hopper until February 14.[53] The late introduction of the proposed law, as well as its bulk (at ninety-nine sections, the second longest bill introduced in the House that year), almost proved to be its immediate undoing. The *Indianapolis Star* reported on February 16 that the health committee, to which the bill had been referred, recommended indefinite postponement since there was not enough time left to consider such a complicated piece of legislation. Bacon and her supporters swung into action immediately; they "convinced the committee members that there was no use shelving it because the time was short, [and] saw to it that it was reported out." Reversing field literally overnight, the committee reported the bill on February 17 with a "do pass" recommendation.[54]

On February 22 the *Star* carried a letter that Cox had written and sent to every member of the House of Representatives. In it he reviewed the history of the "pioneer measure" of 1909, explained the objections that architects and builders had raised against the law, and detailed the subsequent efforts that had been made to "reach an agreement upon a bill that would remove all criticism and also preserve the benefits sought in such a law." Passage of H.B. 578, he argued, would "clear up matters of confusion and . . . [provide] as good a law from the standpoint of health and morals as the former law." Cox closed with the hope that the bill might be approved "without any serious modifications of any of the technical parts, which the official committee of the architects' association says are well prepared."[55]

Whether Cox's letter actually changed any votes is impossible to know, but it certainly seems to have had an effect. The same morning that his missive was published in the *Star* the House took up the bill under suspension of the rules, made one minor amendment, and passed the measure, without debate, by the stunning vote of 82 to 2. Bacon later recorded that "it was all over in five minutes, before I hardly realised what they were doing, and fairly took my breath." The Indianapolis press thought the achievement no less remarkable, one paper referring to the seeming "insurmountable lot of difficulties" the bill faced and calling its passage in the lower chamber a "monument" to Bacon's "indefatigable work."[56]

With such overwhelming support in the House it appeared, in the words of the *Evansville Journal-News,* "fairly certain that it will go through the Senate with flying colors." The bill was introduced in the upper house on February 24, referred to committee, reported back favorably the next day, and read for a second time on February 27. Then, as Bacon put it, the bill "stuck fast" in the face of "the same vicious lobby . . . both inside and out of the legislature" that had opposed the measure two years earlier.[57] Over the course of the next week the bill was brought up for third reading on several occasions, but each time opponents managed to have it postponed. Finally Republican Senator Edgar Durre of Evansville, who was managing the bill for Bacon and her supporters, began "conducting an obstructive policy as a rebuke to the senate . . . for its persistent disregard of the poor and ill-housed." He began questioning the merits of every measure brought up for passage and demanding a roll call in every possible situation. When his colleagues asked him to desist, fearing that their pet measures would not have time for consideration, he replied: "You refused to hear me when I was asking your attention for a bill in which there was nothing for me personally, and now I do not propose to yield to you on measures of local importance."[58]

The staunchest foe of the bill was Senator Levi Harlan (D–Marion County), who argued that the measure should be titled "a bill raising the rent of poor people." "It was a bill also in the interest of contractors, he said, and would drive capital out of the rental business, and prevent further investments along this line." (An Evansville paper observed that Harlan "rents, Mrs. Bacon is told, some of the worst tenements in Indianapolis.")[59] Senator Stephen Powers, a Steuben County Democrat, also spoke against the bill and, in the words of a reporter, "rung in the old-fashioned log house where he was born, and the old-fashioned log schoolhouse where he was educated."[60]

The bill was finally handed down for third reading on March 6, the last day of the session. The proceedings are best described by Bacon herself:

> It was fought off till the night session. That night they could not withstand the pressure, and it came to a vote. Two of our men were sick, one was absent, members who didn't want to offend the party leader ran and hid in the cloak rooms. And yet the vote showed 26 to 17 in our favor. . . . We hurried our bill to the engrossing room, so as to have a copy for the Governor to sign. The senators crowded around to congratulate me. "I'm afraid to take your congratulations," I said, "till the vote is announced." My fears were well grounded. Our enemies stood at the Lieutenant Governor's elbow, and kept him from announcing the vote for an hour, till they could scour the halls and cloak rooms, and get another vote. Finally they got one man to change his vote, and our victory was stolen from us, the last hour of the last night of the session. We asked for the roll, but they said the clerk had stolen the roll, too."[61]

The *Indianapolis Star* headlined its story "HARLAN TRIUMPHS OVER FRAIL WOMAN," and an editorial in the *Evansville Journal-News* suggested that "Infloonces Were at Work." The latter paper blamed the bill's defeat on "wealthy architects, wealthier apartment house owners, monied people who go to Florida in the winter and Bar Harbor [Maine] in the summer on the fruits of $4-a-month rooms in decayed mansions on ash-covered streets. . . . The Democrats," concluded Bacon's hometown paper, "had the power. And the 'infloonces' had the ear of the Democrats." This may have been merely partisan sniping, or support for a native daughter, but analysis of the vote supports the contention. Of the 25 "aye" votes in the Senate, 19 were cast by Republicans; of the 18 "no" votes, 17 were cast by Democrats.[62]

For Bacon "there was nothing to do but to be game, nothing to say but 'thank you,' and 'good-bye.'" She left the capital the following day but, unlike two years earlier, she did not tell anyone that she did not expect to come again. As she rode the train back to Evansville, reading the *Star*'s account of the previous night's events, she "thought of the ultimate effect of this defeat upon the housing movement throughout the state" and judged that it might "give just the touch of sympathy and interest the cause needed." The newspapers had called passage of the bill in the House a "monument" to her efforts. Upon that monument, she reflected, the Senate had written: "Here lies the body of the Tenement Bill, slain March 1911." She resolved to add a second line: "Awaiting the resurrection."[63]

Four

The Homes of Indiana

The biennium between the 1911 and 1913 sessions of the General Assembly was a period of intense activity for Bacon. Her early efforts on behalf of housing reform had been conducted principally (though never exclusively) by means of extensive correspondence. By 1911, however, she was an experienced, increasingly polished public speaker with a growing regional, even national, reputation, and she was much in demand for presentations before various conventions, conferences, and chautauquas. In the months after the bitter defeat of 1911 she used her speaking engagements, as well as her membership in several voluntary associations, to advance the cause closest to her heart. So successful was her campaign that when Bacon and her supporters returned to the legislature in 1913 they "had the help of prominent men all over the state, . . . men of all parties, and women of all beliefs."[1]

Among the various organizations with which she became affiliated, the most important was perhaps the Indiana Federation of Clubs. This statewide federation, composed of women's clubs in virtually every community, became very active in the housing reform movement. This support was indicative of a national trend among many women's organizations during the early twentieth century: a shift from an emphasis on "culture" to a greater concern for "municipal housekeeping." In 1912 Mrs. T. J. Bowlker, president of the Women's Municipal League of Boston, used the pages of the journal *American City* to call on women to "learn to make of their cities great community homes for all the people." The next year, observing the "yeoman work" done by many state federations of women's clubs in civics, civil service, and sanitation, another writer reflected that "it seems incredible that any one can still be found who thinks of this great force for public service as 'Ladies Culture Clubs.'" A few years earlier Ida Husted Harper, a leader in the movement for women's suffrage, noted that a significant number of women had "found that home and children are but the center of an ever-widening circumference which included the whole municipality"; giving women the vote was only logical and proper, she argued, since there was "scarcely a locality in which the women are not becoming recognized public factors."[2]

These developments were, at one level, merely a logical outgrowth of the Progressive-era ethos and the inculcation of a widespread reform impulse that cut across the gender line. But they also highlight the vitally important role of women's voluntary associations as well as the evolution of such organizations in response to societal conditions and their members' needs. As historian Anne Firor Scott observes, although there had been a gradual opening of the professions to women during the latter years of the nineteenth century and the early years of the twentieth, "opportunities for the exercise of ability and ambition, especially for married women, were still comparatively few. Able, ambitious women gravitated to voluntary associations where they could create impressive careers." But Scott also notes that the published statements of the leaders of these associations regarding their motives "reflect the prevailing socialization: since women were expected to be good mothers, and to be compassionate and moral, these qualities were emphasized." As Karen Blair put it in her pathbreaking study of the women's club movement during the Gilded Age and Progressive era, such women engaged in a "struggle to leave the confines of the home without abandoning domestic values." Thus the salience of the term "municipal housekeeping," which, in Anne Scott's words, "conferred an air of respectability upon what might otherwise have been considered unseemly public or political activity."[3]

These national trends were replicated in Indiana, although somewhat later than in leading progressive states such as Wisconsin. Barbara Springer, the closest student of Hoosier women in the early twentieth century, suggests that they were "a bit slower than many of their contemporaries in consolidating their organizations and taking an interest in reform." The Indiana Federation of Clubs (IFC), for example, traced its history only to the turn of the century. As early as 1904, however, an Indianapolis newspaper reported that club women were "awakening to the consciousness of their own power and the forcefulness of organized effort." And Springer clearly documents that, like their sisters in other states, Indiana club women soon were "creating clubs whose purpose was not personal education, but the promotion of philanthropy and reform." Hoosier women retained "conventional ideas about the importance of home and family" but like their counterparts elsewhere who became involved in municipal housekeeping they "expanded domesticity to include their communities, state, and nation."[4]

Bacon's first association with the IFC was in October 1910, when she addressed their annual convention on "The Housing Problem of Indiana."[5] The following June she journeyed to Winona Lake to speak to a summer session, and there, she later recalled, "the Federation opened its arms to me and took me in." Bacon noted that she had "never had time to be a club woman, and this first close view of them was a revelation." She was impressed with the group's dignity and "parliamentary precision," with the earnestness of the members' deliberations and the absence of "small talk or chatter." And when she told them "A Tale of the Tenements" the audience "sat hushed for a moment" and then "rose and pledged support to the housing movement."[6]

The key meeting, however, was the IFC's annual convention held at Indianapolis in October 1911. In an address titled "Women, the Legislature and the Homes of Indiana," Bacon told the story of the legislative defeat suffered the previous winter and asked for the federation's support of future housing reform efforts. She suggested, moreover, that the IFC adopt "The Homes of Indiana" as its slogan. The federation members not only agreed to these requests, they went one step further: they created a standing housing committee and made Bacon its chair. In her words: "It became my part, thereafter, to explain the need and nature of housing reform to the clubs of the state. And so, up and down, from the Ohio to the great lake I went, and back and forth across our state, telling the story of 'The Homes of Indiana.'"[7]

In the fall of 1911 Bacon also helped to form the Indiana Housing Association, the first such state-level group in the country. Modeled after the National Housing Association (of which Bacon was by this time a director), the state group's primary objective was: "To protect and foster the Homes of Indiana by encouraging right housing conditions, and by helping to eliminate those unfit, unsafe and unsanitary conditions which are a menace to morals, health, safety and comfort." The principal officers were all veterans of the 1909 and 1911 legislative campaigns.[8]

Throughout 1912, from one end of the state to the other, Bacon carried the message, serving now not just as a self-appointed spokeswoman but as a representative of the IFC and the Indiana Housing Association. Reporting on the activities of the IFC's housing committee in the fall of 1912 she noted that she had made addresses in thirteen Indiana cities and towns during the previous year, had conducted tours and investigations in nine cities, and had spoken to several institutes sponsored by the State Board of Health. Since the goal remained a *statewide* law, her audiences were not just in the major cities but also in "those quaint old sleepy towns in our state that are as beautiful as bits of Arcady." She felt that it was "almost cruel to wound those gentle hearts with the story I had to bring, but they wanted to know of life in the world outside . . . [and] they had to know, so that their representative should be instructed how to vote properly." Still, it was "a sad business . . . to go about the state, thrusting thorns into tender hearts. 'No one can look at me without thinking of slums,' [she] told them, 'and I almost feel as if my name is Bill, from the constant references to it.'"[9]

In October Bacon once again addressed the IFC annual convention, speaking about "The Housing Problem" and making what she called "my last appeal before the battle is on"—a reference to the next legislative session. She observed that during the past year she and other members of the housing committee had received numerous letters saying, in effect, "we want you to tell us how to help, and what to answer to the questions that we are asked." In this talk Bacon attempted to provide those answers, and she pulled out all her rhetorical and metaphorical stops while doing so. She was able, however, to aid her audience by reducing the complex subject to its essentials:

> The fundamental, vital principle of housing reform is, that every house that is habited shall be sanitary, fit and safe for habitation. Isn't that simple? Who could ask less, who, for shame, could be willing to grant less—that our houses should be sanitary? That they shall not kill the people who rent them, nor make them sick.

And, shrewdly, she tied her topic to other, more traditional, areas of IFC interest and argued that decent housing was a prerequisite to dealing with those other concerns. Referring to the federation's committee on domestic science, for example, she asked "what could domestic science do in these homes, unless housing reform goes ahead of it? How can you teach people to scrub and wash, until they have water? How can you teach them to ventilate until they have windows? . . . And how can you teach the principles of sanitation when what is needed is really to pull the place down, and dig it up, and disinfect the hole where it stood?"[10]

Nor were all of Bacon's addresses to Hoosier audiences. In December she traveled to Philadelphia to speak at the National Housing Association's second annual conference on the topic "Regulation by Law." In this paean to restrictive legislation as an answer to housing problems she maintained that even though more and more people were "coming over to fresh air and sanitation" compulsory standards were still essential. This was the case because:

> There are not enough philanthropists to the square mile.
> Not all the unselfish are wealthy.
> Not all the wealthy are wise.
> Not all builders will refuse to construct houses with dark
> rooms,—"on the contrary."

Thus, the use of the state's "police power" was unavoidable. "In no other way," she argued, "can we maintain our standards than by having them nailed to a pole, and planting that pole so high that it cannot be pulled down, upon the topmost turret of a granite fortress of the law." In the course of this address she also observed that the first lesson learned by "chaperones of a housing bill" is that "legislation is a game of chance; that is, as the pawnbroker's three golden balls are said to indicate, it is two to one that you won't get out what you put in." With that thought in mind, the 1913 session of the General Assembly loomed ahead.[11]

In 1909 the movement for a statewide housing law in Indiana had been little more than a somewhat idiosyncratic, one-woman campaign. But by New Year's Day 1913 a well-organized, politically sophisticated coalition had emerged, and the various elements of that coalition stepped up their activity in the days and weeks immediately preceding introduction of housing legislation for the third time. The Indiana Housing Association, in conjunction with the state's charity organizations, designated January 5 as "Housing Sunday." Charities secretaries distributed a letter from Bacon "To the Pastors" asking that one session of their church services that day be devoted to consideration of the condition of the poor in their city. Enclosed with this letter was a four-part sermonette containing facts and arguments for better housing, organized so that a pastor might substitute his own comments in place of any part.[12]

Dr. Hurty remained committed to the proposed legislation and threw the influence of the State Board of Health behind it. At the board's quarterly meeting on January 10, he urged the members to adopt a resolution "endorsing and supporting the Housing Bill." He noted that he had "examined [the bill] carefully and believe it is all right in every particular" and "certainly has a good deal to do with public health." The board not only agreed to support the measure but ordered Hurty to "have printed a circular concerning the housing problem, the same to be properly distributed in order to further the housing bill."[13]

Various voluntary associations also lined up behind the proposed law. The Domestic Science Club of Evansville, for example, "composed of fifty women, who have made a careful study of sanitation and home making," sent letters of support to their legislators. In Indianapolis a mass meeting was called at the Propylaeum (headquarters for many women's organizations in the capital city) to discuss the housing bill. Bacon, the principal speaker, showed stereopticon views of blighted housing taken in several cities. She was joined by the dean of the Indiana University School of Medicine, an assistant secretary of the State Board of Health, and the presidents of the Indiana Housing Association (Cox), the Woman's Department Club, and the Indiana Federation of Clubs.[14]

Bacon also sought support from influential politicians outside the General Assembly. An important ally was gained when Governor Samuel Ralston declared himself in favor of the tenement bill. Bacon arranged an audience with the governor and took with her the probation officer of Lake County, who described living conditions among the immigrant homes in her district. That evening, addressing a meeting of the YMCA state executive committee called to discuss the association's work among young men and boys, Ralston digressed from his prepared remarks and spoke about young women as well. Alluding to the meeting with Bacon and her supporters, the governor "expressed himself as emphatically in favor of changing housing conditions which tend to retard the moral advancement of young women." Bacon observed that the effect of this speech, "which was in all of the papers, was all we could have asked."[15]

Among the state's major political leaders, there was only one whom Bacon had never met—"Mr. Democracy," Thomas Taggart. When members of both parties recommended that he be consulted, her husband arranged for a brief interview with the former chairman of the Democratic national committee. She discovered, to her surprise, that Taggart was well informed on the history and provisions of the tenement law. One student of the era has described the Democratic boss as a man whose "position on any particular issue, whether for or against a reform, was always a matter of practical politics, not ideology," and his discussion with Bacon supports that assessment. His only question when she used the phrase, "We are asking for this law," was "Who are 'we'?" Bacon enumerated the many individuals and organizations supporting the bill, and Taggart promised to give what assistance he could.[16]

Senate Bill 118, a virtual replica of the 1911 proposal, was introduced on January 21 by Senator Charles B. Clarke (D-Marion County) and reported out of committee in just three days with a "do pass" recommendation.[17] Bacon later recalled that "there was really quite a fight" when the bill came up for final consideration in the Senate on February 3, "enough to rally all our friends to the defence, and call out all our artillery of oratory." The press concurred: an Evansville reporter called the debate "two hours of the hardest fighting of the session," and an Indianapolis paper described it as "a vigorous effort on the part of a hostile minority . . . to pull the teeth of the measure."[18]

Opponents of the proposal pursued two lines of resistance. Senator Franklin Kattman, a Democrat from Brazil, Clay County, moved to amend the bill so that the law would apply only in those communities in which the common council enacted a similar ordinance. Such a provision would, in effect, have permitted any city to veto the law within its corporate boundaries. The proposal "raised a storm of debate," and eventually the motion failed. Senator Kistler, whose home town was Logansport, then proposed that the law not apply to those cities with a population of less than 20,000 at the preceding census. When that motion failed, he tried again with a figure of 19,100 and was again defeated. Although he was obviously operating purely on the basis of local interest (Logansport's population at the 1910 census had been 19,050), Kistler appealed to "party"—arguing that a cardinal tenet of Democracy (that is, the Democratic party) was home rule. Clarke replied that the quality of his Democracy was as good as any man's, "but that he believed in humanity as well and the slightest thought should convince any man that tuberculosis can not be stamped out of the state if Indianapolis and Evansville [the only cities affected by the 1909 law] were to enact drastic tenement house laws while Brazil and Logansport should be permitted to retain disease-breeding tenements." Republican Senator Oscar Ratts, representing Lawrence, Martin, and Orange counties, supported Clarke by observing that no "locality has the right to start a sore on humanity and let it run. This is a social matter," he argued. "If it is good for one place it is good for another."[19]

Following defeat of the proposed amendments by Kattman and

Kistler, several minor changes "not affecting the general force or tenor of the bill" were adopted. One amendment was accepted, however, that did substantially limit the scope of the bill. This was a "grandfather clause" limiting the law to coverage of *new* tenements but not buildings erected prior to the passage of the act. Following this compromise the bill passed by a vote of 36–9. Bacon and her friends found themselves "congratulating ourselves over a rousing victory—there, on that same old ghost-haunted battle ground of other days!" But the battle was not yet over; they still "had to thread the mazes that led to the other House."[20]

The bill was handed down in the lower chamber on February 4 and referred to committee. Two days later, in a column entitled "Our Legislature as Seen by the Outstate Editors," the *Indianapolis News* quoted the *Lafayette Courier*: "The housing bill, which has passed the senate, was an unlooked for piece of progressivism. If the interests which it affects had seen it coming they would have been exceedingly busy. As it is, the house will be literally beseiged [sic] not to pass it." Bacon herself reflected something of a siege mentality as "news poured in . . . from every side of the doings of the opposition." She became especially fearful when the bill stuck in the House committee. At the final hearing a large group of "well known and respected business men" appeared with three typewritten pages of objections. At Bacon's urging they agreed to a separate meeting with her and the Indianapolis building inspector in an attempt to resolve the impasse. Most of the objections were found to be "the result of misinterpretation, or misunderstanding of the effect of certain provisions." In the end there were only three points of contention, and Bacon and her allies considered these relatively minor. They "yielded cheerfully" and sent the agreed upon amendments to the committee for inclusion.[21]

But still the measure languished in committee. In an effort to get it reported out for consideration by the full House, Bacon orchestrated one final, massive lobbying effort. On February 14 the *Indianapolis News* published her lengthy letter entitled "The Housing Bill." She began by enumerating several objections that had been raised against the measure and then, one by one, proceeded to refute each argument. She noted that the legislation, if enacted, "does not mean that anything must be provided which decency does not demand. . . . Simply light and air, water, drainage, provision for waste and a degree of privacy, without which decency is difficult and home life is impossible." But it was not, she stressed, simply a matter of decency or starry-eyed humanitarianism. "Against the great cost [to] the state in caring for crime and de-

Tenement family pictured in Beauty for Ashes: *"Heredity and environment both doing their worst. Mother and two children tuberculous. One child feeble-minded." Bacon,* Beauty for Ashes; *photograph courtesy Indiana Historical Society, C8146*

pendency" the bill represented "one of the few efforts made for preven-tion of the evils whose cure costs the state so much." It was no longer feasible "to let any class live amid conditions that breed disease that endangers the whole community." The debate over the housing bill was, in her view, "simply a question of weighing a little money, belonging to a few people, against the vital interests of all the people of Indiana."[22]

She also called together her Indiana Federation of Clubs housing committee and other IFC leaders, and they "arranged to send word to every corner of the state, that the time had come for their help. How the letters and telegrams came pouring back . . . ," she later recalled, "to the members of the legislature; not only from the club women, but from prominent men whom they had seen, in different communities."[23]

The bill was finally reported out of committee on February 21, but in a manner which indicates that the friends of the measure were just as willing to employ legislative sleight of hand as their opponents had been two years earlier. The bill was advanced to third reading "after being amended according to the recommendations of the committee . . . that several members of the committee didn't know anything about." Four members of the thirteen-man committee (all supporters of the bill) met early in the afternoon and decided to submit a report containing amendments in keeping with the agreement reached between Bacon and those businessmen who had earlier opposed the bill. They then presented their report to the committee chairman and convinced him to sign it and submit it as a unanimous recommendation. One of the absent committee members, who had opposed the measure in 1911 and was "not friendly to the present bill," was "astonished" when the report was issued. The chairman argued, however, that the committee had already expended much effort on the bill, that members were familiar with the proposed amendments, and that the bill had to be reported out to afford ample time for its consideration on the floor.[24]

In fact, when S.B. 118 was handed down for final reading on the afternoon of February 26, its consideration took only minutes. Three minor amendments (one of which postponed the law's effective date until July 1 in order to give those affected time to achieve compliance) were agreed to by unanimous consent. When the bill came up for final vote it was "the first time in the history of [the House that] a bill was put on its passage without explanation." One of the representatives "facetiously called attention to the fact that the bill had not been explained . . . but he added that it made no difference, as every one knew what it was." Bacon "sat unnoticed in one of the side seats, her hands pressed so tightly together that the knuckles whitened, her tense gaze fastened on each member as his name was called." When the bill passed by the remarkable margin of 92–1, a reporter observed that "the sweeping approval of the measure she has worked . . . to place upon the statute books affected her deeply." All that remained was Senate concurrence in the House amendments (which was accomplished the following day) and signature by the governor.[25]

Why did the housing bill succeed in 1913 after its humiliating (if underhanded) defeat two years earlier? A principal explanation, of course, is the spirited lobbying effort mounted by Bacon and her coalition of supporters. She was quick to acknowledge the individuals and groups who had assisted: women's clubs, newspapers, Tom Taggart, the Anti-Tuberculosis Society, the Indiana Housing Association, and Governor Ralston. But from a political point of view, 1913 was an especially propitious time to advocate such a measure. By that year "a general climate of opinion which was receptive to and even expectant of new reforms had settled over Indiana." The deep division in Republican ranks between conservatives and progressives the previous year, and the subsequent formation of a separate Progressive party, reflected the heightened reform spirit. In addition, Hoosiers of all political faiths had noted the electoral gains made by the Socialists in 1912. Indeed, Governor Marshall's valedictory message to the General Assembly in January 1913, called for progressive legislation as a bulwark against potential revolutionary change. Given this backdrop, it is not surprising that Ralston, Taggart, and their lieutenants actively promoted various reforms. The result, in the words of a contemporary observer, was "a body of reform legislation that was most creditable to the State," including the housing bill.[26]

Following a victory dinner at the Denison Hotel, with "flowers and felicitations, pleasant words, and some sad ones," Bacon sped home. The *Evansville Press*, which interviewed her immediately upon her return, praised her efforts by noting that "practically all of Mrs. Bacon's time during the last 12 years has been given to visiting slums and tenement districts and she has lectured in nearly every city in the state in the interest of the bill. She says," the paper reported, "she is glad to be back home."[27]

Bacon's frequent references to her home and family may be understood, at least in part, as the strategic rhetoric employed by many of the Progressive era's municipal housekeepers—the representation of their public work as a simple expansion of traditional domestic activities and concerns. In Bacon's case, however, it was not mere rhetoric. She did draw strength and inspiration from her family, commenting at one point "how much easier it is to do civic work with home as a center and a base." Although she became increasingly comfortable and effective in the spotlight, and took great satisfaction from her accomplishments, she remained a rather private and introspective person and home was often a welcome haven from the growing demands of her public role. As she described the return to Evansville following her first legislative session:

> How good it was to be at home again, to resume my accustomed Identity, to which I felt almost a stranger; to be again a Person, no longer merely a disembodied, homeless Plea! I was avid of all those usual, homely things that all people do, so eager to get back into the same "rut" again that I welcomed even the commonest tasks.[28]

Indeed, without the support of her family Bacon's social activism would have been much more difficult and doubtless more limited.

Hilary Bacon's business career precluded much direct involvement in his wife's philanthropic efforts, especially those activities that took place outside of Evansville. The dry goods firm he had co-founded in the late 1870s, which had evolved into Keck & Bacon by 1887, continued to operate under that name until the late 1890s. In 1898 he formed a partnership with Adolph P. Lahr, and the Lahr-Bacon Company flourished at the corner of Sixth and Main until about 1917 when Lahr sold his interest in the joint enterprise and established his own dry goods firm. At that point Bacon founded the H. E. Bacon Company Department Store, and he continued to do business at the 527–531 Main Street location until his retirement in April 1929 at age 77. In addition, for over thirty years beginning early in the century he served as a director of Evansville's Citizens National Bank.[29]

Although his mercantile affairs took up much of his time and energy, Hilary was nonetheless able to support Albion's work in a number of ways. An obituary noted that while "he seldom actively participated in civic enterprises"—the men's circle of Friendly Visitors was apparently a rare exception—"he counseled and helped Mrs. Bacon in her work." Their youngest daughter remembered him being "busy a hundred percent of the time" but "very supportive, very proud of Mother." Some of that support was, of course, financial. While she sometimes had her travel costs reimbursed when she gave invited speeches, most of the expenses Albion incurred while working for housing reform, and later for other causes, were paid by Hilary. When she first went to the General Assembly in 1909, a state senator who assumed she was a professional lobbyist asked her one day who was covering her expenses. "Why, my husband!" she replied indignantly.[30]

Outside of their limited contributions to the Flower Mission work, the Bacon children likewise had little direct involvement in their mother's philanthropic activities. Margaret had graduated from high school in 1907, just as Bacon became involved with statewide tenement house reform, then spent a year away from home attending a finishing school, and, as we have seen, died unexpectedly in late 1909. Daughter Albion, about two years younger than Margaret, was involved in high school activities of her own and, following graduation, also attended an out-of-state women's college for a year or two. She married George D. Smith in early 1914 and the couple moved into the newly built Audubon Apartments on fashionable Riverside Avenue, not far from the Bacons' place on First Street.

Above: Albion Mary Bacon (b. 1892), the Bacons' second daughter.
Below: Hilary, Sr., holding Joy and Albion holding Hilary, Jr.,
the twins born in 1901. Courtesy Joy Bacon Witwer

Hilary, Jr. and Joy, the twins born in 1901, required a considerable amount of Bacon's attention and energy during the first decade of the century (although in their infancy, and during bouts of illness, hired nurses often provided assistance). Recall Bacon's observation that her early housing correspondence was interrupted "only for household cares or for the children." She later remembered that the twins "played about me or sat as close as possible while I wrote, with little arms about my waist, and I could work better with them near." By the time Joy was in high school she willingly took on significant responsibilities of household management, including planning meals, ordering groceries to be delivered, and training cooks and other help. As she put it years later, "I always felt that Mother had more important things to do. . . . Anybody could do [the routine domestic chores]. Not anybody could do what Mother was doing."[31]

Bacon no doubt welcomed her youngest daughter's assistance. While she clearly cherished hearth and home and sometimes expressed (as quoted earlier) a longing for the "usual, homely things that all people do," there were many domestic activities for which she had neither aptitude nor interest. Joy remembered that her mother very seldom cooked. When necessary "she made the best scrambled eggs of anybody in the world," she prepared an excellent turkey stuffing, and she fixed her favorite dessert, charlotte russe, "to perfection." But "those were her three talents [and] we always had help in the kitchen." Moreover, at least by the time that Bacon became active as a *municipal* housekeeper, she "wasn't interested in talking about laundry problems or kitchen problems or household problems."[32]

Bacon's involvement in social welfare work was not unusual for a middle-class woman during the Progressive era, but the depth of her commitment, the range of her interests, and the level of her visibility— as well as her diffidence regarding many domestic activities—set her apart from most of her peers. As Joy put it decades later, the neighbors "all thought she was wonderful, doing good things. But it was a little beyond them, I think." Joy also claimed that she never heard negative comments about her mother from any of the neighborhood women, even those who "couldn't understand her." But the daughter of one of those neighbors, a woman five or six years older than Joy, recalled the twins as being "holy terrors" who she thought might have been better supervised. She also paraphrased one neighborhood woman's observation (after Hilary, Jr. had gotten into some minor mischief) that "Mrs. Bacon would be better off staying home and looking after her family than running around the country telling other people what to do."[33]

The Bacons' household routine, at least during the twins' childhood and adolescent years, included Bible reading at breakfast and discussion of civic and business affairs at dinner. There was a strict prohibition on gossip during all meals. Hilary believed (because of his Kentucky upbringing, according to Joy) that family members "should come into the dining room and make ourselves charming to each other." Following dinner they often spent time in the parlor or library being "agreeably sociable." On these occasions Albion would sometimes sing Irish and Scottish ballads or African-American spirituals while accompanying herself on the piano, or Hilary would tell the children Uncle Remus stories he had heard during his own youth. These were also times for reading, and Joy recalled that once her mother became involved in social welfare causes "it was always serious reading, it was always studying something."[34]

The family attended church regularly. Joy remembered that she and her brother "grew up in the Amen Corner" of Trinity Methodist and that "it was a very important part of our lives." Her parents, while steadfast in their Sunday observances, were not much involved in the more social aspects of congregational life—church suppers, quilting bees, and the like. Both participated in Bible study groups, however, and Hilary, while less religiously demonstrative than his wife, was a "financial pillar" of Trinity and served on occasion as a church steward.[35]

In her public work Bacon maintained a strict political neutrality, seeking and securing support from members of both major parties. She once wrote her friend Grace Julian Clarke (whose husband, Democratic State Senator Charles B. Clarke, had introduced the 1913 tenement bill) that "I am non-partisan, you know, and never will be anything else, as my work is and will be non-partisan." In a subsequent letter she reiterated the point: "My appeal has never had a political tinge, and, if it had, I don't believe it would have carried." In private life, however, it seems clear that Albion and the other Evansville Bacons were generally Democratic party adherents. Joy, while claiming that her parents "voted only for the person," acknowledged that her father came out of the Solid South tradition and that both parents certainly registered as Democrats.[36]

When one of Indiana's U.S. senators, Benjamin F. Shively, died in the spring of 1916, necessitating an interim appointment, Bacon wrote a personal letter to Governor Samuel Ralston urging that he name Thomas Taggart, the state's Democratic kingpin, to the position. Taggart, she thought, had "done more for his party than any one in the state." (Note, however, that she was careful to say "his party," not "my party" or "our party.") The next year, when Evansville's Democratic mayor Benjamin Bosse was running for reelection, Bacon made what was probably her most public political endorsement. In a signed article—in effect, a guest editorial—on the front page of the *Evansville Courier*, she explained her support of Bosse by enumerating "all the big, splendid things he has done for our city." These included "improvements that civic workers had striven and begged for in vain, through long years": city gardens and forests, parks and playgrounds, and, especially, better housing. Bosse won and, four years later, stood for yet another term. When it became apparent on election night that he had once again been reelected, Democratic revelers paraded through the city. One of their stops was the Bacons' residence in order, as the *Courier* put it, "to show their appreciation of the wonderful work that Mrs. Bacon did for the democratic [*sic*] party here."[37]

Bacon's racial attitudes, while demonstrably more moderate than many of her contemporaries, nonetheless reflected the realities of life in southern Indiana during the early twentieth century. She did not question the appropriateness of residential segregation. The Bacons employed several African Americans as servants over the years, and decades later Joy claimed that her parents considered these individuals "part of the family." At some level that may well have been true. But although the white women who worked as nurses and cooks often lived in the house, the black servants never did so. Even more telling was one of Bacon's observations after a trip to examine housing conditions in northwestern Indiana's Lake County: "We saw negroes and foreigners in the same house, for the latter do not understand our instinct of segregation."[38]

Her social welfare efforts, though, cut across not only ethnic and class lines but also the racial divide, and she gradually became aware of the problems faced by Evansville's African-American residents. As noted previously (see chapter 2), Bacon admitted that the Friendly Visitors Circle in which she had been active rarely assisted black families because such families seldom approached the Associated Charities for aid. Thus, it was some time before she realized just how bad housing conditions were for most of the city's black population. The important point, however, is not her initial myopia but her continuing self-education and her eventual willingness to admit (in print, no less) her previous blind spot. And, for all her desire to eliminate squalid housing, she was also sensitive to specific circumstances. When in 1914 a housing committee recommended razing a large number of dwellings in Baptisttown, the principal African-American residential area in Evansville, few seemed concerned with the fate of those who would be displaced. As the closest student of the Pocket City's black community reports, "Mrs. Bacon and industrialist Richard Rosencranz . . . stood alone in urging gradual change because of the dearth of low income housing in the city." In later years she was a member of Evansville's Inter-Racial Committee. She also served on the county tuberculosis association, in which capacity she urged that Baptisttown's residents not be overlooked or underserved during public health campaigns.[39]

Although Hilary was remembered as a gregarious man who would welcome customers by name as they entered his store, and Albion could meet and greet when the occasion required, the Bacons did not do much entertaining at home. They hosted an occasional small dinner party, and perhaps once a year a large, catered reception, but most socializing was with members of the Bacon and Fellows extended families. During the Christmas season—a "big event" in the household, according to Joy —guests were treated to Hilary's one culinary specialty: the "Bacon egg-nog." This concoction of eggs, whiskey, and sugar, whose creation left whisked egg whites "all over the place," produced a "thick, rich goo" that was "simply marvelous, rich as could be."[40]

Family vacations involved two principal activities: visits with Bacon relatives and stays at some of the religiously and educationally oriented summer resorts popular during the early twentieth century. One of Hilary's brothers, John, had taken over the family homestead in Trigg County, Kentucky, and another brother, Tom, lived in nearby Hopkinsville. The family would take the Louisville & Nashville Railroad to Hopkinsville and then split time between the two sets of relatives. On at least one occasion, Bacon, daughter Albion, and the twins spent a month or so at the famed Chautauqua Institution in western New York State. Young Albion enjoyed dancing and took sailing lessons; Joy was in the Girls Club and took cooking classes; and Hilary, Jr. signed up for elementary woodworking. Bacon, in addition to attending the general lectures and musical performances that were part of the Chautauqua experience, studied song writing with the institution's accompanist and took in a series of lectures on modern drama. On another occasion she and the twins spent time at the Methodist summer colony at Bay View, Michigan (near Petoskey, on Little Traverse Bay). She gave a series of talks as part of the association's Labor and Social Welfare Conference, and the remuneration she received ($50 plus expenses) was enough to cover the cost of taking the children along.[41]

One year, unable to manage an extended stay at Chautauqua, New York, Bacon and a friend took their children and spent a week or so at

The Chautauqua House in Merom, Indiana, which she described as a "*beautiful* spot" with a "wonderful view from the bluffs" overlooking the Wabash River. Two years later she and the twins spent a few weeks at the lakefront resort town of South Haven, Michigan. She wrote Grace Clarke that she needed a rest "from the many civic and other duties that had swamped me." Following their arrival she had "shut a door in my brain, that I have learned to use, upon a little back room where I stuffed all my work and wor[r]y ideas, and sat down in the front room to peaceful thoughts."[42]

The importance of family was also reflected in Bacon's interaction with her sisters. Her relationship with Lura, eight years her senior, is the more difficult to describe. Since they both lived in Evansville and saw each other regularly, they produced no collection of correspondence that might shed light on their dealings with one another. Lura, who bore seven children, devoted herself principally to her family and was never a public figure. But in spite of their differences in age and interests, there is at least indirect evidence that the oldest and youngest Fellows sisters always remained close—and no evidence to the contrary.[43]

The relationship between Albion and Annie was, however, much closer, even though they generally lived far apart. Annie was just two years older, so they shared many childhood experiences. Both were interested in writing. As young adults they toured Europe together, and then returned home for a double wedding. Annie's marriage was cut short after only three years when her husband, Will Johnston, died in 1892 following a lengthy battle with tuberculosis. Left with three stepchildren from Johnston's first marriage—Mary (Mamie), Rena, and John—and little money, Annie began to write professionally in order to support the family. *The Little Colonel* (1895) was the first in a long line of children's books. In 1898 the Johnstons moved to Pewee Valley, Kentucky (near Louisville), the setting for many of the "Little Colonel" stories. Rena died the next year and John's precarious health led them to relocate in the Southwest in 1901. They remained there until John's death in 1910, after which Annie and Mary returned to Pewee Valley.

Throughout their various triumphs and travails over the years, Albion and Annie remained in regular communication. They sent periodic, often lengthy letters to one another. They sought each other's advice regarding writing projects they had underway. They and their children visited each other's homes, and the contents of Annie's annual Christmas box were much anticipated in the Bacon household. During the midst of Albion's housing reform campaign Annie even modeled the character of tenement crusader Mrs. Blythe (read "blithe") in *Mary*

Ware's Promised Land (1912) after her younger sister. There clearly was a special bond between the two; as one student of their relationship has put it, "the sisters were more like twins, with similar interests and abilities." The available evidence supports Joy's memory of her mother and her Aunt Annie as being "very close and very loving and very devoted." Such emotional support, even from a distance, certainly helped Bacon during some stressful times, including the difficult days of legislative lobbying.[44]

❖

However glad Bacon might have been to be home again following the 1913 legislative session, it was obvious she could not remain there long. By then she had become a symbol of the housing reform movement as well as an expert in the field. The success of the Indiana campaign only increased the requests for her aid from various reform groups. Barely a month after her return to Evansville, in the course of a letter of appreciation to Governor Ralston for his support, she noted that she had been asked to speak in several midwestern states and to provide advice on securing statewide housing laws. She was pleased "that Indiana can lead, among these states" in housing reform and wanted the governor to know that "other states are looking to us for help and encouragement, in this matter." But *was* Indiana in the lead? If so, could the state maintain that position? Perhaps little noticed in the wake of her triumph at the General Assembly, but not without significance, was a comment Bacon made casually during her homecoming interview with the *Evansville Press*: "The [1913] housing bill is just the first step."[45]

For all the passion it aroused among both supporters and opponents, the 1913 tenement house law was a decidedly limited piece of legislation. Although it was a statewide law, it applied only to incorporated cities; it did not affect small urban places that had not incorporated, suburban tracts outside city corporation boundaries, or the rural areas in which a majority of the state's residents still lived. In addition, it did not apply to all dwellings in the cities but only to tenements—defined as the "home or residence of two or more families living independently of each other . . . and having a common right in the halls, stairways, yard, cellar, water-closets or privies." Moreover, as noted previously, the law covered only tenements "hereafter erected" or extant buildings converted into multiple dwellings; it did not apply to the many tenement houses already in existence. Finally, in a concession to localism, the law was to be enforced by community building inspectors or boards of health; these

officials were not always well qualified and were certainly more susceptible to local pressure than inspectors from the State Board of Health
would have been.[46]

Bacon was, of course, fully aware of the weaknesses in the 1913 law.
She was also aware that those who had opposed the tenement law
through three successive General Assemblies were not likely suddenly
to disappear. In presenting the report of her housing committee at the
IFC annual convention in October 1913, she thanked the assembled
club women for their support but noted: "We fought to win our victory—we must [now] fight to hold our ground." Reminding her audience that "no law is automatic," she presaged future housing reform
activity when she asked the IFC membership to "Stand by me. Help me
still."[47]

By this time her crowded schedule of traveling and lecturing was
beginning to take its toll. In a letter to Grace Julian Clarke in mid-1914
Bacon apologized to her friend for not writing sooner but noted that
correspondence had been delayed because "it was so hot it took the little breath I had left when I got home. . . . I am getting over a second
spell, since my return, and just beginning to feel alive. I think I am going to take these warnings, and go a little slow. In August I am to lecture in Bay View, [Michigan,] a series of three, and I dread the exertion."[48]

Bacon's various other "exertions" on behalf of housing reform did
not stand in the way of preparations for the next session of the legislature. By December a plan of action for the forthcoming General Assembly was fairly well determined, and in a remarkably detailed and
candid letter to Governor Ralston she set forth "a frank and complete
statement of the subject of proposed housing legislation." The Indiana
"housers" had two goals in 1915: "To take no backward step, and lower
no standards"—that is, to protect the 1913 tenement law from repeal
or weakening amendments; and, "if possible, to take a forward step"
by securing even stronger legislation that would "regulate the classes
of dwellings that now defy the state, county, or local health boards or
building inspectors." Bacon and her colleagues in the Indiana Housing
Association had prepared two separate proposals: a "long bill" that
would regulate all dwellings as the 1913 law regulated tenements, and a
"short bill" that focused specifically on control of dwellings deemed
"infected and uninhabitable." Depending on legislative contingencies
they would try "whichever seems best and wisest, and most hopeful of
passing." She concluded her letter to the governor by observing that she
was "willing to again make a great effort and sacrifice, in the interest of

Albion Fellows Bacon in the gown she wore at daughter Albion's wedding (1914). Albion Fellows Bacon Collection, Special Collections, Willard Library

my state, for all there is a hope of winning, but to do no rash or foolish thing."[49]

The "long bill," which Bacon clearly preferred, would have virtually restated the 1913 tenement law and extended its coverage to every dwelling unit in the state. But she acknowledged that "people will resent being dictated to about space on their lot—the one vital essential, the keystone of the whole law," and conceded that such a measure would be difficult to pass. Politically astute enough to attempt "no foolish thing," she had decided even before the General Assembly convened that passage of the "long bill" was too ambitious a goal and that the "short bill," which would "prepare the way for a future step," was all that could be realistically attempted.[50]

In early January 1915, the *Indianapolis News* reported that Bacon was in the capital to observe the legislative session, that she had been "received with consideration and listened to attentively by every member of the Assembly," and that she hoped "a bill will be passed that will give the state board of health the same power over 'death traps' as the fire marshal now has over fire traps." Senate Bill 61, the "short bill," was introduced by Clarke on January 18. A column in the *Star* headlined "BILL DOOMS GERM TRAP BUILDINGS" summarized its intent: "The measure seeks to confer on the health authorities the same power over dwellings that might be [or would soon become] infested with disease as the present [tenement] law gives the state department of inspection and local building inspectors over structures that are improperly built from an architectural standpoint."[51]

While the "death trap" bill (as it came to be known) began to work its way through the legislature, Bacon and her adherents found themselves struggling to avoid taking a "backward step." As she had foretold, both in her address to the IFC the previous fall and in her letter to the governor, the tenement house law now came under attack. The "point man" in this effort was Representative Willard B. Van Horne, a Republican from Lake and Newton counties, who during the course of the Assembly session introduced several bills to repeal or seriously weaken the 1913 law. Van Horne was clearly acting on the desires of some of his more influential constituents; at a hearing on one of his bills the measure was supported by a Lake County architect (who had apparently drafted the bill), the Hammond building inspector, and the Lake County Democratic chairman.[52]

The "housers" fought back. Jacob H. Hilkene, the Indianapolis building commissioner, expressed surprise at Van Horne's proposals and told an interviewer that the law "certainly governs arrangements whereby the building and sanitary conditions . . . in this city are bettered and are such that they in comparison stand far above other large cities in this country." Bacon also testified against repealing or amending the tene-

Tubercular family pictured in Beauty for Ashes: "Where the White Death throttles its victims." Bacon, Beauty for Ashes; photograph courtesy Indiana Historical Society, C8156

ment law, as did Cox (still president of the Indiana Housing Association) and a spokesperson for the Legislative Council of Indiana Women. The defenders carried the day: none of Van Horne's bills was enacted.[53]

The "death trap" bill was favorably reported by the Senate health committee on January 21, read a second time the next day, and passed by the full Senate on January 27.[54] The following day it was handed down in the lower chamber and referred to committee, whence it reappeared on February 10 with a "do pass" recommendation. Then no action was taken on the measure for a week. During this period an Indianapolis paper carried a short "parable" written by Bacon, an obvious attempt to gain support for the bill. In her story four men meet in an alley, each searching for the cause of tuberculosis in his city. Each has a pet theory—dark rooms, the house fly, polluted water and insufficient food, foul air and dampness—and in one particularly bad house each man finds an example that supports his position.

> "It would be hard for us to disentangle our data," said the bad air man, "when we find each family living under all these bad conditions which we are tracing separately."
> "No need to disentangle them," growled the dark room man. "Call it a case of house, and let's go after the landlord and stop this wholesale murder."

The landlord in the story naturally refuses to make the needed improvements, observing that "There ain't no law to make me do it."[55]

As it happened, there was still no law at the conclusion of the legislative session; the "death trap" bill came up for a final vote in the House on February 17 and was defeated. Summarizing the debate, the *Star* reported that opposition revolved around the "drastic powers" given health authorities to condemn unsanitary residences. "It was argued that the bill, if applied literally, would take his home from many a poor man." Understating the case the paper observed that Bacon "was an interested spectator of the proceedings."[56]

Bacon was, of course, much more than just another interested spectator, and she was deeply disturbed by the defeat of the bill. Although she had been extremely disappointed when the apparent victory for the tenement law in 1911 had been turned to defeat by opponents' questionable tactics, in 1915 her disappointment seemed, for the first time, tinged with bitterness. She had previously been neutral (at least publicly) on the issue of women's suffrage, but an Evansville newspaper reported that the 1915 defeat had made her "the latest recruit to the ranks of the suffragists." "'If all men were like some men,'" she reportedly said, "'the indirect influence of women would be enough and we would not need the ballot. But they are not.'" Several months later she was still describing how the "death trap" bill had been lost in "a general political upheaval."[57]

Determined to see the matter through, Bacon resolved to try again. In the interim she remained active in a variety of housing reform enterprises. She continued to chair the housing committee of the Indiana Federation of Clubs, urging the state's club women to see that the 1913 tenement law was enforced in their communities and to support passage of the "death trap" legislation. Her involvement with the National Housing Association also continued, as did her busy lecture schedule. In mid-May 1916, for example, she made several presentations before a national meeting of "housers" in the Hoosier capital (a meeting presided over by Lawrence Veiller).[58]

She also had occasion to make a plea for housing reform before an international audience. The organizers of the Second Pan American Scientific Congress, which convened in Washington on December 28, 1915, realized in the last months before the meeting that many of the delegates (almost entirely men) would be accompanied by their wives and daughters. Seizing the opportunity, they authorized the formation of a Women's Auxiliary Conference. The idea, according to Eleanor Lansing (wife of Secretary of State Robert Lansing), was to provide a forum for "a Pan American gathering of women to discuss informally questions of common interest to the women of the three Americas." In late November invitations were extended to "a well-chosen list of the prominent women in the United States" to present very brief remarks "pertaining to such general questions as education, civic and social betterment." The presentations were to be kept short in the belief that "informal discussion of the subjects would be more helpful than long papers with less time for an exchange of opinion."[59]

Bacon was one of the "prominent women" invited, and she entitled her presentation on December 29 "'The Powers of Darkness'—The Housing Problem." The wretched living conditions she had encountered in Indiana and the United States, and the disinclination of some people to improve those conditions, were, she observed, "the same with each nation, because human nature is the same everywhere." Since "the homes of the nation are its greatest asset," she called on the delegates to demand that all dwellings have "sanitation, light, air, water, and the disposal of waste. . . . Then we and our children will be safe and the working people strong and efficient." She concluded by expressing a hope that some day there might be a Pan American housing conference where the delegates might "hear what each [country] has done."[60]

Her primary interests remained in Indiana, however, and in January 1917, now as if by habit, Bacon and her allies in the Hoosier state were ready to reintroduce the failed legislation of two years earlier. After the enervating struggles of the previous four assemblies, the 1917 session proved to be almost anticlimactic. House Bill 69, a virtual replica of the 1915 "death trap" measure, was introduced by Representative Donald Jameson (a Republican from Marion County) on January 12 and referred to the Committee on Cities and Towns. The committee reported the bill and four minor amendments on the 24th, recommending passage as amended, and the measure was read for a second time on the 29th. On the morning the bill was scheduled for final consideration, members of the House arrived to find letters on their desks from the Church Federation of Indianapolis (a union of many of the city's Protestant churches) observing that "good morals depend in no small measure upon the housing conditions throughout the entire city" and urging "hearty and unqualified support" for the proposed law. Perhaps the letter swayed a few votes. Or perhaps, as Bacon claimed in the aftermath, there had been "an awakening sense everywhere of the need for better housing." In any event, in striking contrast to the divided House tally of two years earlier, the lower chamber passed the bill by a unanimous vote of 90–0. Even Bacon allowed that the margin of victory "was really a surprise."[61]

The bill was introduced in the Senate the following day and a favorable committee report was submitted within the week. The measure was read for a second time on February 9 and brought up for a vote six days later. The result in the upper chamber was just as convincing as in the House; the bill passed without a single dissenting vote. Regrettably, although appropriately, since she always claimed that housing reform was the most important thing in her life *after* her family, Bacon was not present for the final vote: she had returned to Evansville for the birth of a grandson. When informed by a reporter for her hometown paper that the measure had passed, she expressed "relief and pleasure" that the decade-long campaign was over and that the state's towns, villages, and rural communities "that had hitherto been unprotected by any kind of housing law, might now be protected from the diseases arising from unfit surroundings."[62]

❖

And so the long struggle was over, a struggle that had begun years before when Bacon became convinced that "nothing but a housing law would ever enable us to get relief from the conditions that caused our poor so much misery."[63] As the state and the nation prepared to embark on another crusade—the First World War—Indiana had two housing statutes in place. The first, the 1913 tenement law, regulated the construction of multi-family dwellings; the second, the "death trap" law of 1917, empowered the state's health officers to order corrective action when any dwelling was deemed to be unfit for human habitation. It is well to bear in mind that these laws had no claim to originality. While Bacon was clearly the key personality behind *passage* of the Indiana legislation, the *content* of the statutes owed more to the models prepared and propounded by Veiller. Yet enactment of the two measures stands as a major accomplishment of Indiana's Progressive era social reformers and marks a signal advance in the state's use of its police power.

It is also important to understand that these housing laws were by no means unique. As suggested earlier, reform was "in the air" in the early twentieth century. Bacon and her colleagues in the Indiana Housing Association were not *sui generis* either to or within the Hoosier state. There was in these years a "yearning to purge society of what now seemed its individualistic excesses" (in the case at hand read "irresponsible landlords"), a yearning that led, in one form, to "a new interest in the social and physical environment." The housing statutes, as well as other progressive laws adopted during Marshall's and Ralston's administrations, reflect "the triumph for a few years of the reform spirit which sought to make conditions better, and the recognition on the part of the people and the politicians that the state had some further responsibility than it had exercised in the past." As one student of the era has put it, none "worked harder than the progressives to rationalize and organize what they saw as their chaotic surroundings." For Bacon and other "housers," many of whom had grown to adulthood in rural areas, nothing better exemplified this "chaos" than inadequate, overcrowded housing.[64]

If, as some have claimed, the "fundamental assumption" of Progressive era social reformers was a "deeply held conviction that men and women were creatures of their environment," then it is not hard to understand why housing reform had such a prominent place on their agendas.[65] But the crusade for restrictive legislation (such as Indiana's laws) was not without its limitations. For one thing, it was difficult to sustain the momentum. "Reform movements that are oriented toward the passage of legislation," observes a close student of the subject, "measure enactment as success. Some relaxation of passion is afterwards hard to avoid." Some reformers "assumed that passing a law was equivalent to solving a problem and that government officials could be entrusted to enforce the measure in a progressive spirit. This frequently was not the case."[66] This description does not apply to Bacon, who constantly urged her audiences to see that the laws were *used* in their communities. But it is also clear that Indiana's tenement and housing laws, while they may have ameliorated the most extreme situations, did not eliminate bad housing conditions in the state—in short, that they did not fulfill the expectations of many of their supporters.[67]

Moreover, restrictive legislation could at best prevent or correct bad housing; it could not create additional good housing. By the time Indiana's "death trap" statute was passed the movement for restrictive codes based on Veiller's model laws had crested. Increasingly thereafter the debate in housing reform circles revolved around what could and should be done to *provide* decent housing for those most in need. But this was a step that Indiana, at least the public sector, was not prepared to take on the eve of the 1920s. If the Hoosier state's record of reform legislation during the Progressive era was, as one historian claims, "a large and significant one," it is also true that the record was accomplished in a political climate "compounded of nearly equal parts of conservatism and cautious liberalism, neither dominant for long and each force acting as a check upon the other."[68] The demise of the Progressive party in 1916, preoccupation with American involvement in World War I in 1917–1918, and struggle with a variety of social and economic dislocations in the immediate postwar years marked the beginning of a period of quiescence for the reform impulse in Indiana, at least as reflected in legislative enactments.

Although 1917 marked the completion of her major work on behalf of "the homes of Indiana," Bacon's interest in housing reform continued through the 1920s. She remained active in the Indiana and national housing associations, writing a number of pamphlets for the national organization.[69] She helped to create the Evansville City Plan Commission (see chapter 6) and served as its president for many years. Her wide-ranging social concerns also manifested themselves in other activities, some of which will be detailed in the pages that follow. But it was as a housing reformer that she became and remained well known, in Indiana, the Midwest, and the nation. In a book published two years after passage of Indiana's 1917 law, Edith Elmer Wood, one of the country's leading housing economists, observed that "housing reform in the United States has produced three magnetic personalities." She identified this trio as Jacob Riis, "who first made us care how the other half lived"; Lawrence Veiller, "the high priest of restrictive housing legislation"; and Albion Fellows Bacon, "who won a housing law for her state by sheer, disinterested persistence."[70]

Five

Child Welfare

From the first days of her social welfare activism in Evansville, when she had been concerned with the environment in and around her daughters' school, Bacon had expressed a particular interest in the welfare of children. Following her excursion with Caroline Rein to Old St. Mary's it was the memory of the tenement's youngest residents that remained with her. She subsequently saw many more such cases as she became involved with friendly visiting, the Visiting Nurse's Circle, and the Flower Mission. In a heartfelt passage she later wrote:

> The babies of the slums! Whenever I try to talk of them something rises up and chokes me. It's the thought of one of my own babies setting its little bare feet on those slimy yards, among the sharp cinders. I never see them without a shudder at the thought of all that tender flesh will have to suffer—bruises, aches and illness, hunger and cold—of the coarse, filthy clothing and wretched food. Worst of all, some of them will have oaths and blows, and there will be a bestial life about them, so they cannot grow up innocent or pure.[1]

This concern naturally carried over to and influenced Bacon's work on behalf of housing reform. In her first public address on the subject —"The Homes of the Poor"—she expressed unease about the ways in which youthful character would be affected by "surroundings which sear the mind by reiterated suggestions of evil, which dim the vision of the soul by hideous ugliness, warping it away from ideals of truth and beauty.

What hope is there for the pure child mind to unfold in such a place without a stain?" In her talk entitled "A Tale of the Tenements," later printed as a pamphlet by the Indiana Housing Association, she employed a striking metaphor to describe the slum children whom she had encountered. They "always make me think," she said, "of those gray rubber dolls, that are gray all the way through. It seems they must get that way. I even wonder if their little souls are not gray, from the constant sight of the gray walls, gray floors—the grime that nothing takes out." And in a pamphlet discussing the effects of bad housing she quoted approvingly an unnamed writer: "Every time a baby dies the nation loses a prospective citizen, but *in every slum child who lives the nation has a probable consumptive and a possible criminal.*"[2]

It is thus not surprising that once restrictive housing legislation was in place Bacon became involved with several other efforts to improve the lives of children in the Hoosier state. What may initially seem unusual is that the first of these efforts was an integral part of the state's and the nation's involvement in and reaction to World War I.

❖

It used to be a commonplace among American historians that the Progressive movement of the early twentieth century was sidetracked, if not actually derailed, by American participation in the First World War. Writing in the early 1960s, Clarke Chambers observed that "students of American liberalism have traditionally treated the Great War as the end of reform and the decade between armistice and panic as a great hiatus." As evidence he could have pointed to Richard Hofstadter's renowned *The Age of Reform*, published eight years earlier, which stated flatly that "participation in the war put an end to the Progressive movement."[3]

It is true that a portion of the Progressive agenda was put on hold during the war. It is also true that many Progressives, including some of the most well known, were profoundly disillusioned by the wartime ethos at home, the nature of the peace settlement, and the reactionary events of the immediate postwar years. Yet in answering his own rhetorical question—"What Happened to the Progressive Movement in the 1920's?"—Arthur Link noted over forty years ago that "we must recognize that the progressive movement was certainly not defunct in the 1920's; that on the contrary at least important parts of it were very much alive; and that it is just as important to know how and why progressivism survived as to know how and why it declined."

More recently, labor historian Melvyn Dubofsky has observed succinctly: "War, indeed, was fulfillment for some Progressive Americans."[4]

Some of the Progressives' social welfare goals not only survived the conflict, they were actually advanced during the emergency—sometimes by appealing to (or, depending on one's point of view, pandering to) widely accepted wartime objectives. One of the principal organs of social reform, *Survey* magazine, "played up the ways in which public health, child and infant welfare, and all the other agency services supported the end of national strength and morale." "Social workers," as William O'Neill observes, "could not refuse a chance to put their skills to full use, and the American war effort, while it affronted their traditional values, offered unprecedented opportunities for the conscious exploitation of national power for beneficent ends." And in the words of William Breen, a close student of the World War I home front, women were particularly aggressive "in their efforts to use the wartime crisis as an opportunity to promote various social reforms that had been championed by the prewar women's movement."[5]

Child welfare work is an example of one reform program that women progressives were able to graft successfully onto the wartime agenda. In her recent study of what she calls a "female dominion" in American reform activity during the early twentieth century, historian Robyn Muncy remarks on the "surprising relationship between child welfare reform and war."[6] The mechanism for establishing that relationship was the connection forged between the women's committees of the national and state councils of defense and the federal Children's Bureau. Indiana, which in spite of examples such as housing reform was hardly a bellwether Progressive state, provides an interesting case study of how the process worked. It was a process in which Bacon was centrally involved.

In August 1916, as active American participation in the World War became increasingly likely, Congress authorized the creation of the Council of National Defense and its Civilian Advisory Commission. The council itself consisted of several cabinet secretaries, while the advisory commission members represented such areas of the nation's prospective mobilization needs as transportation, labor, finance, and medicine. Since it had little to do during late 1916 and early 1917, the council focused on replicating itself at the state level. The head of the State Councils Section worked to create defense councils in each state, viewing them as a mechanism through which the national council could "channel information from the different departments and agencies of the administration to the state level and vice versa."[7]

In April 1917, shortly after the formal declaration of war was adopted by Congress, the Council of National Defense belatedly created a Woman's Committee. Headed by the well-known suffragist Anna Howard Shaw, and composed of appointees associated with major women's organizations, the Woman's Committee promptly organized a "Plan of Work" that included such departments as Food Production and Home Economics, Child Welfare, Liberty Loan, and Home and Allied Relief. A "Plan of Organization" was adopted as well. Just as the Council of National Defense worked to establish state defense councils, the Woman's Committee now sought to have its own parallel structure recreated at the state, county, and local levels.[8]

These two federal initiatives bore fruit in the Hoosier state in May 1917, when Governor James Goodrich appointed a State Council of Defense to coordinate Indiana's war effort. The original members of the council—seventeen men and one woman—included Will H. Hays (chairman of the Republican state committee), former Vice-President Charles W. Fairbanks, Tom Taggart (the national Democratic chairman), the president of the Indiana State Federation of Labor, and the well-known humorist and playwright George Ade. The lone woman on the council, appointed to head the Woman's Section, was Anne Studebaker Carlisle, a member of the South Bend wagon and automobile manufacturing family.[9]

During the next eighteen months Carlisle and her small staff, operating out of the State Council of Defense offices in the State House, orchestrated an impressive mobilization of the womanpower of Indiana. They "organized the efforts of thousands . . . in food production, child welfare, sale of Liberty Bonds, soldiers' entertainment and recreation, education and propaganda, motor corps work, Americanization, and the problems pertaining to women in industry." By the end of the conflict some 626,000 Indiana women had been registered for war work, a figure reportedly second only to Michigan on a per capita basis. This furious activity was accomplished by marshaling a wartime spirit of voluntarism—a spirit already present, of course, in many Progressive-era women's organizations. Total disbursements by the Woman's Section from May 1917 through September 1918 amounted to only $8,692, slightly under 8 percent of all expenditures by the State Council of Defense.[10]

The activities of the state councils of defense in general, and the women's sections in particular, have been little noted by historians. David Kennedy's fine survey of the homefront dismisses the state councils with the observation that they were "largely reduced to propaganda organs, occasionally given to fostering vigilantism against local dissidents and 'slackers.'" And while he notes that the Woman's Committee of the Council of National Defense (and, by extension, the women's sections of the state councils) was, "in the eyes of many feminists, the vehicle by which they would perform significant war work," he concludes by quoting a student of the feminist movement: "It became evident that the government viewed the Woman's Committee as a device for occupying women in harmless activities while men got on with the business of war."[11]

Depending on how one defines "significant war work," there is some justification for this view. A cursory glance at the organizational scheme of the Woman's Section in Indiana, for example, suggests that much of its work was an offshoot or expansion of rather traditional "municipal housekeeping" activities engaged in by many middle-class women's organizations during the early twentieth century. The committee names —home economics, child welfare, home and foreign relief, maintaining existing social agencies, health and recreation—are notably similar to the "departments" of the General Federation of Women's Clubs and its state-level counterparts.[12] But William Breen, the closest student of the state councils and of the women's sections that operated within them, argues that "the state councils were extremely varied in their powers, in their composition, in the range of activity they undertook, and in their general efficiency. To emphasize the vigilante aspects of what they did is to distort and minimize their contribution to the mobilization." Likewise, Breen makes the case that while they were "as intensely patriotic as the men, the women were bolder in their social vision."[13]

Breen's thesis is supported by reference to a single division of the Woman's Section of the Indiana State Council of Defense—the Child Welfare Committee. Among the dozen or so committees that comprised the Woman's Section, Child Welfare achieved perhaps the highest profile. This was due in part to the fact that the Child Welfare Committee in Indiana, as in other states, enjoyed a very close relationship with the Children's Bureau in the federal Department of Labor. As we shall see, the professionals in the Children's Bureau set the agenda that the state committees followed. Furthermore, Carlisle had the good judgment to appoint as chair of Indiana's committee a woman of proven ability, energy, commitment to child welfare work, and statewide reputation—Albion Fellows Bacon. Since much of her rhetoric concerning the need for tenement reform was based upon the deleterious effects of substandard housing on children, it is not surprising that

Bacon's name came to the fore when the staff of the Woman's Section went looking for a chair for their Child Welfare Committee. Carlisle offered her the position in early October 1917; Bacon quickly accepted, replying that "it is the kind of work most welcome to me, and nearest my heart."[14]

Richard Meckel, the author of a recent study focusing on American public health reform and the prevention of infant mortality during the late nineteenth and early twentieth centuries, observes that "the overall effect of the war on American infant welfare was not entirely negative. For as was true of the other side of the Atlantic, the war served further to heighten American concern with the conservation of its young." And according to Breen, it was child welfare that was "the most spectacularly successful of the departments of the Woman's Committee." This success resulted, in large measure, from the strong linkage formed between the Child Welfare Department of the Woman's Committee of the Council of National Defense (later known as the Child Conservation Section of the Field Division) and the Children's Bureau. Indeed, the chairwoman of the Child Welfare Department initially prevailed upon Julia Lathrop, the head of the Children's Bureau, to serve concurrently as the executive director of that department.[15]

Lathrop promptly announced that "saving babies is a vital part of fighting the war." In Muncy's words, she "chose to milk the war for all it was worth to the cause of child welfare reform, and it turned out to be worth a lot." The Children's Bureau was therefore able, as Breen describes it, to mobilize "the army of volunteers at the disposal of the Woman's Committee to promote programs designed to educate the public concerning child welfare" and to "undertake a most ambitious project on behalf of the nation's children under the guise of a war measure." The work of Bacon and other state-level chairwomen of child welfare committees was thus more often reactive than proactive. As a rule, they followed the initiatives proposed in Washington.[16]

The first of those initiatives was ensuring that, even with the wartime labor shortage, children of school age remained in the classroom and out of the factory. In late November Bacon advised Carlisle that "the only work detailed us yet from Washington has been the blanks [questionnaires] to discover truancy, and the letter urging that the Child Labor law's enforcement be closely observed, and everything done to keep all children between 6 and 14 in school." Two days later, in a form letter directed to the Woman's Section of each County Council of Defense, Bacon urged immediate appointment of county child welfare committees where they were not already in place. The matter was "urgent," she noted, since the "National Department" was furnishing school attendance questionnaires that were to be completed and returned to Carlisle as soon as possible.[17]

By early 1918 Bacon reported that only sixty of the state's ninety-two counties had appointed child welfare committees, and she urged Carlisle to write the recalcitrant counties with a reminder that "this is not a notion of ours, but that the government requests it, and the great war organization will not be complete if any link is broken or missing." Some counties, she noted, argued that they did not need such a committee, either because they were very rural or because there were already similar organizations in place. Bacon, demonstrating the advocacy that made her such an appropriate choice for her position, would have none of it: "But so long as there is any disease, any delinquency, any contagious cases, Tuberculosis, any vice problem, the welfare of the children of the county is menaced."[18]

In early February, Bacon suddenly had more to worry about than a few stubborn counties. A bulletin from Washington to all the state councils advised that "The Federal Children's Bureau has requested the Council of National Defense to inaugurate in the several states its war-time program for a children's year beginning April 6, 1918." The Children's Year, formally inaugurated on the first anniversary of American entry into the European conflict, was conceived and sponsored by the Children's Bureau as a "war measure." As Lathrop explained in an annual report, "European experience showed that war-time conditions affect children adversely . . . and that the protection of its children is a primary essential to a nation at war." The Bureau, she added, "felt that it could offer no more valuable contribution to the country during the war than to assist in stimulating and coordinating public and volunteer effort for child welfare."[19]

Since a majority of the state-level women's committees had already established child welfare departments, the responsibility for "giving impetus to activities which shall make the program of the Children's Bureau a reality" had been given to the state divisions of the Woman's Committee and, ultimately, their child welfare operations. Bacon wrote Carlisle on February 12 that the Feds had "rolled a mountain over onto the State Council of Defense" and she hadn't "crawled out from under the debris" since receiving the bulletin outlining how state child welfare committees might want to organize for the event.[20]

Bacon's shock was not so much over the existence of the Children's Year campaign per se as it was over the first task that the state child welfare chairwomen were asked to undertake: weighing and measuring, between April 6 and June 6, every preschool child in their states. "Weight and height," explained a Children's Bureau leaflet, "are a rough index of the health of growing children. When these are found to be seriously below the average . . . the test should be followed by intensive care." The Bureau estimated that about 300,000 children under five years of age had died in the United States during the first year of the war, and that half of those deaths would have been preventable with proper care. One goal of the Children's Year, therefore—it almost became a slogan—was to "Save 100,000 Babies." Indiana's quota to "save" from premature death was 2,592.[21]

The Children's Year in general, and the baby weighing and measuring test in particular, were justified as "war measures" in a variety of ways. The *Muncie Star,* in publicizing the first "clinic for baby welfare" in that city, observed that the "examination is ordered by the National Council of Defense and is due to the poor showing made by the draft examination of our soldiers." This claim, though somewhat exaggerated, did have a basis in fact. A disturbingly large percentage of draftees had been rejected as a result of their physical and medical examinations. Some 730,000 men, or 29 percent of those called by the draft, were found to be physically unfit for military duty. Many of the defects apparently resulted from diseases such as scarlet fever and rickets. The Children's Bureau capitalized on these statistics, reminding readers of its Children's Year publications that "We are told that a large proportion of the rejections were for causes dating back to infancy and early childhood." Bacon employed similar rhetoric, writing the county child welfare committees: "Failure to grow and to increase in weight shows something wrong that should be remedied at once. . . . [I]f such a test had been made upon the young men recently examined for the army, many tragic stories of defects would not have been told."[22]

A variation on this theme, and a distinctly martial metaphor, was that the nation's children constituted "our last reserves." Bacon expressed this viewpoint clearly and succinctly: "The saving of our own children has more than military value—and it has that, as they are 'the nation's last reserves.' Our job of registering them will establish their military age, and our work will prevent a loss of fighting force on account of physical defects."[23]

Not everyone was convinced. In mid-April, shortly after the drive had gotten underway, Bacon asked the chairman of the State Council of Defense for some help with publicity. She explained that she needed the assistance because several counties, already exhausted by previous drives of various kinds, "do not consider this war work."[24] And when

Bacon approached the State Council of Defense for formal backing of her plan to use schoolhouses as sites for the weighing and measuring drive, she received a chilly reception. Writing to the Woman's Section two days later she reported that the state council eventually "endorsed my plan for using the school houses . . . but I know they thought whoever put Child Welfare on the Nat[ional] Council of Def[ense] was crazy. I'm glad it was done at Washington."[25]

In spite of the lack of enthusiasm in some quarters, Bacon persevered. During late February and early March she scrambled to get child welfare committees established in the counties where they had not yet been appointed. She advised a member of her Child Welfare Committee in early March that "I have heard from Washington, and they pronounce my plan for Indiana 'excellent.' So we can go right ahead." The next day she wrote the Woman's Section office in Indianapolis that "I bet no other state C. W. [child welfare committee] is as far ahead in the work as ours."[26]

As April 6 approached the major concern was that the printed cards on which the children's height and weight were to be recorded had not yet arrived from Washington. There was much frantic correspondence during the first few days of April, and eventually Bacon simply sent copies of the questions to her county committees with the recommendation that they use blank slips of paper for the time being.[27] Some cards finally arrived on April 8, but only a handful compared with what was needed for the entire state. This produced considerable frustration and by mid-month it began to show as Bacon referred to the baby drive as "the biggest, hardest, meanest job given to the state council." A few days later she wrote to Indianapolis: "It is a relief that the cards are coming in. What a lot of worry that made for every one! It simply wore me to a frazzle, and I am just able to drag about."[28]

Bacon's problem with the cards was, unfortunately, not yet over. During the delay she had written the Children's Bureau and requested that the blanks be sent directly to the counties, rather than to her or the Woman's Section headquarters in Indianapolis, in order to save time. In a typical wartime snafu, however, someone in the federal bureaucracy failed to get the message, and in late May Bacon wrote plaintively to Carlisle: "I have just mailed out, with my own hands, 10,000 cards that were dumped on my sidewalk (in big boxes) from Chicago. I sent them to the most clamorous counties." Three weeks later, after Washington once again promised to send materials directly to the counties, Bacon advised Carlisle that "about half a ton—not much less—of booklets and posters were dumped on my back porch and inside my front hall door.

. . . It was too funny to be tragic, but I laughed rather hysterically and fell on Mr. Bacon's shoulder." Eventually, after the receipt of franked envelopes from the government and with the assistance of neighbors who volunteered for a "mailing bee," she sent the materials on their way to the county child welfare committees.[29]

Another frustration, especially at the start of the Children's Year but continuing in subsequent months, was county child welfare chairwomen who were either completely inactive or failed to report on the results of their activities. Bacon complained about this repeatedly. She wrote the Woman's Section in April that she was "working night and day, now, with such a horrid tangle of counties that are not behaving right." Three months later she observed that "it is maddening to work with county women whom you do not know, and never saw, and have to risk your reputation on their notions to do or not to do what you ask." She became particularly incensed at the chair of the child welfare committee at Bluffton, telling state headquarters that "she lies down on the work, and I hope you will write her county [chair]woman to please appoint a child welfare chairman who appreciates the value of the work, the great opportunity of having government help in saving the lives of the children of their county." A week later she advised her superiors in Indianapolis that she had "written no end of personal letters, in answer to questions, or objections, and, one by one, we seem to be waking up the counties—but some seem dead." And, indeed, the 1918 annual report of the State Council of Defense reported that only fifty counties (out of ninety-two) had turned in results from the baby campaign.[30]

For a woman who claimed in midsummer that she would be "heart broken if Indiana does not lead the Union," such non-compliance must have been hard to accept. For all the difficulties, though, Bacon had no regrets. "It has all shown itself to be worth while," she wrote in June, "on account of defects discovered [in children], operations following, public sentiment awakened . . . permanent clinics started." A month later she advised the Children's Bureau that "we are hearing from counties I thought were hopeless, of some fine work done. You ought to be very, very happy over the idea of the Children's Year, for it is having wonderful results, in hundreds of ways." And in August she remarked that the Children's Year had "opened up wonderful vistas before our country women, as well as our town women" and had demonstrated "the absolute necessity of County Welfare nurses."[31]

The baby weighing and measuring test, while perhaps the most widely noted, was not the only Children's Year initiative. In June and July brochures were sent out from the nation's capital announcing a campaign to maintain and develop recreational activities for youth as a hedge against the wartime increase in juvenile delinquency that European countries had experienced. Bacon approved of the goal, but she received the news with decidedly mixed emotions: "I thought I was just nicely coming out of our baby drive, which has nearly killed me. Now, before we have finished, I am asked to begin a recreation drive." Although she did send a bulletin to the county child welfare committees requesting that a "recreation association" be organized in every community, she worried, correctly, that the drive was beginning too late to get much organized for the summer.[32]

Nor had the logistical problems between Washington and Indiana been solved. When she received only fifty pamphlets detailing the recreation drive Bacon wrote to Lathrop that "We haven't had a fair deal on literature. Food and Liberty Loan flooded the country with theirs. We have not enough even for our township leaders to have one apiece, to say nothing of the mothers." A few weeks later she complained to the Woman's Section that "We have had to make bricks without straw, all year." These impediments exacerbated the mental and physical fatigue inherent in the oversight of a far-flung endeavor that was wholly reliant on volunteers and voluntary compliance. By mid-August the situation was beginning to take a toll. "I feel I couldn't do one more 'lick of work', without a rest, or think one more coherent thought," she admitted in a letter to the Children's Bureau. "In fact, am doing only 'subconscious' work, now."[33]

In addition to her day-to-day responsibilities, Bacon also took on the task of organizing two significant public programs during the year. On May 9, a state conference on child welfare convened in Indianapolis. Carlisle gave the keynote address ("Organization of Women for War Service"), which was followed by several short papers on specific child welfare problems. During the afternoon session, over which Bacon presided, the secretaries of the state boards of health, education, and charities, as well as two representatives from the Indiana Industrial Board, all addressed the topic "What the State is Doing to Protect Her Children." The program concluded in the evening with the chairman of the State Council of Defense speaking on the subject "Defending the Child" and Julia Lathrop, whom Bacon had persuaded to journey out from Washington, discussing the rationale and plans for the Children's Year. (Lathrop observed during her remarks that Indiana was the first state in which the woman's section had called a conference, and said that she was "intensely interested in the sessions in order that I may carry away some suggestions to other states.") Bacon also organized a child welfare session at the annual meeting of the State Conference of Charities and Correction, held in October in Evansville. Besides her own talk, titled "The War Comes Home to Indiana," she had once again arranged for a prominent national speaker to be present: Dr. Jessica Peixotto, who had succeeded Lathrop as chair of the Child Welfare Department, Woman's Committee, Council of National Defense.[34]

It was at this October meeting that the Indiana Child Welfare Committee decided to employ a field secretary who would be able to spend some time traveling around the state to "poke up the slow counties, at first hand." Bacon saw this appointment as essential to the successful continuation of the work. Since no secretarial assistance was provided, she had been typing all her own correspondence, as well as getting out the mass mailings noted above, for a year, and she wrote Carlisle in early November that "I have simply gone my limit and come to the end of my row, physically." On November 16, just five days after the armistice brought a halt to hostilities in Europe, Edna Hatfield Edmondson, an Indiana University–trained social worker and former Lake County probation officer, accepted the field secretary's position. Bacon wrote the Children's Bureau of her "unspeakable relief" at having this position filled, noting that she had been "completely broken down by my office work in July, and was too tired to rest when I went away in August. . . . It took all of the snap and inspiration out of me— work that a $5.00 girl could have done. But now things will be better."[35]

Thus reinvigorated, Bacon fired off a bulletin to the county child welfare committees within days. She announced a new executive committee, which now included representatives of the state boards of charities and health; she announced Edmondson's appointment as field secretary, and explained her duties; and she requested a donation of $20 per county to cover Edmondson's salary and expenses (since the governor had refused to provide money for child welfare work). Finally, she explained that "the close of the war has brought to an end the state council's work, and much of the county councils'. It does not close ours, which we trust is on a firm foundation, that will endure."[36]

Endure it did. The Children's Year continued to completion, and Bacon and Edmondson endeavored throughout the fall of 1918 and spring of 1919 to encourage back-to-school and stay-in-school drives. The Child Welfare Committee, which had been a very small cog in the Indiana State Council of Defense machinery, did not disband, but rather became a separate, non-governmental organization. Writing to Lathrop in mid-April 1919, Bacon noted that she had just returned "from a meeting of our State Council of Defense—the final breaking up of the council. However, our Child Welfare work is going right on—the one green, living shoot . . . of the tree that has just been cut down." Bacon remained as state chairman of the group, Edmondson retained the field secretary's post, and both of them were made special state agents by the Children's Bureau, an appointment that gave them franking privileges for Bureau publications. In addition, Edmondson's travel was partially supported when the Extension Division of Indiana University created a Child Welfare Bureau as part of its Public Welfare Service and engaged her as one of its field representatives. Finally, during the winter of 1919–1920 the members of the Child Welfare Committee adopted a constitution and transformed their group into the Indiana Child Welfare Association, a private organization that continued to work on behalf of the state's children for many years thereafter. The Indiana example supports Muncy's assertion that "child welfare reform was one of the progressive beneficiaries of World War I, and one of the very few whose benefits did not end with demobilization."[37]

The benefits were not achieved, however, without personal cost. Bacon was sharply critical of the "niggardly, measley [sic], inefficient" policy of the State Council of Defense, which provided no financial support for the Child Welfare Committee's work. As a result, she wrote to Lathrop in the aftermath, "I worked with no amanuensis through the thick of the fight to get the state's babies weighed, etc. Last fall I broke down from overwork, and Dr. Edmondson was secured." Eight years later, in a reminiscence prepared for her children, she confided that of all the public work in which she had been engaged "what did me most harm was my work in the State Council of Defence. . . . It was horrible— the manual labor. I've never been the same woman since."[38]

But in spite of the frustrations so evident in her correspondence, Bacon took much satisfaction in what had been accomplished. In two years she had nurtured a small, often overlooked, and sometimes ridiculed component of the state's World War I bureaucracy into a permanent, private, professional association working actively for child betterment in Indiana. And much of value had been accomplished along the way. Although the baby weighing and measuring drive had stalled in many counties, some 100,000 youngsters (about one-half of the state's children under six years of age) were examined, and many correctable abnormalities detected. "Throughout the state," concluded a report of the Child Welfare Committee, "mothers were awakened to the needs of their children and sought intelligent advice."[39] In addition, the back-to-school and stay-in-school drives had kept many children from entering the workforce prematurely and, as we shall see, the 1919 General

Assembly had passed laws positively affecting child welfare. Julia Lathrop wrote Bacon that "all you have done in Indiana is, of course, an astonishingly good result of Children's Year, one of the very best."[40]

On the first page of the first chapter of his examination of American social service and social action between the Progressive era and the New Deal—a chapter titled "Great Expectations: Hopes Deferred"—Clarke Chambers writes that during 1917–1918 "social reformers continued to labor for the uplift of society at home, even as the holocaust of war increasingly consumed the nation's energies, and to plan bold programs for the postwar world." In a similar vein historian Allen Davis has observed that "to their own surprise, many [reformers] came to view the war . . . as a climax and culmination of their movement for social justice in America."[41]

It is only one small example, to be sure, but the wartime activity on behalf of child welfare in Indiana supports such assertions. Although their language sometimes bore a patina of martial rhetoric (the reference to children as "our last reserves," for example), Bacon and her colleagues knew more was at stake in their work than filling some future draft quota. She expressed this nowhere quite so well as in a letter sent to the chairwomen of her county child welfare committees two months before the war's end:

> Month by month this has been borne in upon me. Our work is unlike that of any other department of the Council of Defense. We are not working to supply a temporary need, of food, or money, or workers. *We are building up the state.* Every stone laid, every life saved, every character moulded, makes more secure the foundations of our government.[42]

❖

During the spring of 1919, as Bacon and her colleagues on the Child Welfare Committee were concluding the Children's Year activities and beginning to formulate plans to continue their work following the dissolution of the State Council of Defense, two other events took place that would significantly affect child welfare in Indiana. In mid-March, at least in part because Bacon and her committee had heightened public awareness of the subject, Hoosier legislators created a Commission on Child Welfare and Social Insurance. The five-member commission was charged with making "a careful and systematic study of child welfare and social insurance" in Indiana and other states, submitting findings and recommendations to the governor, and drafting "such bills as may be necessary to embrace and carry out its recommendations" for consideration at the next session of the General Assembly. Then in early May the Children's Bureau sponsored in Washington a national Conference on Child Welfare Standards. Recommendations that emerged from this meeting, slightly modified after their consideration at several regional conferences, were codified into a set of "Minimum Standards for Child Welfare."[43]

Bacon, although invited, did not attend the conference in Washington. She wrote Lathrop that she was "bitterly disappointed" not to be present and was "only missing it because it would mean to sacrifice another member of the family to whom a trip is imperative." Her disappointment reflected an accurate assessment of the importance of the conference; the "Minimum Standards" developed there had considerable impact on child welfare policy nationwide, including the work of Indiana's Commission on Child Welfare and Social Insurance. Bacon, too, had an impact on the work of the commission; doubtless as a result of her wartime work on behalf of the state's youth, Governor James Goodrich named her as one of its members.[44]

Appointing the five commissioners and getting them together to begin their duties proved to be a lengthy process. Bacon knew as early as April that she was to be appointed, advising Lathrop of the fact but cautioning "my name has not been announced, so this is also confidential." The organization of the commission was delayed for months due to the illness of one member. Following this man's eventual resignation, the governor "hunted up and down the state for a successor." "I have been so anxious for it to get started," Bacon wrote at the end of the year, "that I have almost made a nuisance of myself." Finally, in January 1920, the commission held an organizational meeting. The members included, besides Bacon, two businessmen (Harry Wade, J. E. Frederick), a labor leader (J. W. Hays), and the state director of the General Federation of Women's Clubs (Vida Newsom). Frederick, Newsom, and Bacon (chair) constituted a Sub-Commission on Child Welfare. Almost certainly on Bacon's recommendation, the commission selected Edna Hatfield Edmondson, field secretary of the Child Welfare Committee, to be its secretary as well.[45]

Following their organizational meeting in January, the commissioners held four other sessions in Indianapolis during the year as well as "numerous conferences with various persons and organizations in the State." In their report to the governor, submitted in mid-December, the members explicitly thanked the state boards of health, industry, education, and charity for providing help and advice. They also acknowledged receiving "the valuable advice of national authorities in the subjects of [our] study." Many of those authorities, not surprisingly, were on the staff of the Children's Bureau. Edmondson wrote the bureau in late April, explaining the commission and its mandate and asking for "materials you have which would assist us in this work." The acting chief of the bureau wrote back promptly, sending several of the agency's publications (including the recently released *Minimum Standards for Child Welfare*) as well as words of encouragement.[46]

The commission made four principal recommendations in its final report, all of which were described as "matters needing such special attention at this time as to be regarded as emergencies." A second set of suggestions, considered somewhat less vital, dealt largely with providing adequate appropriations for the implementation or enforcement of laws already on the books, and a final set of recommendations enumerated subjects that the commission felt needed further investigation. The bulk of the report, however, concerned the four major recommendations for which legislation was sought: creation of a juvenile commission, a child labor law, providing a strong administrative agency to oversee child labor statutes, and a school attendance law.[47]

The proposal for a juvenile commission, a sort of state-level Children's Bureau, was premised on a belief that responsibility for child welfare had been so balkanized—that is, divided among so many different state agencies, each of which had its own priorities and agendas—that no single entity could deal with the subject as a whole. As the commission summarized the situation: "there is no one board or commission having authority to protect the general interests of all children of all ages, and to prevent dependency, neglect, delinquency, degeneracy, truancy, and illegitimacy." The state boards of charities, education, health, and industry all affected Indiana's youth within their "distinct fields," but none had "the care of all the interests of the child." Even the recently created juvenile court system had proved to be inadequate; although conceived "as a device for dealing with the peculiar social problems of child welfare," it was not working as well as anticipated because it was "grafted upon the regular courts" whose "organization and procedures . . . have been established through long usage." Thus (in language that is almost certainly Bacon's), there needed to be a single state agency "charged with the duty of correcting bad environmental conditions of the children of the state." The juvenile commission being proposed would have the power to recommend changes in the organization and procedure of the juvenile courts, as well as to "investigate and report to the Governor from time to time on condi-tions of child welfare throughout the state."[48]

The commission's second principal recommendation called for the codification and strengthening of the state's child labor laws. The report reviewed and summarized the various statutes then in effect (the earliest dating to 1883) and observed that "the mixing of industrial laws and school laws, the scattering of provisions relating to the same subject, [and] the apparently conflicting statements in regard to the same sub-jects" had led to "an injustifiable confusion and uncertainty" in the minds of all concerned. Moreover, Indiana's guidelines for issuing em-ployment certificates to children did not meet federal standards (specif-ically, those of the Child Labor Tax Board). Unless the situation were remedied, Indiana faced the prospect of having to operate under a dual certification system—an eventuality that would create "great delay and annoyance" both to children entitled to certificates and employers wishing to hire them.[49]

While acknowledging that comparing child labor laws from state to state was difficult, the commissioners averred that "Indiana is not in the front rank" in terms of its requirements. Nor did the state measure up to the "Minimum Standards for Child Welfare" that had emerged from the Children's Bureau conference the previous year. Indeed, the com-mission reported, "the standards set in Indiana law for children in in-dustry are lower in almost every instance than those set in the Mini-mum Standards." For example, Indiana law required that a child (if old enough) must have completed only the fifth grade before leaving school to go to work; the Minimum Standards established completion of the eighth grade as the educational baseline. Thus, Bacon and her col-leagues advised that they had drafted a child labor bill for consideration by the 1921 General Assembly. The proposed legislation would "har-monize the provisions of the present laws . . . concerning minors em-ployed in industry" and "raise the standards in Indiana to meet those set in the federal provisions." The goal was "to place Indiana in the first rank of states and to approximate the Minimum Standards."[50]

The commission based its third major proposal on the belief that the results of good child labor legislation with high standards "must always be disappointing unless the agency administering the laws is both wise and strong." In 1920 the administration of such laws in Indiana was being carried out by a Department of Women and Children located within the Industrial Board. This department had been created by the legislature in 1919, but its status was somewhat uncertain. The bill that had been introduced to authorize the department had been so crippled by amendments that it lost the support of even friendly legislators and failed to pass. Then, at the end of the session, a clause was added to the state's general appropriation bill creating the department and providing for a "competent woman as director." Arguably, however, the authorization would expire when the appropriation bill did—that is, after two years. The commission report detailed the "efficient work" that had been performed by the department during its brief existence, citing this as "evidence of the value of the Department to the state." The commissioners therefore recommended that the Department of Women and Children unambiguously be made a permanent part of the Industrial Board and that its director (who should be a woman) be made a full member of the board.[51]

Finally, the commission took up the matter of compulsory school attendance. "Statutory provisions concerning child labor and school attendance," the report observed, "should go hand in hand, one set of provisions complementing the other." Indiana, as noted, fell far short of the Minimum Standards. The state's requirements were lower for age, length of school term, school grade, and several other indices. The World War I draft had called attention not only to physical defects but to "an astonishingly high percentage of illiteracy among men young enough to have had most of the benefits of the present school system." The laws in effect in 1920 required attendance until the age of 14 as long as the fifth grade had been completed. "With this meager educational training," the commission lamented, "great numbers of children are everywhere in the state leaving school to go to work." Moreover, even the laws that were in effect were enforced haphazardly due to the poor pay, low qualifications, and high turnover of attendance (truant) officers. The commissioners thus recommended (and drafted) a new compulsory school attendance law that would significantly raise the state's standards in this area.[52]

The Commission on Child Welfare and Social Insurance submitted its report to Governor Goodrich in mid-December 1920, with the observation that it contained "definite positive recommendations." Many of those recommendations were considered during the 1921 session of the Indiana General Assembly, which met from January 6 to March 7, and several of them were enacted, although not exactly in the form suggested by Bacon and her colleagues.

The legislators declined to create the full-blown juvenile commission that had been urged upon them. They did, however, agree that the juvenile court system was not operating satisfactorily and took two steps to remedy the situation. First, they created the position of state juvenile probation officer. This individual, to be appointed by the governor for a term of four years, was to prescribe the qualifications of local probation officers, supervise their work, and in general endeavor "to secure the effective application of the probation system and the enforcement of the probation law in all parts of the state." The legislation also provided for a five-member Advisory Juvenile Committee charged with making suggestions and recommendations to the state juvenile probation officer and the governor "in carrying out the probation work of the state."[53]

The commission's call for legislation that would make the Department of Women and Children a permanent part of the state Industrial Board went unheeded by the General Assembly, perhaps because such an enactment was ultimately deemed to be unnecessary. Although the department had been created in a somewhat irregular manner in 1919, its continued existence without the need for subsequent action seems to have been assumed. In the 1921 bill providing the "regular appropriations" of state government, the department is simply listed, without comment, as a part of the Industrial Board. Further, the department's annual reports for 1920 and 1921 make no mention of new legislation being proposed or being necessary in order for its work to proceed. Indeed, the department's efforts on behalf of Indiana women and children employed in industry continued for decades thereafter.[54]

The most important result of the recommendations made by Bacon and her fellow commissioners was passage of a law that combined two of the four principal suggestions of their report. "An act concerning the school attendance and the employment of minors" codified and revised previous legislation on those two subjects and in the process brought Indiana's requirements much closer to the Minimum Standards proposed by the Children's Bureau. The statute created a State Board of Attendance that was given authority to enforce school laws, just as the Industrial Board enforced provisions regarding child labor. With some very limited exceptions, children between the ages of 7 and 16 were required to be in school. Youngsters between 14 and 16 could leave school only if they had completed the eighth grade and obtained a lawful employment certificate (which required proof of age). Except for farm labor or domestic service, employment in any "gainful occupation" was prohibited to those under 14 years, the number of hours that children could work in a day or a week were also limited, and employment in certain dangerous occupations was prohibited.[55]

This measure, a decided strengthening of minimum educational requirements and industrial safety standards, served the state and its children reasonably well. The law was not modified until the end of the decade (and then, in part, to permit minors under age 14 to work as golf caddies!). When the National Child Labor Committee (NCLC) surveyed Indiana's situation in 1927 it gave the state relatively high marks. The organization praised the 1921 law and its report concluded that if the communities sampled were representative, which it believed they were, "Indiana has gone a long way in the solution of its child labor problem." The NCLC's principal criticisms were that the Department of Women and Children had too few inspectors to administer the law properly and that the granting of work certificates to 16 and 17 year olds was not as carefully regulated as it was for 14 and 15 year old children. Still, the proportion of Indiana's children aged 5 to 17 attending school increased from 79 percent at the beginning of the 1920s to 85 percent by the end of the decade.[56]

❖

Bacon's membership on the Commission on Child Welfare and Social Insurance and her role as chair of its subcommission on child welfare were highlights of her efforts on behalf of Indiana's children. But her contributions did not stop there. Once the commission's recommendations were submitted she worked tirelessly to see that they were implemented. She was especially interested in improving the state's system of juvenile justice, and sought advice from the Children's Bureau throughout the summer and fall of 1920 as the commission drafted the bill it would recommend to the General Assembly. Early in the new year she sent a copy of the document to Lathrop, observing that "the bill is not what we want, but we feel it will do a great deal, if it gets through."[57] To ensure that it would "get through," Bacon once again journeyed to Indianapolis to attend the General Assembly. As she reminisced six years later:

> In 1921 I was there a good part of the session, working almost alone, to get the Juvenile Probation Department created. I "personally conducted" the campaign and chaperoned the bill through both houses, as I did the housing laws[,] through the hands of committees, clerks, &c &c &c. No one cared much for it except Sen. [Carl] Holmes & the "father" I chose for it in the house abandoned it & I had to find a foster father. I pulled it through the last hour of the last night of the session & saw it on its way to the Governor.[58]

Just as her work on behalf of child welfare during the war had led to her appointment to the study commission, so her work on the commission and her subsequent lobbying for its recommendations led to yet another public service assignment. When Governor Warren T. McCray selected the members of the newly created Advisory Juvenile Committee (later Commission), which was to oversee the work of the state juvenile probation officer, he named Bacon as one of the five appointees. Her fellow members subsequently chose her as president of the group. Reappointed by a succession of governors, and reelected president by a succession of colleagues, she held this position from 1921 until her death in 1933.[59]

While not involved in the day-to-day operation of what came to be called the Probation Department, Bacon was not a mere figurehead. The advisory committee, which by law was required to meet only once a year, met at least twice and occasionally three or four times annually throughout the 1920s. The whole concept of juvenile probation—an attempt to reform youthful offenders without resorting to incarceration—was then relatively new in the state, and the commission members joined the small staff of the department in attempting to (in the words of an annual report) "sell probation to Indiana." This was done in both formal and informal ways. The former involved, for example, both defending the juvenile probation law in the General Assembly (where there was a serious but unsuccessful attempt in 1923 to abolish the Probation Department) and working to expand the probation system by making its use in every county mandatory rather than optional. An instance of informal proselytizing occurred in early June 1923 when the commission met in Evansville. Following the official session in the morning, the commission held a well-attended luncheon to which area social workers were invited. Later in the afternoon Bacon hosted a public meeting and reception at her home.

Such lobbying paid dividends. When the Probation Department came under attack during the 1923 legislative session it received "splendid support . . . from various outside organizations of women." (Hard evidence is lacking, but it seems likely that Bacon's influence in such groups as the Indiana Child Welfare Committee and the Indiana Federation of Clubs played a role in garnering this assistance.) Gradually, the "probation idea" began to catch on. In 1921 only forty-two (of ninety-two) counties in the state had appointed probation officers; by the end of the decade seventy-two counties had such officers in place. The department's annual report for 1922 claimed 2,731 cases handled by the state's juvenile courts during the year; by 1929 the agency reported 8,359 probation cases involving boys and girls. The precision of these figures, like most crime and criminal justice statistics, is suspect, as the annual reports admit. But they clearly demonstrate the general trend—that the use of probation as a tool in working with juvenile offenders expanded greatly during the 1920s.

Bacon did not originate the idea of juvenile probation in Indiana—a separate juvenile court employing volunteer probation officers was authorized for Marion County (Indianapolis) as early as 1903—but she did play a key role in the creation of a state agency to promote and supervise probation work. As president of that agency's advisory commission for over a decade, she provided guidance as the concept gradually gained acceptance in county after county. It is doubtful that when she accepted appointment to the Commission on Child Welfare and Social Insurance she realized that she would be involved with the issue of juvenile justice for the rest of her life. But it is likely that she welcomed a continuing opportunity to serve the cause of improving the welfare of Hoosier children. Responding during the summer of 1921 to a letter from Julia Lathrop, in which the chief of the Children's Bureau had referred to juvenile court work as "an endless chain of circumstances," Bacon wrote: "Yes, indeed, we do become involved in an 'endless chain' when we begin on Juvenile Court work. . . . And I am in the chain gang—and happy to be."[60]

Six

City Plans and National Housing Standards

During the decade of the 1920s Bacon began to reduce slightly the amount of her public work. She turned sixty in 1925, she had been heavily involved in a plethora of social welfare efforts for over twenty years, and she was plainly tired. She began especially to cut back on speaking engagements, having found the attendant travel to be increasingly debilitating. (As she once explained, her short stature meant that "my feet don't touch anything, neither the floor, nor the opposite [train] seat, without stretching, and I get tired out, just as the children do. The weight and strain is thrown in the wrong places, and a long trip frazzles me out.") After her lobbying effort on behalf of juvenile probation during the 1921 General Assembly, she never again spent significant time in Indianapolis for the biennial legislative sessions. She wrote in January 1927 that "I hope and pray it will not be necessary for me to go up [to the capital] on account of any attack on my housing laws or the State Juvenile Probation Department that I helped create." Referring to her past legislative work she observed: "I do not grudge a moment I have given it, nor loss of flesh and strength. . . . But that's it—it has taken something out of me I can never hope to build up again."[1]

This is not to suggest, however, that she did not continue to be engaged in a wide variety of civic endeavors. As we have seen, she chaired the state's Advisory Juvenile Committee/Commission throughout the 1920s. And she remained involved with many social welfare and community betterment efforts in Evansville. Some of these activities and affiliations were of long standing. The Visiting Nurse's Circle, of which she was one of the earliest members, merged in mid-decade with the Babies Milk Fund to become the Public Health Nursing Association (PHNA). A community health center out of which the association operated moved in 1927 from space in the city's Coliseum to a house donated to the group by local businessman E. Mead Johnson. Bacon, who was a member of the PHNA executive committee, organized the dedication ceremony for the new center, at which she read a poetic "Appreciation" she had written in Johnson's honor. She also chaired or was a member of several other PHNA committees and fund drives during the late 1920s and early 1930s.[2]

Bacon's work on behalf of public health nursing complemented her efforts to combat tuberculosis. This, too, had been an interest for many years, one with obvious links to housing reform. The Vanderburgh County Tuberculosis Association traced its origins to a committee established in 1907 by the Monday Night Club during a meeting at the Bacons' home, and a local newspaper noted in late 1933 that Albion "had retained her membership on the board of directors of the organization through much of the 27 years since that time." She supported the creation of Boehne Camp, a fresh air facility for tubercular patients that eventually became Boehne Hospital, a well-known sanatorium that continued to operate on the far west side of Evansville for several decades. After 1926, when the hospital was taken over by the county and became a separate taxing unit with its own board of trustees, the tuberculosis association refocused its efforts and resources on prevention. Bacon, for example, chaired a committee that established a summer health camp at Inglefield (about twelve miles north of Evansville) for children who were at risk of contracting TB but had not yet developed symptoms. In 1932, in recognition of her many years of service to the organization, the members of the Vanderburgh County Tuberculosis Association selected Bacon as their president.[3]

While her interest in these public health efforts went back many years, the decade of the 1920s also saw Bacon become involved in some new initiatives—most notably, city planning and zoning—that raised her profile in her hometown higher still. And in the early 1930s her national reputation as a housing expert even led to service on a presidential commission.

Writing in the April 1932 issue of the professional journal *City Planning,* Raymond W. Blanchard, executive secretary of the Evansville

City Plan Commission, provided an assessment of the first decade of city planning in the community. Planning, he reported, had experienced "a slow but steady progress" in Evansville. The commission members had managed to overcome the initial "widespread misunderstanding of their purpose" and the feeling that here was "'another useless board which exists only to restrict property development and to overlap existing departments in its activities.'" Now, ten years later, "a general feeling of confidence in the City Plan and a determination to adhere to it have been developed." If Indiana's (then) fourth largest city could "not yet point to any spectacular city planning achievements," the opportunity existed "to make use of the City Plan to develop not only a greater but also a better Evansville." The decade of progress that Blanchard described owed much to the efforts of Albion Bacon.[4]

Although the state of Indiana was not among the leaders in the inauguration of city planning, Hoosiers were not oblivious to the growth of such activity in other parts of the country during the early twentieth century. Reflective of this burgeoning interest, in 1916 the Indiana Bureau of Legislative Information (the research arm of the General Assembly) commissioned Frank G. Bates, a professor of political science at Indiana University, to prepare a short booklet on the subject. Bates's treatment of the topic was factual rather than hortatory; in his twenty-seven pages of text he never actually urged passage of city planning legislation in Indiana. But he definitely made it *sound* like a good idea, defining the subject in his opening sentence as "the science of designing cities or parts of cities so as to make them more convenient, healthful, efficient and beautiful."[5]

It seems likely that the Bureau of Legislative Information had a barely hidden agenda in commissioning Bates's brief, easily understood survey. By 1916 the topic was being widely discussed. Both John Nolen's edited volume, *City Planning*, and Nelson P. Lewis's *The Planning of the Modern City* appeared in that year. And an exhibition of American and foreign city planning endeavors, circulated by the American City Bureau, traveled to several Indiana cities in 1916 in an effort to engender support for state planning legislation. The time was not yet quite right, and a measure authorizing municipalities to engage in city planning failed to pass the General Assembly in 1917. A foundation had been laid, however, and in 1921 the legislature approved "An act providing for the creation of city plan commissions in cities of all classes."[6]

The Indiana planning act authorized any municipality to appoint a commission for the purpose of studying and recommending a plan for its future development. Such commissions normally consisted of nine

members, five of whom were to be private citizens "qualified by knowledge or experience to act in matters pertaining to the development of a
city plan." The other four members were to be representatives of the
common council, board of park commissioners, board of public works,
and city engineer. The plan commission was to have "full power and
authority" to make "plans and maps of the highway and transportation
facilities, the location of [the city's] parks, playgrounds and public buildings." Moreover, the commission had authority to prepare and forward
to the council for adoption proposed ordinances "regulating the height,
area, bulk and use of buildings and the use and intensity of use of land
by districts within the city." Although the latter power was, in effect, advisory only, section 8 of the act empowered the commission to approve
all plats and plans for subdivision made either in or within five miles of
the city. "Thus at least prospectively," observed a student of planning
and zoning in the state, "the commission was in a position to control
and direct city growth and development."[7]

In his 1932 retrospective Blanchard claimed that "there was delib-
erate planning in Evansville as far back as 1817 when the first street plan
was made." A planning movement in any modern sense, however, did
not commence until about 1915. The city's real estate board had taken
"a leading part in the building up of sentiment for city planning . . . and
had much to do with securing the passage" of the state city planning act.
(A major motivation was the realtors' desire for a rational, simplified
house numbering system.) The Evansville Chamber of Commerce also
took an early interest in the subject. Prior to 1920 a committee of that
organization had explored ways to reconfigure several poorly laid out
streets in the city's principal African-American district in order to
improve traffic circulation. Thus, not surprisingly, the community took
advantage of the state's enabling act soon after it became effective. On
October 3, 1921, the common council passed an ordinance creating the
Evansville City Plan Commission; Mayor Benjamin Bosse, a strong supporter of the city planning movement, signed the measure two days
later.[8]

Bosse's five citizen appointees included two women: Bacon and Es-
telle (Mrs. Harry) Joyce, the wife of a local engineer. The three men appointed by the mayor were apparently selected to represent the interests
of the city's manufacturers (William A. Carson), realtors (Henry M.
Dickman), and contractors (Albert J. Hoffman). Bacon, appointed to
an initial four-year term, was unanimously chosen as president by her
colleagues. She was probably the best known of the commission members, and an Evansville newspaper was doubtless correct in observing

that she had been "appointed to the commission in consideration of the work she has taken part in [in] a national capacity."[9]

The organizational meeting took place promptly—October 17, in the mayor's office. Because substantial start-up costs would be incurred in procuring maps and a small professional library, Bosse and the commissioners agreed that the first year or two of operation would require the greatest expenditure. The mayor thus announced that he would request the common council to appropriate from the general fund for the commission's use a sum based upon three mills of the taxables for the remainder of 1921, and eight mills for 1922. According to the *Evansville Courier*, he also "charged the commission that it should realize it is endowed with extensive powers by the law, and has more power in many instances than the common council and more power than the mayor in many respects." Following election of officers, a committee of three was named to obtain information from other cities of Evansville's size concerning their efforts and experiences with city planning. The newspaper reported that this action was to ensure "that all practical information possible might be in the hands of the members before active work starts."[10]

At the next monthly meeting this investigating committee urged the immediate employment of a city planning engineer "to make the necessary studies to evolve a comprehensive City Plan for Evansville." In this they were following the custom of the day. Permanent municipal planning staffs were still the exception; the rule was to contract with an outside planner or planning firm to provide this specialized service. The committee members recommended the selection of Harland Bartholomew, the city planning engineer for St. Louis and founder of a private consulting firm. Bartholomew made a presentation to the commission on November 23, explaining how he would proceed to develop a comprehensive city plan and providing an estimate of costs. Over the course of the next two months the commissioners and Bartholomew gradually worked out the details of a contract, which was ratified early in 1922.[11]

While negotiations with Bartholomew were under way, the commissioners sought to determine the relationship of their fledgling organization to the rest of city government. The mayor's statement regarding their authority notwithstanding, they requested a formal opinion from the city attorney as to whether the City Plan Commission "took away any power heretofore granted" to the common council, board of public works, or park board. "The general idea," the commission's minutes recorded, "was to do everything possible to cause the Commission to get along harmoniously with the various boards." A second inquiry concerned the respective powers of the plan commission and the board of public works in the consideration and approval of plats. The city attorney's response, a model of diplomacy (and thus equivocation), was that "the Commission first pass upon the plat and then refer same to the Board of Public Works, with the added suggestion that the two bodies work together for the best interests of all."[12]

The activities of the Evansville City Plan Commission during its first decade can, for the sake of convenience, be divided into three major categories: routine business, development and publication of long-range plans, and zoning. The first category includes the sorts of operational tasks common to any government agency—preparing budgets, approving expenditures, hiring staff, submitting annual reports, and so on. These details, along with discussion and approval or rejection of proposed plats, comprise the bulk of the commission's minutes.

"Routine" business was not necessarily prosaic. During its first year or two of operation, there were several challenges to the commission's authority. On one occasion a cemetery association apparently attempted to circumvent the commission in seeking approval of a plat. The commissioners found it necessary to go first to the city attorney and eventually to the state's attorney general for confirmation of their prerogatives. In another instance there was discussion of an owner's "method of advertising his [preliminary] plat before getting final approval of same from the Commission, and his intention of going ahead with the sale of lots without first having his plat approved and put on record at the Court House." These procedures were "severely censured" by the commissioners, and the secretary was ordered to "instruct [the owner] by letter of the attitude of the Commission on these practices."[13]

Periodically the commission found itself involved—sometimes quite inadvertently—in a community-wide controversy. When Bacon called the commission into special session on July 21, 1922, for example, she announced that she had requested the meeting "to discuss the proposition of a river terminal, also to answer the challenge of the Press [the *Evansville Press*] in the matter of the City Plan Commission functioning." City officials, it seems, had agreed to lease a substantial portion of the Ohio River waterfront to a private operator of tow boats and barges. The *Press* favored a *municipal* river terminal, and editorialized on July 17 that the plan commission should be actively seeking a site for a facility to be owned and operated by the city. By the time of the meeting four days later the vice-president of the commission had visited the *Press* and come away with a promise that the editors "would desist their lambasting until the City Plan Commission had time to give the matter consideration." The next day the *Press* reported "two important developments": city council leaders had declared themselves in favor of a municipal terminal, and the plan commission had agreed to have its consulting engineer make an immediate study.[14]

William D. Hudson, an employee of Harland Bartholomew and Associates, submitted a "very thorough consideration" of the subject just one week later. His "Preliminary Report on Transportation Facilities" was accepted by the commissioners, who proceeded to endorse most of its proposals. The plan commission concluded that it was inadvisable for the city to build its own river terminal "at this time," and that the structure proposed by the private barge operator would be a "desirable addition to the wharf facilities." On the other hand, the commission members argued that the future needs of the city "demanded a more extended study and survey," which they promised to include in their final report on transportation. In this instance the City Plan Commission acted as a lightning rod for a divisive issue in the community, and was able to defuse the controversy by subjecting the issue to the formal, professional planning process that it was instituting.[15]

The preparation of long-range plans for Evansville's growth and development, though ultimately the responsibility of the plan commission, was principally the work of Harland Bartholomew and his associates. In fact, the City Plan Commission's first executive secretary, Blanchard, was hired in the fall of 1923 from Bartholomew's organization. This pattern was not atypical. As an analyst of his career has observed, "Bartholomew realized that the [city] plan would more likely be implemented if his field man were to become a permanent local fixture. . . . If it was the wish of the contract city to retain its Bartholomew representative on a permanent basis (as it often was) and the latter was agreeable, Bartholomew acted as a kind of sponsor for the union and gave it his blessing."[16]

In selecting Bartholomew, Bacon and her colleagues had chosen one of the pioneers in American city planning, and a man who tended to focus throughout his career on the "big picture." Writing on the eve of his fiftieth anniversary in the profession he recalled that his interest in the field from the beginning "was to produce for every city a true comprehensive plan. This feeling has so dominated my thinking that my family have jokingly remarked on numerous occasions that I should have a middle name, i.e.[,] 'C' for Comprehensive." While not unaware of the need for small-scale studies of neighborhoods and the like, he professed far more interest "in whether there is a basic comprehensive plan which furnishes the framework and substance within which these individual designs can be made."[17]

These proclivities, expressed in the early 1960s, were reflected in Bartholomew's work in Evansville almost forty years earlier. In mid-February 1922 he enumerated for the plan commission a series of studies he proposed to make and their preferred order. These included examination of streets and traffic patterns, transit facilities, railroad and river transportation, and recreational facilities. By April, zoning had been added to the list. On Bartholomew's recommendation Bacon appointed several subcommittees of the commission, each one to focus on a different aspect of the master plan as it evolved. (She put herself on the zoning subcommittee.) In an interview with the *Evansville Journal* six months after the City Plan Commission had been created, Bartholomew itemized several of the city's "neglected problems": the need for new, discrete residential and industrial areas; expansion of the central business district; increased automobile traffic and the tie-ups caused by at-grade railroad crossings; and the city's confusing house numbering system. The *Journal's* headline summed it up: "City Planners Have Many Problems Confronting Them."[18]

Bacon and the other members of the plan commission dealt with those problems throughout the 1920s by authorizing the preparation of essentially what Bartholomew had suggested: a series of reports that ultimately constituted a comprehensive city plan. Researched by his staff associates, presented to the plan commission in preliminary form for discussion, modification, and approval, and finally printed and given wide distribution throughout the community, these "prototype reports" from the "shakedown phase" of Bartholomew's practice "would continue to be the measure of the firm's service to a city in preparing its comprehensive plan."[19]

The Evansville City Plan Commission eventually issued five of these reports. They dealt with plans for the development of a system of major streets (1925) and recreation facilities (1927), suggestions for improving the city's appearance (1927), and plans for railroad and harbor development (1929) and improvement of transit facilities (1930). Produced in an $8^1/_2$ by 11 inch format, these were substantial booklets, not mere brochures. The Major Street Plan, which may be taken as an exemplar, ran to fifty-six pages and included sixteen plates and four appendices. And this was a condensation. The Bartholomew staffer who had principal responsibility for this report explained to the commissioners that "it was felt best to publish a series of maps and diagrams with concise descriptions rather than the fuller text of the original report."

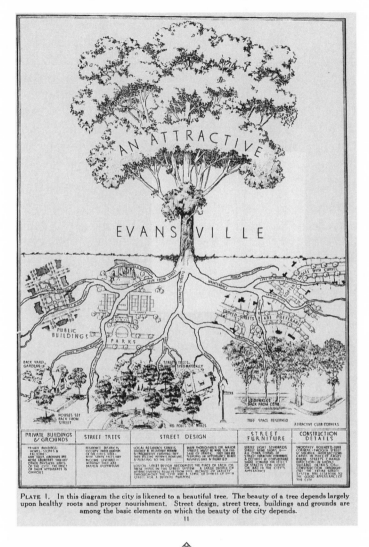

"An Attractive Evansville," illustration from the City Plan Commission's booklet Suggestions for Improving the City's Appearance *(1927). Special Collections, Willard Library*

He also assured commission members, who obviously wanted the city's monies to be expended locally, "that it was intended that the printing should be taken care of in Evansville."[20]

The Major Street Plan, which proposed development of a complete system of heavy traffic thoroughfares, was also important because it included a set of rules adopted by the commission to control the subdivision of land. Such control, Blanchard observed, gave the commission "its greatest opportunity for early and continued accomplishments" and meant that "the practice of subdividing land was gradually elevated to a higher plane." The commissioners themselves expressed confidence that the rules, "which merely carry the fundamental principles of scientific city planning into effect, will meet with general approval." Blanchard, at least, believed that such had been the case:

> The policy of the City Plan Commission in connection with street design has resulted in convincing many citizens who formerly believed that straight, rectangular planning was the only efficient and practical method of street design, that there is a great difference between the requirements of major streets and those of minor residential streets, and that the latter may with distinct advantage be planned as curving streets, which discourage through-traffic and are safer, quieter, and more attractive.[21]

The Major Street Plan went into effect in 1925. In that same year work on the third principal initiative of the commission's first decade, the adoption of a zoning ordinance, also came to fruition. This was the result of a slow, careful campaign that called for considerable public education; its successful conclusion stands as one of the commission's most important achievements during its early years, and it was an effort in which Bacon was centrally involved.

The authority for cities to enact zoning regulations was granted to municipalities by the state legislature in 1921 in a companion bill to the one providing for the creation of city plan commissions.[22] The law prescribed a detailed set of steps communities had to follow in order to pass a zoning ordinance, and a plan commission was an integral part of the process. The sequence of steps began in Evansville in March 1923 when Bacon, who had been reelected president of the City Plan Commission the previous month, announced the appointment of a five-member zoning committee. This group consisted of four of the citizen members of the commission (Bacon herself, Carson, Dickman, William H. Dress); the fifth member, and chairman, was Albert W. Hartig, the city council's representative on the commission.[23]

This committee appears to have been inactive during the remainder of 1923; at least there is virtually nothing regarding zoning in the commission minutes for that period. Early in 1924, however, Bartholomew associate Earl Mills addressed the commission on the subject. As reported in the minutes, "He emphasized the necessity of thoro[ugh] publicity, especially thru neighborhood meetings and discussion before clubs and public organizations." Mills also urged the creation of a citizens committee and noted that newspaper articles "on definite phases of the subject would be of great value in bringing home to people the need for zoning."[24]

Precisely who drafted the Evansville ordinance is not clear. Blanchard, as executive secretary, probably took a leading role, with advice from Bartholomew and Mills and consultation with the zoning committee presumably part of the process. The measure took some time to prepare; it was not until late summer that the draft of a proposed ordinance, including both text and maps, was reported out of the zoning committee and passed on to the full City Plan Commission for consideration. The commission, after making a few minor amendments, voted unanimously to approve the zoning committee's report, and then heard Blanchard detail "an outline for [the] publicity procedure for the Zoning Ordinance" that he and Mills had prepared. As a first step in that direction, the commissioners agreed to invite the entire city council to their next regular meeting "in order to permit thorough official discussion of the aims and methods of zoning before commencing to explain the proposed ordinance to the public."[25]

This meeting, attended by the mayor, eight councilmen, and the city building inspector, took place a month later. Blanchard presented an overview of the ordinance, including the boundaries of the proposed use districts, and Bacon and the other members of the zoning committee all made brief presentations in favor of the measure. Building Commissioner Edward Kerth also spoke on behalf of the proposal, using a recently erected factory as "an example of a well-constructed building wrongly placed." He observed that a zone ordinance would allow him "to refuse a building permit . . . not only on grounds of faulty construction but also in case of invasion of factories into home neighborhoods." He also appealed to the elected officials' civic pride, noting that of all the cities that sent representatives to the most recent national conference of building inspectors only two—Evansville and Flint, Michigan—were still unzoned.[26]

Then in mid-December the commission held a public hearing "to consider all suggested revisions of the zone ordinance before submission of same to the City Council." Newspaper reports indicate that the council chamber, where the hearing took place, was "almost filled with representative business and professional men, practically all of whom signified that they were heartily in favor of a zoning system here." Bacon presided over the meeting, using her well-practiced rhetorical skills to good effect. She counseled that the proposed ordinance was "so vital to the welfare of present and future generations in Evansville that its passage or failure are matters of life or death." Employing the medical metaphors that had characterized her housing reform lectures, she observed: "Lack of a zoning system is causing our city to become congested, and congestion is as dangerous to a city body as congestion of the lungs to the human body." At the request of the mayor, Hartig read the section of the proposal that established a board of zoning appeals—an obvious attempt to allay the fears of those who assumed there would be no recourse if a zoning decision went against them. Proponents were also careful to point out that the ordinance would not be retroactive. Although the mayor took no public position on the draft ordinance, he reportedly commented that "some kind of an ordinance in this respect will have to be passed."[27]

The scene of action now shifted to the city council. This was in accordance with the state enabling act, which mandated that after the plan commission had drafted the ordinance, held hearings on it, and submitted it to the council, the common council was to repeat the process and conduct its own hearings on the proposal. According to one analyst, this seeming redundancy resulted because the drafters of the state law "were convinced of the desirability of protecting the interests of private persons so far as possible and were committed to the proposition that the zoning act should be as fair and reasonable as it could be made."[28] Thus a committee of the council spent the first half of 1925 reviewing the commission's work and conferring with the city attorney to ensure that there would be no adverse legal ramifications.

The council's public hearing was conducted on August 3, and the results mirrored the commission's hearing eight months earlier. Two hundred persons were present and the newspapers reported that "sweeping approvals" of the ordinance came from the Chamber of Commerce, a voters' and taxpayers' league, the Real Estate Board, and prominent individuals. Two councilmen expressed concern over restrictions on factories and compensation for factory owners who might be affected. Carson, who at Bacon's request had assumed the presidency of the plan commission in April (she became vice-president), explained once again that current factories were protected by a grandfather clause: "Once a factory, it may continue to be used as a factory." Thus reassured, and no doubt noting the strong support for the measure by those in attendance, the council unanimously approved the ordinance at its regular meeting two weeks later. The *Courier* observed, correctly, that the action "followed more than a year of intensive preparation through the city plan commission and the city's zoning engineer."[29]

The ordinance quickly proved its worth. Blanchard wrote in the early 1930s that since the adoption of zoning "inestimable good has resulted throughout the city." He conceded that occasionally an individual "has had to abandon an intended property use which would have netted him a greater financial return than that permitted" by the ordinance. But in "scores of cases" neighborhoods had been protected from "misplaced commercial or industrial developments, buildings protruding beyond the average building line, and other damaging construction." He gave much credit to the board of zoning appeals, which made the system work by "smoothing the rough places and relieving cases of really unnecessary hardship." Only nine amendments to the zoning ordinance had been approved by 1932, most with the agreement of the City Plan Commission. Only once did the council lower a district classification contrary to the advice of the commission.[30]

During the 1920s, therefore, Evansville was able to implement successfully a process of ongoing, professional city planning. A permanent office to concentrate on the issue was established as part of the municipal government (it has evolved into today's Area Plan Commission); a respected consultant was engaged, and he and his associates assisted with the technical aspects of the work for many years; a series of reports, which combined to create the community's first comprehensive city plan, were researched, written, and widely distributed; and a zoning ordinance ensured continued attention to and differentiation of land use as the city developed. Blanchard, who was in the midst of most of this activity, reflected at the end of ten years that success had resulted from "cooperation with numerous agencies, both public and private"; from "repeated services and courtesies to individuals, such as working out more profitable as well as more orderly subdivision layouts, conforming to the City Plan"; and from "continual educational work as to the economy, the health and safety factors, and the convenience and increased livability of the city" that resulted from the planning process. He noted, with obvious pleasure, that when a small group on the city council made an effort in 1928 to eliminate the City Plan Commission's appropriation from the budget, the Real Estate Board, Rotary Club, Kiwanis Club, Tax Conference Committee, and Chamber of Commerce all came to the commission's defense. The council eventually approved the commission's levy as usual because, as Blanchard put it, "the community's civic leaders had made it plain that they desired the benefits of city planning."[31]

While Bacon's role in these developments was not quite as central as it had been in the local and state initiatives on behalf of housing reform, she was nonetheless an important player in the implementation of city planning and zoning in her hometown. She served for over three years as the first president of the Evansville City Plan Commission, and subsequently was the group's vice-president throughout the 1920s. Decisions made and actions taken under her leadership established the agency as an integral and accepted part of city government. She was particularly energetic in her efforts to have zoning adopted in the Pocket City, and her forceful public statements supporting the concept—especially given her reputation for promoting progressive measures—no doubt helped sway some residents who initially had reservations about additional government control on the use of private property.

She also aided the cause of city planning in her community by helping her colleagues and neighbors understand that the efforts of the City Plan Commission were part of a much larger movement for metropolitan improvement of which (she argued) Evansville must be a part. As early as May 1922, she urged that the commission send a representative to a meeting of the National Conference on City Planning. After some initial reluctance (the minutes simply record that the mayor and members who represented city departments "felt differently"), the commission voted unanimously to send Dickman to the meeting "at its expense" and to take out a membership in the national organization.[32] Two years later the commissioners agreed to underwrite the expenses for any member who wished to attend the second annual Indiana Conference on City Planning, which was held at Lafayette and sponsored by the Purdue University School of Civil Engineering. Bacon did attend (she was apparently on the program) and reported back on the "fine spirit and the enthusiasm shown by delegates from all parts of the state" as they described the activities of their planning commissions. She also, the minutes record, "modestly announced" her selection as vice-president of the state conference.[33]

It seems likely (although solid evidence is lacking) that Bacon's position on the executive committee influenced the decision to hold the next state conference (1925) in Evansville. The publicity that resulted from this conclave served to further endorse the City Plan Commission's work. In a front-page story headlined "Indiana City Plan Groups Gather Here" the *Evansville Journal* reported on a discussion of local activities during which "the [prospective] new zoning ordinance was explained and officials complimented on its efficiency." In addition, the Evansville city plan and its proposed studies were detailed in a presentation by Harland Bartholomew. Bacon, who was reelected as vice-president of the state group, was said by the *Journal* to be "recognized as one of the most prominent leaders in the city planning movement in Indiana." Attending members, the paper proudly observed, had accorded "unanimous approval of the work done by Mrs. Bacon and Albert W. Hartig . . . in city planning work here."[34]

This bonanza of free, favorable publicity strengthened the City Plan Commission's hand and served as a springboard for its accomplishments into the early 1930s. As with so much else in early twentieth century Evansville, Albion Bacon was centrally involved.

❖

Despite her attempts to cut back on her public obligations and to focus more of her attention on her hometown, as well as her desire to spend less time traveling and lecturing, Bacon could be lured away from Evansville by events that had a high profile, that dealt with topics that remained close to her heart, and that seemed to her likely to achieve positive results. It was also hard to say no when the request came, directly or indirectly, from federal officials and was couched in terms of service to the nation. That had been true in 1916 when she participated in the women's auxiliary conference held in conjunction with the Second Pan American Congress. It had been true in 1917–1918 when she viewed her work on behalf of child welfare, even though at the state level, as an integral part of the country's war effort. And it was true once again in the fall of 1931 when she accepted appointment as a delegate to a presidential conference, an assignment that required her to make repeated trips to the nation's capital.

In August of that year Herbert Hoover welcomed to the White House a planning committee that he charged with arranging a President's Conference on Home Building and Home Ownership. He had determined, he told his guests, "to undertake the organization of an adequate investigation and study on a nation-wide scale of the problems presented in home ownership and home building." The president was doubtless preaching to the converted when he told the assembled experts that "adequate housing goes to the very roots of the well-being of the family, and the family is the social unit of the nation." Given the state of the American economy in 1931, as the Great Depression began to spread and deepen, he was unrealistically optimistic when he asserted: "It should be possible in our country for anybody of sound character and industrious habits to provide himself with adequate housing and preferably to buy his own home." Hoover knew, however, that what he called the "national ideals of homes for all our people" were, in fact, far from being realized. The purpose of the presidential conference was thus to collect information regarding the current situation, "followed by a weighing and distillation of these facts and the formation of collective judgment of the leaders of our country in this special knowledge."[35]

The members of the planning committee held two subsequent meetings and decided to appoint twenty-five "fact-finding committees," each of which would study a particular topic relevant to the conference theme. An additional six "correlating committees" were to deal with broader "questions of aim and method" common to many of the fact-finding groups. All thirty-one committees were asked to complete work by early autumn so that their reports and recommendations could be printed and ready for distribution prior to the conference in December.[36]

A few weeks later the Evansville newspapers reported that Bacon had accepted an invitation from Secretary of Commerce Robert Lamont to serve on the Correlating Committee on Standards and Objectives, "one of the most important committees in connection with the conference." Precisely how her appointment came about is not certain. Harland Bartholomew, who by this time had held contracts with the Evansville City Plan Commission for almost a decade, was a member of Hoover's planning committee for the conference and he may have suggested her name. Even more likely is that she was recruited by the chair of the Standards and Objectives Committee, Lawrence Veiller, who was now the director of the National Housing Association. He had known Bacon for over twenty years, ever since she sought his assistance during her first efforts to secure housing reform legislation for Indiana. In any event, as the *Courier* noted, she was "considered an authority on housing questions and laws" and since her initial forays into the subject some two decades before she had "kept in touch with whatever progress has been made along this line."[37]

The Committee on Standards and Objectives held its first meeting in Washington on September 25, 1931. Eleven members, including Bacon, were present. James Ford, a prominent housing authority, executive director of a group called Better Homes in America, and a member of the conference planning committee, also attended, and he began the proceedings by outlining the general purpose of the conference and summarizing the work assigned to the twenty-five fact-finding committees. Veiller then explained to his colleagues that their task was two-fold: "welding together" the committee's own conception of standards and objectives for housing and home building in the United States; and, to the extent possible, correlating the reports of the fact-finding committees insofar as they related to standards and objectives. Ford agreed, requesting that the committee be prepared to present a "unified statement" to the full conference. This was obviously a tall order, made even more so since the conference was scheduled for early December, just ten weeks away.[38]

Bacon joined the discussion by proposing her own set of "chief objectives" for housing:

> that a home should be a shelter and a protection, a retreat from the world with privacy and quiet, it should be safe from danger to life and limb, from fire, from intrusion, and from moral hazards; it should not be overcrowded; it should have outlook; it should have dryness, absence of dampness and foul odors; it should be kept in repair; and it should have convenience, comfort and beauty.

Veiller, ever the practical technician, responded to this enthusiastic wish list by observing that it was a "splendid" enunciation of goals and that the committee "might safely use [such a] general statement for objectives." He warned, however, that "we should be more specific in drawing up standards." To begin the process of doing so, the full committee agreed to break into subcommittees of one. Each individual was assigned one or two of the specific topics being considered by the conference and asked to "report back after having formulated standards and objectives" for that subject. Bacon, at her request, took on "Kitchens and Other Work Centers" and "Household Management."[39]

The committee reconvened in Washington on October 12 for a two-day session. Drafts of seventeen reports had been completed, and according to the secretary "the entire time of these meetings was taken up with the detailed consideration" of just eight of the documents— including both of those prepared by Bacon. Unfortunately, the specifics of those discussions did not make it into the minutes; there are no copies of Bacon's drafts or details regarding the constructive criticism to which they were presumably subjected. At the end of the second day Veiller arranged for a clean copy of each report, as revised and amended, to be sent to members of the committee prior to the next meeting.[40]

That third meeting took place, again in Washington, on October 28 and 29. The members scrutinized and revised nine more reports.

They also formulated procedures for presenting the final report that Standards and Objectives would make to the full conference. They decided to divide the two hours they had been allotted into five segments, each of which would group together related topics. For each segment there was to be a principal speaker (ten minutes), a secondary speaker (five minutes), and discussion from the floor (six minutes). Her colleagues chose Bacon as one of the principal speakers.[41]

There was a fourth gathering of the committee on November 16 and 17. Although the minutes for that session seem to have been lost, the members presumably followed the same procedures as in their previous two meetings and completed work on the remaining drafts. Then, apparently, Veiller took the revised versions, crafted the committee's final statement, and sent copies to all the members for their reaction. Bacon cabled the committee's secretary on November 30: "Will approve Mr. Veiller's report without meeting."[42]

The President's Conference on Home Building and Home Ownership met December 2–5, 1931; the Correlating Committee on Standards and Objectives, with Veiller presiding, made its presentation on the afternoon of the 4th. Bacon was responsible for summarizing the committee's conclusions on home information centers, home furnishings and decorations, household management, kitchens, and homemaking. As she explained: "I have five subjects to cover in ten minutes. I will scramble them all together." She also noted that the topics she was discussing were "intended to apply to a higher class of our citizens, that large number that are struggling to own and to make and to keep a home."[43]

This brief presentation—Veiller thanked her at the end for concluding three minutes ahead of schedule!—was vintage Bacon, reflecting both her environmental determinism and her more ethereal proclivities. She began by stressing, in language that harked back to "The Homes of Indiana" days, that the country had "thousands of dwellings of the poor so wretched, so overcrowded, so unsanitary, so uncomfortable, so inconvenient that the children growing up in them can never know the meaning of home." She called on homemakers (clearly understood to be women) to exercise care in painting, papering, furnishing, and decorating their dwellings. "Let us urge them," she charged her audience, "to have beauty always, [since] it costs no more than ugliness." One should avoid, for example, "provocative and inflammatory colors," as in "wallpaper that makes a sick person's fever higher, and I have known such."[44]

That the report was aimed toward a "higher class" became apparent in Bacon's discussion of household management. "It is very much simpler," she explained, "when there is a servant in the house . . . or even a part-time servant. With a servant you need more brains than strength." For most Americans in the early 1930s, this was not a useful observation. In fairness, however, she went on to stress that women should set priorities, budget time and strength to ensure adequate rest and relaxation, and not permit "the spirit of home" to be destroyed by "the demon of housekeeping."[45]

The need for adequate space in the home, for both physical and emotional reasons, was another theme that recalled the rhetoric of her housing reform heyday. It was, she claimed, an "essential of homemaking. . . . Crowding kills family life." She ridiculed the notion that a kitchen need be no larger than 7 feet by 8 feet and that if there were a child who needed to be watched during meal preparations he or she could be put with playthings at one end of the room. "There isn't," she insisted, "any end to a room eight feet long; it is all middle." She also called, although she did not use the phrase, for "a room of one's own"—private spaces where father could smoke, mother could read and sew, and children could play. "When people get on each other's toes, they get on each other's nerves." There must be, she concluded, "those conditions that make for mental health as well as for physical health."[46]

The final report of the Committee on Standards and Objectives was published the next year. The introduction (unsigned, but presumably by Veiller) asserted that a home "must be something much more than shelter" and decried the fact that "the great majority of the homes that are being built in this country today are not worthy of the American people." It was necessary, therefore, to clearly spell out objectives ("the ends sought to be attained by effort in the Housing field") and the standards required to achieve those objectives. This the report proceeded to do, in fifty detailed pages that blended definite injunctions ("the therapeutic ultra-violet rays of the sun . . . will freely enter all rooms") with flights of imprecision (the home should be a place of "safety, wholesomeness, health, cleanliness, order, cheerfulness, tranquility, comfort, restfulness, attractiveness, spaciousness"). The latter quotation (which seemingly appropriated Bacon's rhetoric) reflected a noble dream, especially in 1932, as she and Veiller certainly knew. "It is fully realized," the introduction admitted, "that all of these standards cannot be achieved at once. It is also equally realized that for many families in America these standards today seem to represent a counsel of perfection."[47]

And, indeed, the President's Conference on Home Building and

Home Ownership had little immediate impact, especially regarding housing standards. Its published reports were issued as the country approached the nadir of the Great Depression and as the electorate prepared to repudiate the man who had convened the meeting.[48] Many Americans were less concerned with the niceties of furnishing and decorating their homes than with whether they could keep from losing them. (Non–farm foreclosures rose from about 68,000 in 1926 to 250,000 in 1932.) It was also hard to improve standards when few new homes were being built. Construction of residential property dropped by 95 percent between 1928 and 1933, remained low throughout the 1930s, and then virtually stopped during World War II. The Housing Act of 1937, which made possible some low-cost public housing, was a significant piece of New Deal legislation, but it had little to do with what many of Hoover's conferees—and certainly most members of the Standards and Objectives Committee—were discussing in 1931. The publications of the conference were quickly relegated to the shelves of research libraries, little read and soon forgotten in the midst of severe economic depression and world war.[49]

For those interested in Albion Bacon's public activities, however, the 1931 conference is important in a number of respects. It allowed her to revisit one last time, in a highly visible venue, many of the themes and issues she had felt so keenly and articulated so forcefully in the earliest days of her social welfare work. Much had happened since her first visit to Old St. Mary's tenement almost thirty years earlier, but her participation in the Washington conference and the language she employed when discussing homes and homemakers indicates that she was still held by "the clutch of the thorns." The Washington meetings also provided an opportunity to work once again with old friends—especially Veiller. By the late 1920s, however, his restrictionist solutions to housing problems (which Bacon had emulated in drafting Indiana's legislation) had largely run their course and had begun to be superseded by other approaches. In that sense the Washington conference can be considered a denouement for the two old comrades.

But Bacon's involvement in the conference also represents a culmination. While her role in the proceedings was not large—she was, after all, one of over 500 committee members—simply being invited was recognition of her past achievements and her national reputation. It is especially noteworthy that she was recruited for the Standards and Objectives Committee, whose charge required both broad vision and concern for detail. By the early thirties Bacon's health was beginning to fail—five trips to Washington in ten weeks probably did not help—and thereafter her travel and public activities became increasingly restricted. Her participation in the President's Conference on Home Building and Home Ownership thus served as both a capstone and a valedictory. It also fulfilled a pledge she had made in 1913, soon after Indiana's statewide housing law had been enacted. When a friend asked what she intended to do next, she replied: "Housing reform. Housing till I die." [50]

Seven

Prose, Poetry, and Pageants

In the midst of her social welfare activities, and often linked to them, Bacon continued to engage in a pursuit that had attracted her since childhood: writing. Soon after she began her public work she set up a modest study, little more than a desk and typewriter, in her bedroom. Some years later she had a space on the third floor remodeled into what she called her "tree top typery." She spent countless hours in these two locations; "when she was busy," daughter Joy remembered, "she stayed with it." Her literary efforts took many forms, from the nonfiction tracts of a housing reformer to epigrammatic poetry, from devotional pieces to children's stories. Some of this work, especially some of the poetry, was produced principally for personal satisfaction and was not intended for circulation. Much of what she wrote was published, however, and some of it reached a national audience. It is Albion's sibling Annie Fellows Johnston, author of the "Little Colonel" series of children's books, who is usually considered to have been the "literary" Fellows sister, and that is true in the sense that after Annie was widowed she made her living with her pen. But Bacon was a prolific author as well, and she took the responsibilities of authorship seriously. In the memoir she wrote for her children in the late 1920s she recalled that as she grew older "I had the natural ambition that goes with writing and other creative work. I wanted it to be 'good', to be recognized by my peers." Her own judgment was that she had "excelled more in writing than in any other field."[1]

The Bacons' house on First Street as it appeared ca. 1985. Albion's
"tree top typery" was on the third floor. Robert G. Barrows

Since much of her adult life was devoted to social reform efforts, it
is no surprise that Bacon's writing was often didactic rather than creative. The first of her many publications dealing with housing reform
evolved from a talk she gave in October 1907, when the Indiana Conference of Charities and Correction met in Evansville. The organization's bulletin printed the talk—"The Homes of the Poor"—the next
year. It is a short article, only about five pages, but in this small space
Bacon introduced several themes that were to recur in her later work.
In the first paragraph, for example, she commented on "the stupidity of
builders and the cupidity of landlords." She continued with graphic descriptions of some of the worst housing conditions in her hometown.
"I am sorry to expose Evansville," she told her readers, but warned that
"if you have any poor folk and any old houses you may look to find some
of these conditions."[2]

Two other hallmarks of her writing concerning housing are present in Bacon's initial publication dealing with the subject: a strong belief in environmental determinism and an assertion that reform efforts were not only philanthropic but also defensive. She made both points in just a few sentences:

> There is a psychological question to be considered here—the effect of the environment on character. What a terrifying thought is that of lives set among surroundings which sear the mind by reiterated suggestions of evil, which dim the vision of the soul by hideous ugliness, warping it away from ideals of truth and beauty. What hope is there for the pure child mind to unfold in such a place without a stain? . . . Just as surely as an apple grown in a bottle takes the bottle's shape, so surely are these people molded by their environment. We might stand by and look on with indifference, if we dared, only for one thing—whatever threatens them threatens us. The civic edifice is no stronger than its foundation. What avail beautiful pillars and domes if the substructure be of rotting wood?

To prevent such civic deterioration she called for sanitary plumbing, an adequate water supply, and windows to furnish both light and ventilation, as well as the laws needed to ensure their provision. She advanced the proposed Evansville tenement ordinance on which she had worked as a model for other Indiana communities.[3]

"The Housing Problem in Indiana," Bacon's first article in a publication with national circulation, appeared in late 1908 in the periodical *Charities and the Commons*. One historian has written that this magazine, renamed *The Survey* the following year, "provided the major links between a wide variety of reforms and the new profession of social work." Bacon's article evolved, once again, from a talk she had given at the Indiana charities conference. The piece described the findings of the statewide housing survey she had undertaken during the summer of 1908, a survey conducted principally by means of questionnaires mailed to local charities secretaries but that also relied upon her own travel and observations. Typical of much of the writing she did in this vein, the article is detailed, graphic, and full of exhortations to "head off the slums" (in Riis's words) while there was still time to do so. She was explicit (and ahead of her time for Indiana) in arguing that this was not a metropolitan problem, but one that also affected the state's small towns: "Let us take down our telescopes trained to find the outward signs of big city slums, and put on our spectacles to see clearly what Indiana's housing problem is today."[4]

Two years later *The Survey* ran another short article by Bacon, "The Awakening of a State." This was a report on the 1909 campaign to get a tenement law enacted for Indiana—a description of how she and her allies had gone about "waking up" the state and, especially, its legislators. This was both a "how-we-did-it" piece and a strong suggestion to the magazine's readers that it was an action that probably needed to be undertaken in their own states and communities. In her second paragraph Bacon threw out a challenge: "I am so convinced that our Indiana problem is, in the main, the problem of all states in the Union . . . that I want you [readers] to tell me if our conditions are not typical." She stressed, as she had two years earlier, that abysmal housing was not confined to big cities. She acknowledged that the Hoosier state's "little unpretentious slums" could not compete with those of New York or Chicago, and thus "the hardest thing to teach the public" had been that "slums are not a matter of size."[5]

In the wake of her legislative defeat in 1911, Bacon stepped up efforts to attract others to the cause of housing reform. She later described "A Tale of the Tenements," a speech she first delivered that summer, as "a true and simple story of life in the slums of our Indiana towns." This piece was unabashed propaganda, consciously aimed at the heart as well as the head; she admitted that she made the story "just as bare and sordid and miserable as I found it." As noted previously, this was the talk she gave to a summer session of the Indiana Federation of Clubs that helped to win the support of that organization. So effective was her description and her plea for assistance that the Indiana Housing Association issued a revised version of the talk in pamphlet form the next year.[6]

The introduction to this essay is vintage Bacon, contrasting a naturalistic ideal with the realities of life experienced by some Hoosier residents.

> All over the state of Indiana today is summer and sunshine, bloom and verdure. Harvests are ripening, fruit is turning gold. . . . With so much room, so much sunshine, so much beauty, so much bounty, it would seem that no one in our state could be crowded, or stifle for lack of air, that no one could be hungry or unhappy, in all this wide domain.

> But it is not all country. There are towns. . . . Towns full of mills that weave up human lives. Towns made up of what men call houses. Some of them are homes, but too many are no more than prisons, boxes, traps. . . . And here women grow sickly, babies droop and die,

and tuberculosis cuts down one in every seven. The shadow of Death and the curse of Sin is on our towns, in our big, free, bountiful Indiana.

I wish my story were to be of the hills and fields, that God made, rather than of the towns, that man made. But some one must tell it, or men will never know the truth about "How the Other Half Lives" in Indiana.

And tell the tale she did, at length and in explicit detail. "I want you to see the poor as they are," she told her listeners and readers, " . . . and to see that their conditions make them largely what they are." She then recounted example after example of those conditions. And, once again, she concluded with the message that ameliorating such conditions was not just charitable but also prudent. Life in the tenements "touches you in your home, because your fortunes are bound up with your community." A partial solution to the problem was, of course, the housing law for which she would be crusading in 1913, a law "stronger than greed, and avarice, and selfishness, and ignorance."[7]

Bacon published many more essays and articles concerning housing—so many that they cannot all be described and discussed in detail. Some of these were first presented as papers at the annual conferences of groups such as the National Housing Association, the National Conference of Social Work, and the National Conference of Charities and Correction, and subsequently appeared in those organizations' proceedings. Professionals working in the various social welfare fields comprised the principal audience for these works. Some of Bacon's articles graced very small, localized journals—*Illinois Health News* and the *Iowa State Board of Health Bulletin*, for example; other pieces were published in national magazines, such as *The American City* and *Municipal Engineering*, that focused on urban affairs. Two small bulletins that she prepared for the National Housing Association—*What Bad Housing Means to the Community* and *Housing—Its Relation to Social Work*—had a wider circulation, especially after finding their way onto the reading lists of college and university courses.[8]

Bacon's most important publication regarding housing, and arguably the most significant thing she ever wrote, was *Beauty for Ashes*. This story of her growth from ingenue to municipal housekeeper also started life in *The Survey*, appearing as a series of articles that began in December 1913 and continued through the early months of the next year. Whether Bacon contacted the magazine with the idea for the series or the editor(s) approached her is not known. By late in the summer of 1913, however, she had the manuscript well underway. "I am making good progress with my story," she wrote her sister Annie in early September. "Mr. Kellogg [editor of *The Survey*] sent those sketches you revised, and part of the third . . . to Jacob Riis, and he made some generous comments." Final copy for the early installments was due in October, and she lamented that she had "been sitting up late at night to write, for my interruptions are nothing short of 'fierce.' If I didn't have the story so well in my head, I'd go crazy."[9]

As she labored with the writing, she also struggled to find an appropriate title. Since the backbone of the narrative was to be her "journey" from sheltered youth to public crusader, the use of "road" as a metaphor suggested itself. She considered and then dismissed "The White Road" and "The Road to Jericho." Kellogg suggested something along the lines of "From an Indiana Threshold," which Bacon rejected out of hand as too provincial. "I want to appeal to the whole country," she wrote Annie, "and have extended my work all over the U.S. . . . Besides, I'm sorry to say that the average Indiana threshold doesn't sound specially nice to me." She thought about and quickly abandoned "An Awakening" and "The Shadow," although the latter did become a chapter title. Finally, in late September, she told her sister: "I want to use 'Beauty for Ashes' as a title, for it fits every chapter. But Mr. K. isn't satisfied yet." Kellogg apparently overcame his reluctance, however, and the series ran with the title Bacon had settled upon. It was, as Kellogg admitted in an editorial accompanying the first installment, an apt choice, being one of the "familiar phrases which begin that great chapter of Isaiah in which the prophet tells of his mission."

> [T]o comfort all that mourn . . . to give unto them beauty for ashes, the oil of joy for mourning, the garment of praise for the spirit of heaviness. . . . And they shall build the old wastes, they shall raise up the former desolations, and they shall repair the waste cities, the desolations of many generations.[10]

Although by this time Bacon was used to seeing her words in print, she had never done anything on this scale before and seems to have been a bit overwhelmed by it all. When Kellogg sent her copies of two "wonderful" letters elicited by the series—one from Jacob Riis, the other from a professor who was an "authority on immigrants"—she wrote Annie that she was becoming "all stuck up." She reported, too, that Survey Associates (the organization that published *The Survey*) had written expressing appreciation and making her a life member. "I don't know just what I've 'jined,'" she told her sister, "but it's Jane Addams and Graham Taylor, and that ilk. I told Hilary I hope it means dividends and not dues."[11]

As early as September 1913, when the manuscript was still far from complete, the editors at *The Survey* suggested that it had the potential to be reissued in book form after running serially in the magazine. Since Annie was accustomed to dealing with publishers, Bacon asked her for advice. "Oughtn't I to reserve all rights?" she inquired. "Or what should I say[?] You know I'm not getting a cent [for the series in *The Survey*]." In early December she reported that a staffer at the magazine had written that a "Mr. Chase of Dodd, Mead & Co. was interested in my story & that he would put him in communication with me if I liked. I said 'all right' in effect." Chase apparently acted swiftly, for when Bacon wrote Annie on New Year's Day 1914, she referred to a letter she had received from him before Christmas. He wrote that he had read three chapters and found them most interesting and forceful. He explained that he was speaking only for himself, not yet making a formal offer for Dodd, Mead, but that he was sufficiently impressed to pass the chapters on to the firm's selection committee for its consideration.[12]

Bacon's reaction to Chase's letter reveals an intriguing blend of insecurity, pride, and ambition. The letter struck her, she wrote Annie, as "patronizing, without meaning to be. That he spoke to me as one would to an inexperienced person, who had no idea about publishing books." In truth, however, she *didn't* have much personal experience with book publishing, and once again she asked her sister for advice "by the earliest mail" on how to reply. She explained that she did not want to be "airy or resentful, neither do I want to scramble to fall in with his good impression, or anything that he might offer. I don't want to be churlish, nor do I want to be too anxious. Nor do I want to lose a good chance." In the meantime she continued to work on the manuscript, convinced that Chase and Dodd, Mead's committee would find "lots more in the book and like it better if they saw more of it."[13]

Bacon produced additional installments for *The Survey* during the spring of 1914, complaining to Annie at one point that "I am writing night and day, because I can't train my family as you do, and I have no end of interruptions." Although she had hoped to send drafts to her sister for comment (as she had done earlier), she was now forced to rush them to the magazine's editors "hot off the griddle, as they are pushing me a little." During the first few weeks of the year she also seems to have struck a deal with Dodd, Mead. In mid-February she wrote that the New York publisher wanted her "to make the book a little longer than 10 chapters"—a statement that assumes that there was going to *be* a book. In May she was still working on the last chapters, and expressed concern that she would not get them completed prior to several planned summer trips. She finally sent off the finished manuscript on June 6.[14]

Dodd, Mead & Company published *Beauty for Ashes* in the fall of 1914. The 360-page volume, priced at $1.50, is divided into twelve chapters and includes some two score illustrations. The book performs several functions. It is, first, an autobiography—not a full-scale or complete one, to be sure, but rather one with a specific focus on, as Bacon put it, "the evolution of a housing reformer." In describing that evolution, however, she has a great deal to say about growing up in McCutchanville, living in Evansville in the late nineteenth and early twentieth centuries, and her early involvement with the city's philanthropic organizations and activities.

Secondly, the book is a detailed description of the passage of Indiana's first housing laws, a very personal account of Bacon's 1909, 1911, and 1913 campaigns in the General Assembly. (One wishes sometimes that she had waited a while before preparing, or at least completing, her manuscript, so that it would have included the developments of the next few years.) She goes into great detail in these chapters describing the effort and frustrations, the defeats and victories, the friends and foes of her legislative endeavors. This section of the book was intended, at least in part, as a kind of how-to-do-it manual.

Finally, *Beauty for Ashes* is propaganda. It attempts to convince readers of the need for housing reform, as well as to assure them that they, too, can effect such change in their cities, towns, and states. This goal is quite explicit in the final chapter, entitled "Looking Forward," where Bacon writes: "In order that this story shall not fail of its purpose, let me say . . . that it has been my intention to show that if any one so timid, and so physically unfortified for hard marching and fighting [as I], could stand the strain and meet with some success, surely no one else should fear to try."[15]

The Dodd, Mead files for this period apparently are not extant, so many details that would be of interest regarding the volume—press run, sales figures, royalty arrangements—are not known. The press run likely was modest, a conjecture based on the assumption that the publisher probably did not envision a large market and the fact that very few copies seem to have survived. (Libraries in Indiana, including the major research repositories and libraries in Evansville, have remarkably few copies of *Beauty*, and the author of this study, after many years of looking, has never found the volume in a used book shop.) While there were royalties, Bacon's youngest daughter remembered them as not "substantial enough to be of big influence" in the family's finances.[16]

Critical assessments of the volume were complimentary. A brief summary in *The Outlook* concluded with the observation that the author "tells her story with spontaneous wit and deep feeling." An equally brief notice in *The Nation* commented that "Mrs. Bacon manages to be earnest without becoming hysterical." The "novel feature" of the book, according to *The Nation*'s reviewer, was its "revelation that the slum is by no means a unique possession of New York or any other of our largest cities." The *Boston Evening Transcript* praised "the literary charm of [the book's] vivid and ingenious narrative" and opined that "the awakening of the uninterested will be Mrs. Bacon's real achievement." The author of a lengthy review in the *Springfield* (Mass.) *Republican* judged that *Beauty for Ashes* "deserves a place on the best shelf of social welfare volumes, along with Riis, Spargo and other apostles of social uplift."[17]

Bacon herself wrote surprisingly little about her most substantial publication. In early December 1914 she confided to Annie that her publisher was "disappointed with Evansville sales." ("I am not," she added, "knowing Evansville.") Dodd, Mead reported that they were getting sales "by sending the book on approval. *Of course*," Bacon joked to her sister, "every one who sees it is crazy about it." She had resolved not to worry, convinced that the book "will sell some day." It does seem to have reached one of the audiences for which it was intended: students of "social work," broadly defined. She remarked years later that her disappointment at never having been able to attend college was salved when she learned that *Beauty for Ashes* was being used as a text in several universities, including Union Theological Seminary.[18]

❖

In his sketch of Bacon for *Notable American Women*, Roy Lubove notes that "her career drew strength and inspiration from her Methodist training, with its emphasis on social service as a religious duty." Elsewhere Lubove has written that "if one does not understand her profound religious impulse, one understands neither Albion Fellows Bacon nor the essentially religious genesis of Indiana's first housing laws."[19]

Familiarity with Bacon's own words—not to mention her deeds—underscores Lubove's observations concerning her deep religiosity. She introduced her unpublished 1926/1927 memoir with the explanation that "I feel that I have a few things to pass on, especially, and most of all, a great and unusual faith in God and in immortal life." In an article she had prepared a decade earlier for *The Bookman*, part of a series solicited by the editor on the theme "what the day's work means to me," she noted at the outset: "I could not possibly make clear all that my work means to me without stating, simply, that it has grown from an act of religious consecration." And she recounted in *Beauty for Ashes* that a link between her spiritual life and her social welfare concerns had begun to be forged in her youth. Biblical injunctions to aid those less fortunate, invoked by her childhood minister in McCutchanville, caused her concern. "Suppose," she worried, "I died before I encountered any poor to visit and to minister to? For years the thought hung over me like a threatening shadow."[20]

Her religious impulses and her belief in doing "good works" are at least implicit (and often explicit) in many of Bacon's speeches and articles regarding housing reform and other social service endeavors. The focus of such pieces, however, is on the reform activity itself. But she did publish several items that speak directly to the question of her religious faith. The first of these was, once again, a brief article in *The Survey*. "The Divine Call: Follow Me" begins with a discussion of the apostles who abandoned their former lives to follow Christ. Jesus' object in keeping the disciples near him during the years of his ministry was "to train them for service, to carry on His work in the world." We too, Bacon argues, are subject to this divine call. And service, she suggests, is a condition for both spiritual growth and spiritual knowledge; upon these "two great fundamental truths of service . . . any one can build the temple of a beautiful and happy life."[21]

Christ's will is "to save and to heal and to bless." When we are called, she asserts, "He sends us out with that same commission. . . . He commands us to clothe the naked, to minister to the sick, and to visit those in prison." And why so much emphasis on ministry to the poor when all alike face life's trials? "No one will ask that question who is much among the poor," as she had been. "Poverty makes every trouble worse." Much social welfare, in her view, was thus "the rightful work of the church, more than of charity or philanthropy." Such efforts by the churches, however, should go beyond teas, bazaars, and committee work, "a wholesale kind of service, not so personal and intimate as the service to the Master we give to His poor." For those unsatisfied with their spiritual life, Bacon had this suggestion: "Stop arguing and searching, *go to work*, begin to do His will, and the truth will begin to dawn upon you; . . . you will have the joy and the peace that comes to those who are in the current of all good purposes."[22]

In 1928 Bacon published a longer and more formal statement of her religious creed. She had apparently been working on this document for some time, for in the fall of 1926 she referred to a "little book" she had written—she called it "Finding God"—that she described as her "last testament." Harper & Brothers issued the 76-page tract with the title *The Path to God*. No one would mistake this work for a profound theological treatise, but that is not what Bacon intended it to be. The book is, rather, a personal account of spiritual growth, written with the hope that in bearing her own witness she might help others who were "groping, blindfold, toiling up steep and rocky ways to find God." She believed it was a "duty to pass on our vital spiritual experience."[23]

Bacon wrote *The Path to God* during the maelstrom of the fundamentalist-modernist debate of the 1920s, a debate exemplified by the famous 1925 "monkey trial" of John Scopes for teaching the theory of evolution in a Tennessee classroom. She seems to have accepted the modernist position that science and the scriptures could coexist. "It is not my province or purpose to try to reconcile the Bible, the higher criticism and science," she wrote. "We are told, and I am willing to concede, that portions of the Bible may rest upon traditions and other parts may be legendary in character." Ultimately, however, she was not much interested in the controversy: "It makes no essential difference . . . whether the 'days' of creation were of twenty-four hours or twenty-four aeons; whether man was created in millions of years of evolution . . . or was made complete in a moment of time. . . . Either demands a God of infinite power."[24]

This, for Bacon, was the crux of her religious faith. There was a God because there *had to be*. While she recognized that "the miracles of the Bible are a stumbling block to many," for her "the most incomprehensible miracle would be a world without a Divine Cause." Her faith thus began "at the place where Science, because it can go no farther, stops. I believe that my God is the 'Most probable Cause,' and the higher critics have thus far offered no other."[25]

For proof of a Creator, she argued, one need merely observe the beauty and regularity of the natural world. "Even those who do not know God feel a sudden quickening of the heart at the ineffable beauty of a sunrise." The laws of light, color, chiaroscuro, music and harmony "are as enchanting as magic, yet as exact as mathematics." These "fine and subtle forms of truth . . . appeal to the ignorant as well as to the learned," and all may discern in them "intimations of the Divine Spirit."[26]

She stressed, however, that belief in God was not enough. One must also experience the "personal intuition" of the divine brought about through the agency of prayer. In this she practiced what she preached. Her daughter Joy recounted that every morning after breakfast her mother read the Bible, meditated, and prayed for thirty to sixty minutes. And then "she got up and put her hand in God's and knew it was going to be a good day. Never doubted it." Bacon herself wrote that it was a conception of God as "the Comforter" that had often sustained her.[27]

The comfort provided by her faith helped Bacon cope with the greatest tragedy of her life—the sudden and unexpected death of her daughter Margaret in 1909. This experience led, years later, to yet another publication, one that she hoped would bring solace to those who had suffered a similar loss.

In mid-June 1921 Bacon wrote a letter addressed to the "Editor of the Atlantic Monthly." She enclosed no autobiographical information, but merely began: "I am sending you with this [letter] a sketch called 'Consolation,' which deals with a very unusual experience that came to me with the death of my daughter, some years ago. It is absolutely true. I have analyzed it most carefully, so that nothing I say may be misleading. I have been driven to write it because of the great mourning in the world during these last years, and the fantastic things that are written about death." She was offering the manuscript, she explained, for potential publication as both a magazine article and a short book.[28]

Ellery Sedgwick, editor of the *Atlantic Monthly*, responded promptly, observing that he had read the piece "at a time of acute personal distress, and feel very strongly its tender and wholesome message." It "ought to be printed," he told Bacon; he would be "very glad to make a place for your main thesis in The Atlantic." He was also potentially interested in publishing the material in book form, but was not yet ready to make a commitment to do so. "Would it not be a wise plan," he counseled, "if we were to publish the paper I outline in The Atlantic, and then act in regard to the book upon the indications which will follow the appearance of the paper."[29]

Bacon found this proposal acceptable, and in response to Sedgwick's editorial suggestions she set about reorganizing and abridging her manuscript for use in the magazine. She also wrote to Dodd, Mead & Company to ensure that subsequent publication of this material in the form of a "small brochure" (language proposed by Sedgwick) would not violate the clause in her *Beauty for Ashes* contract to give that firm the right of first refusal for her "next book." Dodd, Mead quickly waived its rights, and the project proceeded. "Consolation" appeared in the December 1921 issue of the *Atlantic*.[30]

The article begins by recounting the delivery to the Bacon household, early one morning, of a telegram that read simply: "Margaret is very ill. Come at once." (Recall, from chapter 3, that she was in Texas to serve as a friend's bridesmaid.) A second telegram, several hours later, announced her death. The tragedy was compounded by being so completely unexpected, and the Bacons were devastated by the news. "My brain reeled," Albion recalled. "Thought seemed to stagger, to faint, to rouse and fall, exactly as it does when recovering from an anaesthetic or a blow. . . . That impression of the anaesthetic persisted for days—the feeling of dull stupor, with sudden sharp stabs of pain, as realization came at times."

Then, all at once, came the "clear thought" that her daughter was with God, that "she *knows* what we two have so often wondered about." As Bacon described the experience:

> Suddenly it seemed that Margaret was with me. She seemed to take my hand and draw me up, a step higher, while she stood close to me, a little higher, still holding my hand. . . . I do not know how long we stood. It was so wonderful that I found myself smiling, though I stood there, at last, alone. . . . The beauty and glory of that experience stayed with me. It left an exaltation that lasted for months. It left, too, a deep conviction that Margaret was in a realm of love and happiness and beauty, infinitely transcending ours.

She was at pains to point out that she was not a spiritualist and did not believe in "communications" with the deceased. She stressed that in the event she was describing "there was no appearance, no voice, no touch, no thrill of contact . . . no illusion." The experience did not seem supernatural but "to be of the texture of thought, as if I had a strong thought of her being with me. . . . It gave me unspeakable comfort and assurance."

During the funeral, and in the weeks, months, and years that followed, Bacon's grief was assuaged not just by her belief in God and an afterlife, but by a conviction that Margaret was a continuing presence, "a living part of our daily lives." Her love of nature was enhanced by a sense that her eldest daughter was "immanent in all beauty, as a living part of it—in sunset or moonlight, in garden walks or woodland paths." Her assurance on this point is underscored by the fact that five years later she dedicated *Beauty for Ashes* not to the *memory* of her daughter, but simply "To Margaret."

The December issue of the *Atlantic* actually appeared in late November, and within a month Sedgwick advised Bacon that the many letters he had received in response to "Consolation" convinced him that "a version in more permanent form will be treasured in many lonely households." He had reread the original manuscript, rearranged some of the sections, and now had a few other changes for her to consider. Bacon replied that she was gratified by the reaction to the magazine article, which made her "feel justified in laying bare so intimate an experience to the public." Although by and large she approved of Sedgwick's editorial work, she also thought that "in making the surgical operations, a few arteries are untied, and some of the real life blood of my message . . . is lost."[31]

In a series of letters during the next few weeks, Bacon and her editor resolved their minor differences, agreed on the format of the book, and settled financial arrangements. She made it clear that her main object was to get her message into the hands of those who might be helped by it. And Sedgwick made it clear that, while he believed strongly in the project, it was unlikely to be a money-maker. He offered $100 "for the privilege of publishing the book" and a royalty of 10 percent on the gross price (75 cents) after the first 2,500 copies had been sold. Bacon found the offer "generous" and "most thoughtful," since it covered "all possibilities in a very satisfactory and practical way." The book-making process proceeded with dispatch, and Sedgwick forwarded one of the first copies of *Consolation* in early March 1922. The author replied that she was "delighted with its appearance" and hoped that the volume "may justify your kind belief in it."[32]

Consolation seems to have been somewhat more successful as a commercial venture than Sedgwick expected. Five months after its publication, in response to a query about the earlier magazine article, an *Atlantic* staffer wrote that "many thousand copies" of the volume had already been distributed.[33] In early September, Bacon acknowledged receipt of a royalty check for $56.18. Given the terms of her contract, it appears that roughly 3,250 copies were sold in the six months following publication. Four more royalty payments between March 1923 and September 1924 totaled almost $120, indicating the purchase of another 1,600 copies. By the latter date, however, sales had clearly tapered off, and there is no evidence of further royalties.[34]

Critical response to *Consolation* is hard to assess, in part because

Illustration by Billie Chapman for the story "More About Goldilocks"
in Bacon's The Charm String

such a modest volume did not engender much reaction. *Book Review Digest* summarized the "little book" in one sentence and offered no evaluation; the *Boston Evening Transcript* merely quoted key passages without comment. For her part, Bacon derived great satisfaction from the enterprise. Four years later she described the work as her "best contribution."[35]

❖

The Charm String was unique among Bacon's writings, her only work intended specifically for children. Issued in 1929 by L. C. Page &

Company, the same firm that published Annie's "Little Colonel" books, the 204-page volume included twelve stories.

The origin and part of the content were rooted in Bacon's own childhood. As she explained in her introduction:

> Once upon a time, three little sisters [Lura, Annie, Albion] lived with their mother on top of a high hill, crowned with cherry trees [McCutchanville]. . . . The oldest sister told many fairy tales and poems to the younger sisters. Then when the two little sisters went to bed, they "made up" fairy tales, and told them to each other. . . . These tales made them so happy—I know, because I was the littlest sister— that they told them often to other children.[36]

Bacon presumably told some of these stories to her own children, probably expanding and polishing them a bit over the years. The impetus to write them down, however, apparently came as she began repeating them to her grandson, George Bacon Smith (her daughter Albion's only child). The volume is dedicated to the memory of George, who died in 1926 at age eight, "the dear child who loved these stories best."[37]

The stories clearly seem to have "worked" as children's literature, giving free rein to youngsters' imaginations. Compared to many of the "classics" of the genre (not to mention the Saturday morning cartoons on television), they are free of any hint of violence. This was not accidental. As Bacon's youngest children observed in their preface to a 1970s reprint, the stories in *The Charm String* "were written for her grandson by a woman who felt that even the classic GRIMM'S FAIRY TALES were too full of terrors and anxieties for small children."[38] To give but one example: In "More About Goldilocks" the story begins where the traditional tale ends. Instead of Goldilocks fleeing the bears' cottage in fright, she and Baby Bear become best friends; the two families subsequently pay social calls on one another and occasionally have picnics together in the woods. That Bacon could advance such a plot line at the same time she was grappling with the details of housing laws and zoning ordinances underscores the breadth of her intellectual interests and abilities.

❖

Reminiscing in 1926 Bacon recalled that "at times, in childhood, and in my later years, a passion for writing poetry would come over me."[39] As noted earlier (see chapter 1), she had produced passable verses while still a schoolgirl; she continued to do so, with varying levels of intensity, for the rest of her life. In the mid-1880s she began keeping a poetry journal (referred to hereafter as her "Verses" Journal) in which she copied more-or-less final versions of her efforts. The last poem in this notebook is dated 1930, and there are several from the early twentieth century, but the 1880s and 1890s (except for the period of her illness) were the years of her greatest productivity.[40]

During the eighties Bacon was clearly writing with publication in mind. Many of the poems in her "Verses" Journal have marginal notations indicating either that the piece had been submitted to a newspaper or magazine or that it had actually been printed somewhere. Publications in which her poems appeared include the *DePauw Monthly*, the *Washington* (Ind.) *Democrat, Current*, the *Indianapolis Journal*, the *Evansville Courier*, and *American Magazine*. Rejections are noted from *Harper's, McClure's, St. Nicholas*, and the *New York World*. In addition, a number of poems written in these years appeared in *Songs Ysame*, the collection that she and Annie jointly published in 1897 (see chapter 2).

After about 1900 she seems to have written much less poetry, and little of what she wrote was published. Most of her poems during the 1900s and 1910s were what one might call "special occasion" verses intended for a limited audience—pieces written for a birthday, anniversary, or family reunion, for example, or for a philanthropic organization's fundraising event. There were several reasons for this greatly reduced output. Most obviously, she became heavily involved in social welfare activities after the turn of the century, had less time to write, and, as we have seen, devoted most of her writing energies to advancing the reform causes with which she was associated. In addition, there was the effect of her daughter's death. "After Margaret died," she later recalled, "I never felt like writing poetry. What I tried was heavy . . . the lightsomeness was gone. My heavy cares of public work crushed me, too, as well as grief." Finally, she feared that being known as a poet would undermine her credibility as a reformer. As she wrote in *Beauty for Ashes* regarding her work at the legislature in 1909: "It was my care to avoid sentimentality, and to stick to the practical issues, in a practical way. . . . I wouldn't have let one of those men know that I had ever written a verse!"[41]

By the late 1920s the poetic urge had returned, but obstacles clearly remained:

> If I could get away from my work and cares, the little round of housekeeping and servants, my civic meetings, so endless and tiring, I feel I could write. If I could go to some lonely, lonely shore, some island in

the sea, and rest and rest, and sit watching sunsets, and feel time was not pushing or pulling me—*then* I could write poetry.

Some of her poems came to her in a sudden flash of creativity—"all in a breath," as she put it. One, she remembered, "came, word for word, while I walked down stairs to the hall door. 'The old house' came while I rode a few blocks on the streetcar." In another instance a verse came "word for word, after I had gone to sleep at night, with no such thought in my mind, and wakened wide and wrote it down."[42] Regardless of whether poems came to her in this instantaneous manner or were the products of a more protracted creation, she often kept tinkering with them. Many of the entries in her poetry journal have words or lines that have been changed, or marginal notes regarding possible alterations.

Although, as indicated earlier, Bacon found some "modernist" ideas acceptable in the realm of religion, she was less flexible where poetry was concerned—another reason, perhaps, why she was less published in the twentieth century. "I can't be satisfied to write free verse," she confided in her memoirs. Poetry that did not have a rhythmic meter seemed to her "lazy—like wearing an unhemmed dress, only basted. Or like frowsy hair. It's not tidy." Bird songs, waves, even human respiration had "evenly recurring metre—not like free verse. It's shaggy. Sloppy."[43]

As her public service activities (or at least her out-of-town travels) slackened a bit in the late 1920s, her interest in poetry, and especially a desire to see her best work collected and published, seems to have revived. Some of the emendations in her "Verses" Journal probably date from this period. And she carefully read and reread her works, many of them written decades before, and drew large Xs through those that did not measure up. A note placed at the beginning of the journal directed that "The crossed out poems must *not* be published." Daughter Joy remembered that her mother rejected the idea of self-publication, proclaiming that "if your writings aren't worth somebody's buying, never have them published yourself." But she very much wanted her poems to be printed eventually, and gave them to Joy before she died with the hope that her daughter could arrange for their appearance. That hope was not realized, and thus several of the poems that follow as samples of Bacon's work have never before been published.[44]

Much of Bacon's poetry, especially that written while she was a young woman, is serious, even melancholy, and deals with themes such as love, death, loss, and nature. Indeed, she seems to have believed that one of the poet's principal tasks was to plumb emotional depths and then to express the results of that search in verse. Her thoughts on the value of poetry and its place in the literary spectrum are revealed in a short piece entitled "History, Fiction and Poetry":

> How happy is the man whose ready pen
> Records the words, the deeds, the lives of men!
> Thrice happy he who with a heaven-born skill
> Can create worlds and people them at will.
>
> But he alone doth reach beatitude
> Who can express his own heart's changing mood—
> Pour out its longings, love and grief reveal,
> And voice for others what they can but feel.[45]

Bacon composed the following poem—"Stranded"—while sailing to Europe in 1888. It suggests a growing awareness of the vagaries of life and, significantly, seems to anticipate the environmental determinism that was to be a hallmark of so much of her writing about housing reform and other social welfare concerns. Just as a ship that is well-built may still be wrecked if unforeseen or uncontrollable forces conspire against it, so too may human lives be damaged by the caprice of circumstance.

> We found a wreck cast up on the shore,
> Battered and bruised, and scarred and rent,
> And I spoke aloud, "Here was worthless work,
> And a barque unfit to the sea was sent."
>
> But he said, my friend, in his gentle mood,
> "Nay, none may say but the barque was good,
> For none can tell of the seas it sailed,
> Of the waves it braved and the storms withstood."
>
> Then we spoke no more, but I mutely mused
> And thought, oh, heart and oh, life of man
> That we find wrecked! we may never know
> How brave you were when your course began.[46]

Although Bacon's poetry and her interests in social reform seldom intersected, there are exceptions to that general rule. The most notable example, "Poverty's Children," is undated, but was almost certainly written after she had begun to examine housing conditions in Evansville and elsewhere.

> All through the city, on every side,
> Poverty's children are scattered wide.

Poverty, she is a cruel mother,
But she has more children than any other.

Little she gives them to eat or wear—
Rags and tatters, and bones picked bare.

Toys both gruesome and strange have they,
Gleaned from the refuse and cast-away.

For Poverty turns her children out
To play in the gutters round about.

Naught for their good does Poverty care,
Cheats them of sunlight and common air.

Crowds them together in filthy pens,
Herds them in stifling, unwholesome dens,

Dingy walls that are gray with grime,
Sodden yards that are thick with slime—

Is it a wonder, such homes within,
Poverty's child is a child of Sin?[47]

Bacon's poetry was not all serious and somber, however. Many of her poems—including most of those that have probably held up best over the years—are lighthearted, even irreverent considerations of human foibles.

"Don't Forget"
You're just as odd to other folks
As they are odd to you,
For blue's as different from red
As red is unlike blue,
And two is just as far from one
As one is far from two,
So, as you judge of other folks
Be sure they're judging you.[48]

"The Family Tree"
I'm glad a grand old family tree
Has come to flower at last in ME.
I'm glad my forefathers were such
They don't disturb me very much.
But as for all this Chinese way
Of worshipping ancestors—say,
They'll keep all right, and, great or not,
Our pride don't alter them a jot.

157

I'm thinking of Posterity,
That when they climb our tree to me
They will not scorning say, *"That limb?"*
What reason to be proud of *him?*[49]

We even learn from one of her short poems about an apparent health
problem that she discussed nowhere else.

"Go, bury thy sorrow"
I've colitis, known as "spastic"
So I think I'd better mastic-
ate my food till it is plastic.
Spastic troubles: Hard to carry 'em
All emotions seem to harry 'em
But I'll try this one cure—barium.

(bury 'em)[50]

An entry in Bacon's "Verses" Journal, dated March 21, 1902, reads:
"Henceforth I will devote more attention to epigrams. I believe they are
my forte." Such poems are, by definition, concise, deal "pointedly and
often satirically with a single thought or event," and often end "with an
ingenious turn of thought." She *was* good at them, even using the
epigrammatic form to provide her own evaluation of the form itself.

"The Epigram"
Those who are easy to amuse
May feed on humor as they choose
But only epigrams are fit
To serve to epicures of wit.[51]

Her "Verses" Journal includes several examples of epigrams (some of
which are also included in a file of her unpublished poems at the Willard
Library in Evansville). Some representative selections:

"Gossip"
The hospitals would all be full,
The ambulance would run all day,
If merely flesh were bruised and gashed,
Or bones were broken by "they say."[52]

"Forbearance"
We crave forbearance for ourselves,
   But there the matter ends,

For, as a rule, the more we need,
    The less we give our friends.[53]

"Conceit"
Conceit still dogs humility,
For think how it would grieve us,
When we confess our inmost faults,
To have the world believe us.[54]

"Faith"
No need, if prayer avail for naught,
    To take kind Heaven to task, for
Full half who pray would be surprised
    To get the things they ask for.[55]

"Poverty"
It isn't just the pinch and pang
That tries our spirits so,
It's missing what the others have,
And knowing that they know.[56]

"Capital to Labor"
The case stands thus—none but the rich may shirk,
So I must keep you poor to do my work.[57]

A fitting conclusion to this discussion of Albion Bacon's poetry is a verse she called "The Spires." Dated September 9, 1933, three months before her death, it is one of the last things she wrote, and probably her last poem. The title refers to the twin spires of Trinity Methodist, the church her father had under construction at the time of his death and which she attended from her high school years onward. The poem touches on several themes that were important to her: religious faith, love of nature, and detestation of the physical and psychological harm caused by shortsighted and greedy industrialists and slumlords. It seems especially appropriate as her final poetic offering.

Oh, I laugh when I look at the spires,
All slender and silver and slight,
Threading their needles with clouds,
So lovely and useless and light.

And my laugh is in triumph to think
They have stood unmolested so long,

Unprotested, unnoticed, perchance,
By those who are stupid and strong.

Oh spires that the swallows salute,
Those men who have levelled our hills,
Who have blackened the earth with their mines,
Who have builded their hideous mills,

Who have crowded the poor in their slums,
Without windows for light or for breath,
Who have counted their profits on space,
But not counted our losses on death,

They might speak, if they thought:
                          "What's the use
Of a spire? It's a waste—an abuse.
Now, the church—you can sit in the pews,
You can preach from the pulpit, but how could you use
That comical, conical, pointed affair?
Why, it wouldn't have room for a desk or a chair,
Near the top. It won't do for a silo or bin,
It's no use for a granary,
Store house or cannery.
Come! Cut it off! Take it down!
It's no use to the church, it's no use to the town."

But hush! Lest some practical man
Overhear me. I fear me 'twould be
As it was when they pulled down the spires
In that dark, tragic land over-sea

When they tore down the bells from the towers,
And over the altars they trod.
When they burned sacred missals and fled
And left it—a land without God.

How much we would miss them—our spires!
What they mean to the rover, who sees
At the turn of the road, going home,
'Gainst the sunset, that point 'midst the trees.

What it means to us all that they hold
High aloft our ideals, and keep
Such beauty for man, and such Grace,
That they pray while the City's asleep.[58]

Trinity Methodist Episcopal Church (ca. 1910). The church's twin towers inspired Bacon's last poem, "The Spires." Karl Kae Knecht Collection, Special Collections, Willard Library

In addition to her articles, pamphlets, and books dealing with social welfare issues, her statements of religious faith, her children's stories, and her poetry, Bacon authored several pageants—a form of popular entertainment and education that enjoyed a brief vogue during the early twentieth century. She wrote the text, and in some cases the music, for a number of these productions, and later recalled her efforts fondly. "I can never tell how my pageants have *rested* me—and cheered me, and made me feel *human* again," she wrote in early 1927. "They are so wonderful, so beautiful—they are so big & overwhelming—they catch me up into an ecstasy over light and color, groupings, beauty of line, chiaro-scuro—stirring scenes &c."[59]

Historian David Glassberg observes that at the height of the pageantry movement "thousands of Americans in hundreds of towns . . . joined in civic celebrations by acting out dramatic episodes from their town's history." The craze turned out to be ephemeral, fading away in the mid-1920s. "After all," notes another student of the phenomenon, "[isn't] it common knowledge that pageants were silly, trite productions, full of ridiculous poses and terrible dialogue?" Well, yes. But if they left something to be desired in terms of dramaturgy, pageants nonetheless provide a useful window on progressives' use of history. And in none too subtle ways, the productions often served to advance progressive causes. As Glassberg puts it, pageant organizers in the early twentieth century believed "that history could be made into a dramatic public ritual through which the residents of a town, by acting out the right version of their past, could bring about some kind of future social and political transformation. . . . Essential to the progressive appeal was the use of historical imagery to discover or invent an appropriate tradition in support of reform." The Russell Sage Foundation even provided significant financial support for a 1911 Vermont production in order to learn "whether or not the pageant may be used successfully as an agent in social advancement."[60]

Bacon became involved in the pageant movement in 1916 as part of the centennial of Indiana's statehood. The Indiana Historical Commission (now Bureau), created to plan and supervise appropriate celebrations of the anniversary, decided to decentralize most commemorative activities to the county level. Many of the county celebrations were highlighted by a pageant that portrayed aspects of state and local history. By one count there were forty-five separate pageants produced in Indiana during the centennial year. Among them was an exemplary presentation by Vanderburgh County/Evansville that "pointed the way for the [other] counties of the [southwestern] Pocket district."[61]

This Evansville State Centennial Pageant was presented May 10–11, 1916, in conjunction with the state encampment of the Grand Army of the Republic. Bacon wrote the pageant and it was directed by "pageant master" Carl Dreisch, another local resident. Held outdoors at Bosse Field, the city's newest and largest athletic facility, it was, by all accounts, a stunning success. The Historical Commission's summary of the event referred to the "spirit and beauty of the pageant" and described it as "a great, impressive spectacle." It also repeated Bacon's claim that nearly 4,000 people participated in the production in some way. The Evansville newspapers were equally enthusiastic. The *Courier*, estimating a crowd of 6,300 the first night, acknowledged Bacon's efforts and opined that "had the details not been worked out by her the most glorious affair Evansville has ever seen would likely not have been staged."[62]

In seventeen episodes performed over two evenings, *The Pageant of Indiana* was intended (in Bacon's words) "to portray the most important facts of [the state's] history and her progress, as well as her products, her industries, and all for which she is famed." Many of the episodes dealt with predictable subjects: "Indian Scene," "Pioneers," "1861" (the Civil War), "Industry." However, consistent with the observation that some pageant organizers used their creations to help advance a reform agenda, the final episode dealt with "Education, Social Welfare, Health and Charities." Bacon, who was at the time deeply involved in her housing reform crusade, seldom passed up an opportunity to proselytize on behalf of the social welfare and cultural causes she supported. In her own synopsis of the pageant she described its conclusion as follows:

> The advance of Education is shown, accompanied by the Advanced Ideas that follow Education, Child Welfare, Social Service, the Playground movement, Sanitation, Vocational education. As these appear in the pageant procession there are seen grouped below Indiana, the spirits of Child Welfare, Social Service, Health and Sanitation, Poesy [Poetry], Music, Literature, Art, Education, Science, Invention, and Fame, who holds a roll of our great and honored names.[63]

The collaboration of Bacon and Carl Dreisch was revived two years later, but with results that reflect the anti-German paranoia of the World War I years. In early September 1918, Bacon wrote to the Woman's Section of the Indiana State Council of Defense regarding the child welfare work she was overseeing. In the course of this letter she mentioned that plans for a "Play Week" in Evansville had been disrupted. The local War Mothers organization, she reported, "broke up the pageant I was preparing for them, by objecting to the pageant director" on the grounds of his Bavarian origins. Since he had been naturalized and "no one has presented any proof of his disloyalty," Bacon "did not dream that he was other than a most valuable citizen, nor do I yet." But because Dreisch was "the only one that we could depend on" to serve as pageant master, plans for the performance had been dropped.[64]

Another of Bacon's pageants reflects the pacifist fervor that swept the country in the years after World War I. She prepared *A Pageant of War and Peace* for presentation on Armistice Day. Although the typescript in her papers is undated, a biographical entry for which she provided information records that it was originally produced in 1920 and revised for production in Washington, D.C., in 1925. However that may be, it was definitely presented to a packed house in the Evansville Coliseum on November 11, 1921, as part of that year's Armistice Day celebration.[65]

As reported in the *Indiana Magazine of History*, "the subject of the pageant was Disarmament, and [it] was written for the express purpose of showing the horrors of war and the blessings of peace." The central character in the first act is War, attended by Death and Famine. Various other personifications—Commerce and Industry, Art and Agriculture, the Nations of the World and the War Mothers—take their turns beseeching an unmoved War to release his grip on the world. In the second act Peace has become the central figure, "enthroned on the earth surrounded by smiling nations and happy flower-laden children." When this joyous state of affairs is suddenly threatened by a possible resumption of warfare, and the nations implore Peace to stay, she replies "very impressively, and slowly": "If Peace is to remain and bless the world, You must disarm! You must disarm! Or of a certainty War will return!" In the concluding scene Peace sings to a contingent of the American Legion:

> Ye gallant men, who heard your country calling,
> "To arms, to arms," and went so bravely then,
> The cause of Peace demands that you resign them,
> "Lay down your arms," your country calls again.

Whereupon, to the strains of "The Star-Spangled Banner," the Legionnaires promptly stack their weapons.[66]

To modern sensibilities both the ideas advanced in this production and the manner of their expression seem naive, unsophisticated, hokey. But Bacon was not out of step with the temper of her times. During the 1920s, in the words of a noted diplomatic historian, "treaties for the avoidance of war and treaties of disarmament were the American prescription for world peace." In a coincidental but delightfully appropriate conjunction of events, on the same day that *A Pageant of War and Peace* was presented in Evansville representatives from several nations began meeting in Washington at a conference devoted to the limitation of naval armaments. (Following the pageant the commander of an Evansville American Legion post sent a telegram to the U.S. delegates at the conference noting that thousands of Evansville residents had that day "demonstrated their support of the limitation of armament.") Later in the decade there was much popular support in the United States for the Kellogg-Briand Pact, an (unenforceable) international agreement by which signatories agreed to "renounce [war] as an instrument of national policy in their relations with one another." Bacon's antiwar and pro-disarmament pageant is thus properly seen as a local, as well as personal, expression of sentiments that had wide currency during the postwar decade.[67]

A 1923 *Program for Citizenship Day*, which seems to have been Bacon's last pageant, was sponsored by the Department of American Citizenship of the General Federation of Women's Clubs. Indeed, Bacon dedicated the program to Mrs. Percy V. Pennybacker, a former chair of that department and past president of the federation, who had promoted the preparation of such a pageant for many years. This project demanded the full range of Bacon's creativity. In addition to writing the text, she provided detailed suggestions regarding staging and wrote both the words and the music for several songs that were an integral part of the production. Although abbreviated versions were presented in many small towns during June and early July, the first full-scale production of the pageant premiered on July 20 at the Chautauqua Institution in western New York, where portions of it were also filmed.[68]

As was true of her earlier efforts—and of most pageants—*Program for Citizenship Day* relied heavily on symbolism and personification. The cast of characters included Columbia (that is, the United States), Justice, Liberty, Opportunity, and History. Depending on local circumstances, the program could employ the Boys of '76 (a fife and drum corps) as well as an American Legion assemblage. In a departure from the norm, the pageant made use of a responsive reading that engaged the entire audience in a ritual affirmation of patriotism. This was followed by ceremonies in which two groups—"young men and women, 21 years of age" and "the foreign born"—took oaths to support the Constitution.

Bacon took pains to offer suggestions for the most effective use of stereopticon projections, music, and lighting, but she did not want producers to worry if they did not have the most sophisticated technical equipment or professional expertise. Her notes stressed the adaptability of the script to the circumstances of any community. She wanted the program to be "an inspiration, not a bar, to the celebration of Citizenship Day," and she thus emphasized that since "the main features are the ritual, and the administering of the oaths, all else may be adapted as the facilities of the community require."[69]

Albion Fellows Bacon's name is seldom mentioned (and never mentioned prominently) in discussions of Indiana's literary heritage. As an adult she did not write fiction (unless one counts the children's stories in *The Charm String*) and her designation as a "mediocre poet" by a scholar of Indiana literature is probably warranted.[70] Her pageants, like the pageantry craze itself, have faded into obscurity. Her devotional pieces, *Consolation* and *The Path to God*, were not widely noticed when published and are essentially unknown today. Even her most substantial and significant publication, *Beauty for Ashes*, is difficult to find and rarely read.

Bacon was not, of course, a professional author, and she should not be judged by the standards one might apply to someone claiming that status. What is noteworthy is that she was able to sustain her strong childhood interest in writing throughout her life, to produce interesting, effective, and affecting works in a variety of genres, and to do so while simultaneously engaged in social welfare activities that consumed great quantities of time and energy. That she was able to write as much as she did as well as she did for as long as she did is a testament to her creativity, mental agility, and self-discipline. It is also a testament to her ability to employ her skill with the written word in the service of her other interests. "I could not bear to write just for money," she observed in the late 1920s. "Nor to write just for Art's sake. Nor for anything that would not make the world brighter or better, wiser or happier."[71]

Eight

Municipal Housekeeper and Inadvertent Feminist

Albion Fellows Bacon was 68 years of age when she died at home early on the morning of Sunday, December 10, 1933. Although she had seemed to be in reasonably good health until the last few months before her death, there was some prior evidence of physical decline. A decade earlier she had spent time in a sanatorium. She wrote her friend Grace Julian Clarke afterwards that she had not been ill and had gone only for "a regular looking over." That this attempted reassurance may have been disingenuous is suggested by the length of her stay (two months) and her offhand comment that the doctor "was well satisfied with my condition, as far as my organs were concerned." A year later she advised Clarke that she would not be able to attend a General Federation of Women's Clubs meeting in Los Angeles at which a film of her Citizenship Day pageant was to be shown. Although it was a great disappointment not to go, she felt she was "not strong enough to take the long trip, and run the risk of getting sick, so far away from home." She was being cautious because "I have not been quite well all winter, and even my short little trips, on state business . . . have just finished me, each time." In her later years she suffered some gallbladder problems. Near the end, when she was unable to eat and her doctor proposed feeding her artificially through a tube, Hilary adamantly refused to permit it. "He wouldn't want that done to himself," Joy recalled, "and he wouldn't have it done to mother." The official cause of death was recorded as arteriosclerotic heart disease and chronic nephritis (that is, a combination of coronary artery disease and kidney failure). Joy put it less technically but perhaps no less accurately: "Mother just burned herself out."[1]

While she had slowed down a bit during her last few years, and traveled less than she once did, Bacon was still involved with numerous agencies and organizations working for social and cultural betterment. The obituaries in her hometown newspapers printed long lists of her past and present memberships and benefactions. One paper recalled that in January 1930, on the occasion of her receipt of the Rotary Civic Award, she was president of the Evansville City Plan Commission, the Vanderburgh County Tuberculosis Association, and the Advisory Juvenile Commission of the state's Probation Department. At the same time she was also on the board or executive committee of the Vanderburgh Child Welfare Association (president in 1930), the Family Welfare Association, the Public Health Nursing Association, the Southwestern Indiana Historical Society, the Society of History and Fine Arts, and the Indiana Mental Hygiene Society, as well as being a member of the National Probation Association, the National Housing Association, and the International Housing and Town Planning Association. No wonder, then, that the *Evansville Courier* observed in an appreciation: "Her interests were amazing in their catholicity; her talents were bewildering in their versatility." Conspicuously absent from the recountings of her affiliations, however, are groups that focused primarily on women's issues, including women's suffrage.[2]

❖

Students of the Progressive era have long recognized the considerable overlap of social welfare history and women's history during the first decades of the twentieth century. They have struggled, however, when attempting to find appropriate language to "locate" a particular individual within the matrix created by that overlap. Bacon's life and her de facto career highlight the difficulty. For example, even by the definitions of her own day, and certainly by the definitions of ours, it is impossible to describe Bacon as a "radical" feminist. A more difficult question is whether it is historically accurate to associate her with feminism at all.

Bacon seldom used the word "feminist" in her writings, and she never applied the term to herself. To the extent that the word implies belief in the existence of some degree of female subjugation, it is questionable whether she even accepted the premise. And if one hallmark of early twentieth century feminism was insistence upon at least the *political* equality of men and women, then Bacon was a late and somewhat ambivalent convert to the cause. The evidence to support these assertions is limited, but that fact itself is a form of evidence. Issues relating to suffrage and feminism were of sufficiently low priority that she seldom wrote or spoke of them.

Given that the public policy and social welfare issues with which she was involved were sometimes contentious, Bacon seems to have enjoyed remarkably cordial relations with most of the (usually male) administrators, legislators, and businessmen with whom she came in contact. Writing in 1914 she recalled a hearing before the Evansville Common Council five years earlier at which the proposed appointment of a building inspector for the city was being discussed. She and her supporters "were given the kind and cordial reception which I have invariably received from councils." The experience left her wondering "why women are afraid to go to such meetings. Women deal with the same men in the grocery, the bank or the coal office, and come out ahead. Why, then, should they feel timid about meeting them in session?" She concluded that if women approaching public officials would "only not, *not* be belligerent and antagonistic, but simply pleasant, persistent, and always watchful, they will generally win."[3] Twelve years later, in a memoir that was not written with publication in mind, she echoed these sentiments:

> I have worked with men since I first reported in Court and took depositions. Later, in my public work, I have encountered every kind of men, of every walk of life. I sit on boards and commissions and in committees composed largely or most entirely of men. It is always the same—courtesy, deference, and, what is best, a good fellowship, as if I were a man, with a give & take of opinion. And never a glance, a flicker of an eye lid, never a word, of a personal nature that is used in society. It is great! fine! splendid![4]

This is not to say that Bacon was above adopting a persona when she felt it was a pragmatic necessity. Especially while lobbying the General Assembly she consciously adjusted her behavior to fit her perception of men's expectations. "It was a point of pride with me," she wrote, "to avoid all the little things that cause the reproachful remark 'That's just like a woman,' and to take all the fates of war, at least outwardly, in the calm impersonal way men do." She refused to express doubts about eventual success, recognizing "the value of a confident bearing." She endeavored "to avoid sentimentality, and to stick to the practical issues, in a practical way." And, she recalled, "I wouldn't have let one of those men know that I had ever written a verse!"[5]

Bacon, unlike some women who were her contemporaries, was not an opponent of suffrage, but neither was it a priority for her. As her youngest daughter put it, "mother had her own irons in the fire, and suffrage wasn't one of them." In the wake of her 1913 legislative victory a friend asked if she would now turn her attention to the extension of the franchise; no, she replied, she would continue to focus on housing. At one point, in fact, she saw the passions aroused by the suffrage debate as inimical to her own work. Joy remembered that when a woman who had a reputation as a militant suffragist volunteered to support housing reform, her mother felt that it would be "a kiss of death."[6]

When Bacon eventually did come out publicly in favor of women's suffrage her decision had less to do with ideology than with political realities. It was only after the failure of the "death trap" housing bill in 1915 that an Evansville newspaper described her as "the latest recruit to the ranks of the suffragists." If all men were as reasonable and right-thinking as her supporters, the *Press* quoted her as saying, then "the *indirect* influence of women would be enough and we would not need the ballot." But since they were not, evidenced by her bill's rejection, she had concluded that women's votes would be necessary to advance the reform causes in which she and others were interested. Her pragmatic, gradualist approach to the issue is evident, however, in a letter she wrote Grace Clarke (a strong suffrage proponent who was then out of town) during that 1915 legislative session:

> Dr. [Amelia] Keller [president of the Woman's Franchise League of Indiana] is standing out for all suffrage or none. . . . I tell them to get *something* in quickly, or they will lose everything by delay. I think school [board] and municipal suffrage would be an entering wedge, and see what political power it would give us, what leverage! We would be so much better off, and appear so much more reasonable.

So while she came, finally, to support women's suffrage, it was less out of a belief in abstract rights than it was a matter of hard-headed practicality. Women's votes were, for Bacon, a means rather than an end. Once the franchise had been attained, however, it comes as no surprise that she took this civic responsibility seriously. According to Joy, her mother "never missed a vote."[7]

So what do we *call* Bacon? Her beliefs and activities seem, at first glance, to place her in a category some historians have referred to as "social feminism." The term was first employed by William L. O'Neill, who used it "to group together women who were municipal civic reformers, club members, settlement house residents, and labor activists concerned about working women and child laborers," and to contrast such women with so-called "hard-core" feminists whose principal goals were suffrage and the expansion of women's rights. The social feminist rubric has since been used widely "to designate women's public activism of the late nineteenth and early twentieth centuries." J. Stanley Lemons, for example, adopted the terminology in his 1973 book *The Woman Citizen* to distinguish between those who "put women's rights and women's emancipation above all other considerations" and those (the social feminists) who "also wanted emancipation but tended to subordinate this to social reform."[8]

By the late 1980s, however, the "social feminist" label had come under attack, most notably by historian Nancy Cott. In an insightful essay she protested "rhetorical overuse" of the word feminism and its various composites "to signify all the notable things that women have ever done." She conceded that "the concept of social feminism made strides toward expressing the way that women raised their own public stature and responsibilities by asserting themselves on behalf of others, on behalf of reform causes." But, she argued, since the term "lumps together virtually all the public activities of Progressive Era women in social welfare, education, and labor reform" its use "is calling on one conceptual category to do too much." The crux of the matter, in Cott's view, was that "the usage *social feminism* leaches out meaning from the word *feminism*." Surely, she declared, "feminism should designate something more specific than women's entrance into public life or efforts at social reform." The problem, in short, was that social feminism's inclusiveness "blots out the rise of feminism as a discrete, self-named movement in the 1910s."[9]

For Lemons, however, the delineation between feminism and other social currents of the day was not so clear cut, the distinctions among them not as sharp at the time as Cott would have it in retrospect. And, in his view, the synergistic relationships benefited all parties. As he summarized it: "The point is that as various women and organizations worked for a broad reform movement to civilize, democratize, and humanize the American system, as they worked for progressive reform, they advanced the status of American women. And as they fought for women's rights, they pushed progressivism along." Moreover, Lemons was apparently unmoved by critiques of the term that he, O'Neill, and others had popularized; when *The Woman Citizen* was reissued in 1990 (a year after Cott's article appeared) he wrote in the preface that "nearly everyone accepts 'social feminist' as a useful and appropriate term."[10]

Lemons's riposte to the contrary, it is not difficult to understand Cott's concerns. Words do (or should) have meaning, and as she notes "much of what Lemons catches in the net of social feminism might as easily be considered alternative, or even opposed, to feminism." Hence her conclusion that a phrase used in this study, the Progressive era's own "municipal housekeeping," or the more recently coined "civic maternalism," are both "more precise and successful terms" to describe "organized women's efforts to assure public health, sanitation, and children's welfare." Particularly if one accepts the notion that a woman could be a feminist in the early twentieth century only if (to quote Cott) she "protested male domination and attempted to redefine gender hierarchy," then Albion Bacon is indeed more accurately identified as a municipal housekeeper than as a feminist, social or otherwise.[11]

As Cott acknowledges, however, the reality of women's lives in the early twentieth century was doubtless more complex than can be suggested by such "totalizing, either/or questions" as "was she a feminist or not?" Cott's criteria notwithstanding, could one be a feminist without meaning to be? Put another way, in the movement to expand women's rights and opportunities could what one *did*—the example one set—be as important as what one *believed*? Cott herself offers an extreme but intriguing example: women who actively opposed suffrage. Antisuffrage agitation by women was "certainly *not* feminist," she observes. But might one say "that insofar as female antisuffragists engaged themselves in the political arena where men ruled, sought to define women's political responsibilities for themselves, and refused to cede those definitions to men, they joined the battle to alter gender hierarchy even while they said they were defending women's traditional place?" In short, asks Cott, "did their activity have a feminist *aspect*?"[12]

If one's answer to this rhetorical question is yes, then Bacon serves as an appropriate case study to support the claim that feminism might sometimes have been unintentional. As we have seen, she was at best a tepid proponent of women's suffrage and she expressed no conscious desire to "redefine gender hierarchy." Yet she certainly did so, even if in limited ways and as a by-product of seeking to achieve other goals. While it was not the intent of her housing reform work to advance women's rights, her efforts did lead to her very visible engagement in "the political arena where men ruled." So did her presidencies of the state's Advisory Juvenile Commission and the Evansville City Plan Commission, both high-profile appointments that were sometimes politically sensitive. In pressing the cause of housing reform she challenged the economic interests of many landlords (usually men) and while she sought to ameliorate the lot of all those who lived in substandard dwellings she seems to have been especially sensitive to the plight of women and their children. She was sympathetic, too, to the working conditions faced by many women, a concern that manifested itself in her directorship of the Working Girls' Association and in her repeated calls for female factory inspectors. Finally, during her service with the President's Conference on Home Building and Home Ownership she purposely focused her efforts on formulating standards for kitchens and household management. Although she clearly assumed and accepted that these were topics of interest almost exclusively to women (no redefinition of gender roles here), she also thought that her insights regarding these issues were more likely than those of her male colleagues to improve women's lives. Thus, while Bacon may not qualify under a strict definition of "feminist," it is clear that much of her public work did have, even if unintentionally, a "feminist aspect." While she herself might well have rejected the term, it does not seem inappropriate or inaccurate to think of her as an *inadvertent* feminist, as someone whose actions (if not rhetoric) provided a model of public participation that advanced the cause of women's emancipation and equality.[13]

If Bacon was unwilling, as her daughter put it, "to fight men for women's rights," she apparently was not out of the mainstream, at least in Indiana. As discussed earlier, many women of the municipal housekeeper ilk found it strategically useful (and perhaps psychologically necessary) to describe and defend their public activities in terms of traditional roles. Barbara Springer, the closest student of the Hoosier state's activist women during the Progressive years, has dubbed them "ladylike reformers" and concludes that, as a group, they "did little to change the popular image of women as wives and mothers." Indeed, to support her contention that "Indiana women reformers continually reiterated that their first duty was to family and home" Springer cites a newspaper profile that identifies one of Bacon's "pet horrors" as being perceived as "a big masculine woman who is interested in everything but her home duties."[14]

The concept of inadvertent feminism gains some support, however, from Springer's further observation that "despite their lip service to domesticity, it may be that [the women reformers'] actions spoke louder than their words in influencing the next generation. Progressive women were not the first females to agitate for change in Indiana, but they made such agitation acceptable, in part because of their professed 'ladylike' behavior." The language of domesticity aside, these women "were often tough, pragmatic, and strong-willed" and "had what amounted to unpaid careers"—a description that certainly fits Bacon. And "beyond what they did for their state and as role models for the next generation, progressive female reformers found that their work enriched their own lives." Springer supports this assertion with, once again, a quote from Bacon:

> We all realized how much our abundance had gone to waste for lack of ways to spend it. Not money, not goods, but richness of experience, fullness of life, love lavished on a few, hoarded in our own walls. It was a relief to open the channels and let it flow out.[15]

If Bacon was an inadvertent feminist, she clearly was not an inadvertent Methodist. Roy Lubove, the only historian to have previously assayed her life, observed that she was "a complex woman with a simple, trusting religious faith." She was, he concluded, "a distinguished exemplar of the social gospel," a Progressive era effort to apply Christian doctrine to the nation's social, economic, and political problems.[16]

As discussed in the preceding chapter, Bacon articulated her religious beliefs and shared them with others in some of her publications. "The Divine Call: Follow Me" and *The Path to God* bespoke her deep (if theologically unsophisticated) religious sensibilities. And the profound comfort her faith provided her in the aftermath of her eldest daughter's death is obvious in *Consolation*. But Bacon's religion—and, more specifically, her Methodism—was not only contemplative (though for her it was that too). It also served as the wellspring for her social service activism. During the midst of her housing work she commented that her reform efforts grew out of "an act of religious consecration."[17]

Bacon's religious upbringing and her lifelong membership in Methodist churches may not have been the sole causes of her reform efforts. They were, however, a significant part of the context within which her social consciousness was raised as well as an influence on the particular direction her activism took. While there is no direct connection between the two events, it is nonetheless noteworthy and indicative of the temper of the times that just two months after Bacon's 1907 talk describing "The Homes of the Poor" in Evansville the Methodist Federation for Social Service was organized as an unofficial group allied with the national church. Its stated purpose was "to deepen within the Church the sense of social obligation and opportunity to study social problems from the Christian point of view, and to promote social service in the spirit of Jesus Christ."[18]

Kevin Corn, a recent student of Indiana Methodism, has noted that by the early twentieth century the denomination had begun to move away from "a voluntarist model of reform that focused on the individual"—activities, for example, such as the friendly visiting and Flower Mission work in which Bacon had initially been engaged. "In its place they adopted a strategy more focused on society as a whole, and more reliant on cooperation with the state. As such, they became increasingly ready to enforce their vision of a respectable Christian society by means of legal coercion"—such as the restrictive housing legislation and child labor laws Bacon espoused.[19]

Methodists were not unique in this regard. Many Progressives (who were largely Protestant) were animated by strong religious convictions. (Think, for example, of Theodore Roosevelt's assertion to his Bull Moose followers in 1912 that "We stand at Armageddon, and we battle for the Lord.") The reform movements of the early twentieth century owed much to men and women of a variety of religious persuasions who sought careers or avocations that, in Robert Crunden's fine phrase, "offered possibilities for preaching without pulpits." But as Corn observes, in a passage that seems written with Bacon in mind, "more than most other religious groups, Methodists put an emphasis on action, and took much of their particular denominational identity from the things they did, or attempted to do, in the larger society."[20]

❖

Following Bacon's death her hometown newspapers all referred to her as Evansville's "best known and most loved woman." The lengthy obituaries quoted the presidents of most of the city's social welfare institutions, all of whom "paid tribute to her memory, not only with words of sorrow, but with utterances of gratitude for her leadership and praise for her accomplishments." Her colleagues on the City Plan Commission (several of whom served as pallbearers) convened a special meeting at noon on Monday to adopt a memorial resolution in her honor.

The funeral service was held on Tuesday at Trinity Methodist, the church her father had under construction when he died, the church where she had been married and which she had attended for some fifty years. Hundreds of pink roses covered the casket and banked the altar. Trinity's minister, the Rev. Herbert A. Keck, noted in his funeral sermon that "her reputation as a social worker was state-wide, nationwide" and that "through her influence much progressive social legislation was written on the statute books of Indiana. . . . She was vibrant, dynamic, she literally spent and was spent in the service of humanity." Keck recalled, too, her devotion to her family and the strong religious faith—"the mainspring of her life"—that motivated her social work. Fittingly, he recited one of Bacon's poems, "The Torch," which she had written on Easter Sunday 1910:

Make me to be a torch for groping feet
Down Truth's dim trail; to bear for wistful eyes
Comfort of light; to bid great beacons blaze
And kindle altar fires of sacrifice.

Let me set souls aflame with quenchless zeal
For great endeavors, causes true and high.
So would I live to quicken and inspire,
So would I, thus consumed, burn out and die.[21]

Bacon was buried in Evansville's Oak Hill Cemetery in a family plot that really *was* on a low hill shaded by an oak tree. Her daughter Margaret and her grandson George Bacon Smith were already interred there. Hilary died just over two years later, in February 1936, and was buried next to his wife. Their daughter Albion (d. 1962) and her husband, George D. Smith (d. 1955), also rest in this spot. The twins, who had been born in 1901, both lived long lives. Hilary, Jr., who attended Johns Hopkins University and then remained in the Baltimore area, died in the mid-1980s. Joy attended Radcliffe College, married Edwin C. Witwer in 1926, and lived thereafter in the South Bend, Indiana–Niles, Michigan area; she died in 1995.

As the news of Bacon's passing spread beyond her hometown, other individuals and institutions weighed in with tributes. Grace Julian Clarke, a friend since the early housing reform days, used her column in the *Indianapolis Star* to lament the "untimely" death. She recalled Bacon's first appearance before the Indiana Federation of Clubs, "how small and frail she seemed, and how her earnestness and determination roused us to go the limit in helping her with her housing bill." On a more personal level Clarke remembered that her friend "was peculiarly gifted as a letter writer, her sense of humor was keen and the marginal illustrations to her epistles were often eloquent." Beyond this, however, was "a certain fine spiritual quality impossible adequately to describe. . . . Her fragile form . . . seemed to be the envelope of a soul destined for ampler regions."[22]

Another old friend, Amos Butler, former secretary of the Board of State Charities, headed a committee that prepared a memorial resolution adopted in the fall of 1934 by the Indiana State Conference on Social Work. He reminisced that Bacon "came into this Conference some thirty years ago and won us all by her charm." He enumerated her specific accomplishments—in housing reform, child welfare, juvenile probation—but he also noted that she had been interested "in all phases of social welfare work represented by this Conference." Butler and his colleagues agreed that they would all miss "one whose presence and speech were not only an inspiration to us but were felt as a peculiar power wherever she went throughout this broad land."[23]

The shortest tribute to Bacon and her achievements was no less heartfelt for its brevity. The journal of the National Housing Association ran a black-bordered obituary in June 1934. Although unsigned, the notice was undoubtedly prepared by the journal's editor, Lawrence Veiller, who had been one of the first "housers" Bacon read when she became interested in the subject and whom she had brought to Indiana as an expert consultant when her 1909 housing law was being revised and expanded for submission to the 1911 General Assembly. The pair had last worked together in December 1931, when they served on the same committee as part of the President's Conference on Home Building and Home Ownership. Veiller informed his readers of Bacon's death by centering her name and the date she died on the page, as they might appear on a gravestone.[24] And then he observed:

> Thus passed away one of those who contributed much in her own state and outside it to the Cause of Housing.
>
> A great leader and a valiant warrior in the fight against evils of all kinds—against Slums, against poverty, against child oppression.
>
> A gay blithe spirit forcing her frail body to perform miracles beyond her strength. Everywhere and at all times she gave
>
> Beauty for Ashes.

NOTES

Introduction

1. Vincent P. DeSantis, *The Shaping of Modern America: 1877–1920*, 2nd ed. (Arlington Heights, Ill., 1989 [1973]).

2. Anne Firor Scott, *Natural Allies: Women's Associations in American History* (Urbana and Chicago, 1992), 155, 3.

3. Albion Fellows Bacon, "What the Day's Work Means to Me," *The Bookman*, 42 (October 1915), 201.

4. *Evansville Courier*, December 11, 1933.

5. *Evansville Journal*, April 10, 1925.

6. Nancy F. Cott, "What's in a Name? The Limits of 'Social Feminism'; or, Expanding the Vocabulary of Women's History," *Journal of American History*, 76 (December 1989), 809–811, 818–819, 820–821.

7. James H. Madison, *The Indiana Way: A State History* (Bloomington and Indianapolis, 1986), 222.

1. The Sheltered Life

1. *Evansville Daily Journal*, March 4, 5 [6], 1865. The child was born April 8, 1865, and named after *both* parents: Albion Mary Fellows.

2. Roy Lubove, "Albion Fellows Bacon and the Awakening of a State," *Midwest Review* (1962), 63, n. 1; "The Iglehart or Igleheart Family; The Levi Igleheart (1786–1855) Branch, Including Descendants of his Eight Children" (1961) [photocopy in possession of the author; hereafter cited as "Iglehart/Igleheart Genealogy"]; Methodist Episcopal Church, *Indiana Conference Minutes* (1865), 15–16.

3. "Iglehart/Igleheart Genealogy"; Annie Fellows Johnston, *The Land of the Little Colonel: Reminiscence and Autobiography* (Boston, 1929), 12.

4. Johnston, *Land of the Little Colonel*, 17, 21, 23–24.

5. Ibid., 26–30; *Indiana Conference Minutes* (1913), 204.

6. Fort Wayne College eventually evolved into Taylor University and moved to Upland, Indiana. See William C. Ringenberg, *Taylor University: The First 125 Years* (Grand Rapids, Mich., 1973), esp. chapter 3.

7. "Iglehart/Igleheart Genealogy"; Mary Fellows Cavanaugh, *The Fellows Family* (n.p., n.d.) [copy in the Albion Fellows Bacon Collection, Willard Library, Evansville, Indiana]; *Indiana Conference Minutes* (1865), 15–16; 1860 U.S. manuscript census of population, Boonville, Boon Township, Warrick County, Indiana, dwelling number 1243; Evansville city directory (1863).

8. Evansville city directory (1865); Gordon Thompson, *Beacon Lights of Trinity Methodist Church* (Evansville, Ind., 1966), 2.

9. Evansville city directories (1868–69, 1870–71, 1871–72); 1870 U.S. manuscript census of population, Evansville (2nd ward), Vanderburgh County, Indiana, dwelling number 414; Johnston, *Land of the Little Colonel*, 63.

There is some confusion, even mystery, concerning the number of children born to Reverend Albion and Mary Erskine Fellows. Most sources indicate that there were three daughters: Lura (born 1857), Anna/Annie (1863), and Albion/Allie (1865). One of the couple's grandchildren (Albion's youngest daughter, Joy Bacon Witwer) claimed in a 1988 interview that she had no knowledge of her mother having other siblings. In the 1860 manuscript census of population, however, there is a four-year-old child named Ella recorded immediately following Albion and Mary on the census schedule. The next line records two-year-old "Laura" (an obvious misspelling of Lura), which makes it appear that the enumerator was recording Ella as the eldest child. Moreover, a Fellows family history, prepared circa 1919 by Rev. Fellows's youngest sister and based on her personal knowledge as well as family papers and correspondence, mentions four daughters and lists Ella as the oldest. One possibility is that this child died soon after the summer of 1860 and that Rev. Fellows and Mary never discussed the loss with their other children. To complicate matters further, the 1900 census asked women how many children they had borne and how many of those children were still living. Mary's answers to those questions (or at least the answers that *someone* gave the enumerator) were "six" and "three." And in an autobiographical reflection late in her life, Albion referred to her mother as "having lost my father and three children." Assuming that there was a daughter named Ella who died young, and assuming that the census data and Albion's reminiscences are accurate, apparently there were two other children who were stillborn or died in infancy. This supposition is supported by Rev. Richard Hargrave, who knew Rev. Fellows and prepared a brief biographical sketch of him. According to Hargrave, Albion and Mary Fellows "were blessed with six children—four daughters and two sons. The sons died in infancy." Hargrave also claimed, however, that the eldest daughter (Ella) died shortly after her father at age thirteen. That is highly improbable, since it would mean she was born in 1852—two years prior to Rev. Fellows's graduation, ordination, and marriage. See Joy Bacon Witwer oral history interview, September 23, 1988 (hereafter cited as Witwer interview #2), 11–14; 1860 manuscript census of population, Boonville, Boon Township, Warrick County, Indiana, dwelling number 1243; Cavanaugh, *The Fellows Family*, 20; 1900 manuscript census of population, Vanderburgh County, Indiana, enumeration district 84, sheet 4, line 21; Albion Fellows Bacon, 36-page manuscript "auto-biography" written for her children over a several month period in late 1926 and early 1927 (the original manuscript, which is currently in possession of the author, will be deposited in the Bacon Collection, Willard Library, where a copy is already on file; hereafter cited as Bacon "Autobiography"), [8]; William P. Hargrave, ed., *Sacred Poems of Rev. Richard Hargrave . . .* (Cincinnati, 1890), 347–348 (thanks to Bill Bartelt for this citation).

10. Johnston, *Land of the Little Colonel*, 37; Albion Fellows Bacon, *Beauty for Ashes* (New York, 1914), 1–2.

11. Bacon, *Beauty for Ashes*, 2–5; Joy Bacon Witwer oral history interview, August 13, 1988 (hereafter cited as Witwer interview #1), 57.

12. Kenneth P. McCutchan, *From Then Til Now: History of McCutchanville* (Indianapolis, 1969), 100, 102.

13. Johnston, *Land of the Little Colonel*, 42. A red brick building, erected on the site a decade later, continued to serve the religious needs of many members of the community. With some subsequent alterations and additions, it functions today as a chapel for the local United Methodist Church. National Register of Historic Places nomination form for the McJohnston Chapel of the McCutchanville United Methodist Church (copy obtained from the Division of Historic Preservation and Archaeology, Indiana Department of Natural Resources, Indianapolis).

14. Bacon, "Autobiography," [2–3]; Annie Fellows Johnston and Albion Fellows Bacon, *Songs Ysame* (Boston, 1897), 29–30 (reprinted in McCutchan, *From Then Til Now*, 104).

15. Bacon, "Autobiography," [2]; Bacon, *Beauty for Ashes*, 11.

16. McCutchan, *From Then Til Now*, 49–50; Johnston, *Land of the Little Colonel*, 77.

17. Bacon, "Autobiography," [23–24]; Bacon, *Beauty for Ashes*, 5; Johnston, *Land of the Little Colonel*, 78.

18. Bacon, "Autobiography," [9]; Bacon, *Beauty for Ashes*, 12, 5; Johnston, *Land of the Little Colonel*, 64, 51, 52–53.

19. Bacon, *Beauty for Ashes*, 10, 12; Witwer interview #1, p. 23; Bacon, "Autobiography," [8]. Contrary to what one might assume, the family's straitened circumstances did not result—at least not directly—from the fact that Mary was the widow of a poorly paid minister. Albion observed that her father "was an unusually good business man. He left property around what is now Evanston, Ill. that should have made us very wealthy. But my mother, with no business experience, took the advice of men she trusted, sold the land, and invested in western land that never even paid the taxes. So we were always poor." Bacon, "Autobiography," [13].

20. Bacon, *Beauty for Ashes*, 5–6.

21. Ibid., 12–13; Johnston, *Land of the Little Colonel*, 38, 40–41.

22. Bacon, *Beauty for Ashes*, 12, 9; Johnston, *Land of the Little Colonel*, 80–81.

23. Grade school copybook (untitled), Box 3, Bacon Collection, Willard Library.

24. Johnston, *Land of the Little Colonel*, 81–83; Evansville city directories (1882, 1883); *Evansville Daily Journal*, June 13, 1883; Bacon, "Autobiography," [24]; Annie Fellows, "Diary, 1880–1885," Annie Fellows Johnston Collection, Willard Library (entries for October 19, 1882, January 12, 1883, April 23, 1885).

George P. Heilman, Lura's husband, was the son of William Heilman, a wealthy businessman and U.S. congressman, and the older brother of Charles F. Heilman, mayor of Evansville from 1910 to 1914. Karl J. Heilman, Jr. and James E. Raudabaugh, *Our Heilman Family* (n.p., 1991), 358–363, 374–375, 428.

25. Bacon, "Autobiography," [24]; Bacon, *Beauty for Ashes*, 14; *Evansville Daily Journal*, June 16, 1883.

26. *Evansville Daily Journal*, June 13, 1883.

27. Ibid., June 13, 16, 1883.

28. Witwer interview #1, p. 6; Bacon, "Autobiography," [24].

29. Bacon, *Beauty for Ashes*, 15; Bacon, "Autobiography," [25]; *Evansville Courier*, November 17, 1888 (column headed "A Graceful Compliment" that reprints an article from the *Phonagraphic* [sic] *World*).

Judge Asa Iglehart (as he preferred to spell it, although other family members and many other sources rendered it "Igleheart") was Mary Erskine Fellows's maternal uncle and one of the most prominent attorneys in Evansville. Born in Kentucky in 1816 or 1817, his parents brought him to Warrick County, Indiana, in 1823. He studied law while farming and teaching in a country school, was admitted to the Indiana bar in 1848, and moved to Evansville the next year. A common pleas judgeship in the 1850s conferred the title by which he was known thereafter. Iglehart maintained a private practice until shortly before his death in 1887 and was, as one biographical sketch put it, "a man of means and affairs and successful in accumulating property." *Biographical Cyclopedia of Vanderburgh County, Indiana* (Evansville, 1897), 115–117 (quotation, 116); John E. Iglehart, "The Life and Times of John Shrader," *Indiana Magazine of History*, 17 (March 1921), 41–42.

30. Evansville city directories (1881–1887). After moving to Evansville in 1881, Mary and her daughters made regular (and sometimes lengthy) visits to McCutchanville. Annie's diary for 1880–1885 contains several references to "visiting in the country." In her entry of October 13, 1883, for example, she recorded that "Allie and I made a three weeks visit in the country this summer. . . . We were invited out to spend the day to nearly every place in the neighborhood." Annie Fellows, "Diary, 1880–1885."

31. "Complete Record of Young Ladies Foreign Missionary Society, 1878–1904," Trinity United Methodist Church archives, Evansville.

32. Johnston, *Land of the Little Colonel*, 83–84.

33. Bacon, "Autobiography," [26]; "Miscellaneous Poems" file, Box 3, Ba-

con Collection, Willard Library; *Evansville Courier* and *Evansville Daily Journal*, September 20, 21, 1887.

34. Bacon, *Beauty for Ashes*, 14; Witwer interview #1, p. 29.

35. John E. Iglehart, ed., *An Account of Vanderburgh County from Its Organization* (Dayton, Ohio, 1923), 491–494; *Evansville Courier*, February 17, 1936 (Hilary Bacon obituary); Witwer interview #1, pp. 3–4.

36. "Pioneer Merchant Once Worked for $25 a Year," *Evansville Press*, March 18, 1928; *Evansville Courier*, February 17, 1936; Iglehart, ed., *An Account of Vanderburgh County*, 493.

37. *Biographical Cyclopedia of Vanderburgh County*, 65–66; Iglehart, ed., *An Account of Vanderburgh County*, 491–493; Evansville city directories.

38. Iglehart, ed., *An Account of Vanderburgh County*, 493; Witwer interview #1, p. 4.

39. *Evansville Courier*, February 17, 1936; Evansville city directories.

40. Witwer interview #1, pp. 6–7; Johnston, *Land of the Little Colonel*, 86.

41. Albion Fellows Bacon, 84-page manuscript diary of her European trip during the summer of 1888 (hereafter cited as "Grand Tour Diary"), 1–4. The original diary, which the author was permitted to photocopy in September 1988, was then in the possession of Bacon's youngest daughter, Joy Bacon Witwer.

42. Bacon, "Grand Tour Diary," 4, 8, 5.

43. Ibid., 9; Johnston, *Land of the Little Colonel*, 86.

44. Bacon, "Grand Tour Diary," 21.

45. Ibid., 36, 17.

46. Ibid., 37–48.

47. Ibid., 49, 51; Johnston, *Land of the Little Colonel*, 86–87.

48. Bacon, "Grand Tour Diary," 55–58 (quotations, 55, 57); Johnston, *Land of the Little Colonel*, 87–88.

49. Bacon, "Grand Tour Diary," 59–73 (quotations, 70, 73).

50. Ibid., 78–83 (poem, 80); Johnston, *Land of the Little Colonel*, 87.

51. Bacon, "Grand Tour Diary," 84; Johnston, *Land of the Little Colonel*, 87–88; Bacon, *Beauty for Ashes*, 15.

52. *Evansville Daily Journal*, October 12, 1888.

53. Evansville city directories; Bacon, *Beauty for Ashes*, 16–17.

2. The Clutch of the Thorns

1. Roy Lubove, "Albion Fellows Bacon and the Awakening of a State," *Midwest Review* (1962), 64–65; Albion Fellows Bacon, *Beauty for Ashes* (New York, 1914), 16.

2. Bacon, *Beauty for Ashes*, 16–17, 18.

3. Joy Bacon Witwer oral history interview, August 13, 1988 (hereafter cited as Witwer interview #1), 40–41; Bacon, *Beauty for Ashes*, 18–19. The "White Road" is a metaphor for the course of Bacon's life, which now seemed to her to be barricaded.

4. F. G. Gosling, *Before Freud: Neurasthenia and the American Medical Community, 1870–1910* (Urbana and Chicago, 1987), 15, 79, 9; Tom Lutz, *American Nervousness, 1903: An Anecdotal History* (Ithaca, N.Y., 1991), 19. For a European perspective on the malady, see Anson Rabinbach, *The Human Motor: Energy, Fatigue, and the Origins of Modernity* (Berkeley and Los Angeles, 1990), esp. chapter 6, "Mental Fatigue, Neurasthenia, and Civilization."

5. Gosling, *Before Freud*, 9–11, 56 (first Cleaves quotation); John S. Haller, Jr., "Neurasthenia: The Medical Profession and the 'New Woman' of [the] Late Nineteenth Century," *New York State Journal of Medicine*, 71 (February 15, 1971), 475 (second Cleaves quotation).

6. Lutz, *American Nervousness*, 32.

7. Gosling, *Before Freud*, 111.

8. Ibid., 98; Haller, "Neurasthenia: The Medical Profession and the 'New Woman,'" 478.

9. Gosling, *Before Freud*, 80–81, 15.

10. Lutz, *American Nervousness*, 25.

11. Allen F. Davis, *American Heroine: The Life and Legend of Jane Addams* (New York, 1973), 24–25, 30.

12. Ibid., Chapter II (quotation, 24); Jane Addams, *Twenty Years at Hull-House* (New York: Signet Classic paperback edition, 1961), 67, 59.

13. Addams, *Twenty Years at Hull-House*, 94.

14. Hall is quoted in Haller, "Neurasthenia: The Medical Profession and the 'New Woman,'" 480, n. 60.

15. Jane Addams, *Democracy and Social Ethics* (New York, 1902), 87.

16. Bacon, *Beauty for Ashes*, 17; Bacon, "Autobiography," [18], [26], [17].

17. Lutz, *American Nervousness*, 30.

18. Evansville city directories.

19. Annie Fellows Johnston and Albion Fellows Bacon, *Songs Ysame* (Boston, 1897), 27–33, 49, 109.

20. Ibid., 125, 123.

21. Bacon, *Beauty for Ashes*, 20; "Treasurer's Book of the Woman's Foreign Missionary Society" and "Ladies and Pastors Union" ledger book, Trinity United Methodist Church archives, Evansville, Indiana.

22. Bacon, *Beauty for Ashes*, 21–22, 17.

23. Ibid., 23–27 (quotes, 26).

24. Ibid., 24, 26, 27–28.

25. Ibid., 29–30.

26. Ibid., 35. Bacon refers to Rein's employer as the "Charities Organisation"; city directories identify it as the Associated Charities of Evansville (organized in 1897). This appears to have been part of the Charity Organization Societies (COS) movement that flourished toward the end of the nineteenth century. See Robert H. Bremner, *From the Depths: The Discovery of Poverty in the United States* (New York, 1956), 51–53, and John D. Buenker and

Edward R. Kantowicz, eds., *Historical Dictionary of the Progressive Era, 1890–1920* (New York, 1988), 65.

27. Lawrence M. Lipin, *Producers, Proletarians, and Politicians: Workers and Party Politics in Evansville and New Albany, Indiana, 1850–87* (Urbana, Ill., 1994), 77, 85; Darrel E. Bigham, *An Evansville Album: Perspectives on a River City, 1812–1988* (Bloomington, Ind., 1988), 16. See also James E. Morlock, *The Evansville Story: A Cultural Interpretation* ([Evansville], 1956), esp. chapter 8.

28. Bacon, *Beauty for Ashes*, 36–37.

29. Ibid., 37–40 (quotations, 38, 39). "Old St. Mary's" was originally a Marine Hospital built for rivermen in the mid-1850s by the federal government. The building was later sold to the Daughters of Charity, who operated the facility as St. Mary's Hospital from 1872 until 1894. Bigham, *An Evansville Album*, 5.

30. Bacon, *Beauty for Ashes*, 40–44 (quotations, 40, 44).

31. Ibid., 38, 40, 45. Bacon titled Chapter III of her book "The Clutch of the Thorns."

32. Ibid., 46–47. "Friendly visiting," an integral part of the Charity Organization Societies' method of operation, bore some similarities to the better-known settlement house movement, minus the settlements' residential component. Historian Robyn Muncy's description of female settlement workers as "women trying to fulfill existing social expectations for self-sacrificing female service while at the same time satisfying their need for public recognition, authority, and independence" seems to apply to many friendly visitors as well. See Muncy, *Creating a Female Dominion in American Reform, 1890–1935* (New York, 1991), 30. For a critique of friendly visiting, in which he observes that "it was impossible to establish satisfactory *personal* relationships between 'superior' volunteers and 'inferior' dependents," see Walter I. Trattner, *From Poor Law to Welfare State: A History of Social Welfare in America*, 4th ed. (New York, 1989), 91–94.

33. Bacon, *Beauty for Ashes*, 48–49.

34. Ibid., 51–52.

35. Ibid., 50, 53.

36. Ibid., 63–68.

37. Ibid., 62.

38. Ibid., 69–71.

39. Ibid., 81.

40. Ibid., 83. Hilary, Jr. was, of course, named for his father. To have a companion name for Hilary, which Bacon said meant "hilarity," they christened the other twin Joy. Witwer interview #1, p. 1.

41. Bacon, *Beauty for Ashes*, 84.

42. Ibid., 85–91 (quotation, 91); Witwer interview #1, p. 33.

43. Bacon, *Beauty for Ashes*, 87–88, 91–92.

44. Ibid., 119, 99.

45. Ibid., 101–103.

46. Ibid., 103–104.

47. Ibid., 104–105, 107–108.

48. Ibid., 106, 108. For a recent study of working girls' societies, especially in the East and Northeast, see Priscilla Murolo, *The Common Ground of Womanhood: Class, Gender, and Working Girls' Clubs, 1884–1928* (Urbana and Chicago, 1997).

49. Bacon, *Beauty for Ashes*, 101–111, 113, 124–125.

50. Ibid., 121–122, 123.

51. Ibid., 124; Evansville YWCA, Board Minutes 1911–1925, meetings of March 11, April 3, 1911, June 1913. Bacon's position on the YWCA's board was to expire in 1914; by late summer 1912, however, when new printed stationery began to be used, her name was not listed among the officers. While no record of her resignation from the board was found in the minutes, it is possible that she may have done so sometime in 1912. As we shall see, this was a period when she became heavily involved in other social welfare activities and was frequently out of town. She may have left the board early because she felt she could not devote the time or energy necessary to be a productive member.

52. Bacon, *Beauty for Ashes*, 114.

53. Ibid., 115.

54. Ibid., 120.

3. Ambassador of the Poor

1. Albion Fellows Bacon, *Beauty for Ashes* (New York, 1914), 154.

2. Ibid., 160.

3. Ibid., 160–162.

4. Ibid., 163 (emphases in the original).

5. Arthur S. Link and Richard L. McCormick, *Progressivism* (Arlington Heights, Ill., 1983), 2–3, 22.

6. Clifton J. Phillips, *Indiana in Transition: The Emergence of an Industrial Commonwealth, 1880–1920* (Indianapolis, 1968), 95–97, 99, 110, 120–121; Richard John Del Vecchio, "Indiana Politics during the Progressive Era, 1912–1916" (Ph.D. diss., University of Notre Dame, 1973), 42–43; John D. Barnhart and Donald F. Carmony, *Indiana: From Frontier to Industrial Commonwealth* (4 vols., New York, 1954), II, 369; Jacob Piatt Dunn, *Indiana and Indianans* (5 vols., Chicago and New York, 1919), II, 778–779.

7. Robert C. Brooks, "A Bibliography of Municipal Problems and City Conditions," *Municipal Affairs*, 5 (March 1901), esp. 99–107.

8. Robert W. DeForest, "A Brief History of the Housing Movement in America," *Annals of the American Academy of Political and Social Science*, 51 (January 1914), 8.

9. Roy Lubove, *The Progressives and the Slums: Tenement House Reform in New York City, 1890–1917* (Pittsburgh, 1962), 140–142, 248; DeForest, "A

Brief History," 10; Lawrence M. Friedman, *Government and Slum Housing: A Century of Frustration* (Chicago, 1968), 36.

10. Bacon, *Beauty for Ashes*, 163–164.

11. Ibid., 164–166.

12. Ibid., 167–168; Bacon to Annie Fellows Johnston, November 20, 1906, Annie Fellows Johnston Collection, Willard Library, Evansville, Indiana.

13. Bacon, *Beauty for Ashes*, 168–169.

14. Annie [sic] Fellows Bacon, "The Homes of the Poor," *Indiana Bulletin of Charities and Correction* (June 1908), 47–52; Bacon, *Beauty for Ashes*, 169–170.

15. Bacon, *Beauty for Ashes*, 170–171.

16. Ibid., 171–173.

17. Ibid., 173–174, 180–181; Albion Fellows Bacon, "The Awakening of a State—Indiana," *The Survey*, 25 (December 17, 1910), 471. Asked if some of the drudgery of correspondence could not have been alleviated by a secretary, Bacon responded: "In a city of our size? A mother and a housekeeper doing so much public work that she had to employ a secretary! That would have been a scandal, indeed, almost as bad as to have an office!" Bacon, *Beauty for Ashes*, 181.

18. Albion Fellows Bacon, "The Housing Problem in Indiana," *Charities and the Commons* (later *The Survey*), 21 (December 5, 1908), 376–383 (reprinted in *Indiana Bulletin of Charities and Correction* [June 1909], 212–219); Bacon, *Beauty for Ashes*, 184–185.

19. *Annual Report of the Commercial Club of Indianapolis . . . 1891* (Indianapolis, 1891); "Articles of Association" of the Indianapolis Commercial Club (copy in the pamphlet collection, Indiana Division, Indiana State Library, Indianapolis).

20. Meeting of June 16, 1908, Directors' Minutes, November 1906–June 1909, p. 287, Indianapolis Commercial Club Records, Collection M422, Indiana Historical Society Library, Indianapolis; meetings of July 1, September 30, October 12, 1908, Committee Reports, May 1908–July 1909, pp. 23, 42, 46, ibid.

21. Bacon, *Beauty for Ashes*, 186–187; handwritten report by Dunn dated October 26, 1908, Committee Reports, May 1908–July 1909, p. 52, Indianapolis Commercial Club Records; meeting of November 17, 1908, Directors' Minutes, November 1906–June 1909, pp. 330–331, ibid.

22. Bacon, *Beauty for Ashes*, 188.

23. Ibid., 179, 188–190.

24. The measure was designated House Bill 3 in the lower chamber and Senate Bill 51 in the upper house. Although both bills received consideration in both chambers, attention came to focus on the House measure and action on the Senate bill eventually ceased.

25. Bacon, *Beauty for Ashes*, 192–197; *Evansville Press*, January 20, 1909; *Indianapolis News*, January 20, 1909.

26. *Indianapolis Star*, January 20, 1909; *Indianapolis News*, January 20, 1909;

meeting of January 18, 1909, Committee Reports, May 1908–July 1909, p. 80, Indianapolis Commercial Club Records; Bacon, *Beauty for Ashes*, 197.

27. Bacon, *Beauty for Ashes*, 199–200; *Indianapolis News*, January 21, 1909; *Indianapolis Star*, January 22, 1909.

28. Bacon, *Beauty for Ashes* 175–176. One of her hometown newspapers, with a mixture of pride and embarrassment, remarked that "Mrs. Bacon has hung out Evansville's 'dirty wash on the line,'" and observed that "an interested crowd of statesmen and 'just common people' is always gathered" around the pictures. The article was headlined: "PICTURES OF OUR BACK YARDS ADORN (?) STATE HOUSE WALLS." *Evansville Press*, January 22, 1909.

29. Bacon, *Beauty for Ashes*, 201.

30. Ibid., 203, 206–211. Throughout this and the following chapter the political affiliations and districts of legislators are drawn from Rebecca A. Shepherd et al., eds., *A Biographical Directory of the Indiana General Assembly* (2 vols., Indianapolis, 1980, 1984).

31. Meeting of March 1, 1909, in Directors' Minutes, November 1906–June 1909, Indianapolis Commercial Club Records; Hurty to Bacon, July 29, October 10, November 18, 21, December 8, 24, 1908, January 9, 1909, Hurty to T. B. Pearson, January 30, 1909, Hurty to Dr. Frederick Green, February 15, 1909, and Hurty to Eliza Wilson, February 18, 1909, all in Dr. John Hurty Letter Books, Records of the State Board of Health, Archives Division, Indiana Commission on Public Records, Indianapolis.

32. *Indianapolis Star*, February 1, 1909; *Indianapolis News*, February 4, 1909; Indiana *Senate Journal* (1909), 423–429. The *Star*, February 5, reported that the Kistler amendment passed by a "rising vote" of 22–18; the *News*, February 4, and the *Senate Journal*, 426, both give the count as 30–18. S.B. 51 was subsequently referred to the House, where it did not come out of committee until February 26. No further action was taken on the Senate bill, however, as attention shifted to H.B. 3, the companion measure introduced in the House.

33. *Indianapolis News*, February 4, 1909; *Indianapolis Star*, February 16, 1909; Indiana *House Journal* (1909), 361, 501–502.

34. Hurty to T. B. Pearson, January 30, 1909, Hurty Letter Books (emphasis in the original); *Evansville Press*, February 5, 1909.

35. Bacon, *Beauty for Ashes*, 213–214, 216–218 (emphases in the original).

36. Ibid., 219–222; *Indianapolis News*, February 27, 1909.

37. Indiana *Senate Journal* (1909), 1391; *Indianapolis News*, February 27, 1909.

38. *Indianapolis Star*, February 28, 1909; Indiana *Senate Journal* (1909), 1404; Indiana *House Journal* (1909), 1206–1217, 1299; *Laws of Indiana* (1909), chapter 47. Bacon and her supporters considered this bill a nonpartisan measure and certainly worked both sides of the aisle in their efforts to secure its passage. In the House the bill's support did come from both parties; of the 62 "aye" votes on final passage, 33 were cast by Democrats and 29 by Republicans. Of the 27 representatives voting "no," however, 21 were Democrats. In the Sen-

ate the division was sharply along party lines; 24 Republicans and 2 Democrats voted in favor on the final roll call, while 19 Democrats and 1 Republican voted against the measure. For the roll calls, see Indiana *House Journal* (1909), 502, and Indiana *Senate Journal* (1909), 1404.

39. *Evansville Press*, March 4, 1909; *Evansville Journal-News*, January 18, 1909.

40. *Indianapolis News*, February 4, 1909; *Evansville Journal-News*, March 3, 1909.

41. Bacon, *Beauty for Ashes*, 228–229.

42. The Albion Apartments (sometimes referred to as Albion Terrace or Albion Flats), originally proposed for the corner of Seventh and Vine, were actually constructed at the intersection of Seventh and Division (now Martin Luther King, Jr. Boulevard and Court Street). Apartments were a relatively new type of housing in Evansville ca. 1910, and "The Albion" was so successful that Rosencranz put up two more apartment buildings in the same area "as fast as the ground could be acquired." *Evansville Courier*, July 31, 1909, July 17, 1910.

43. Witwer interview #1, p. 35; *Evansville Courier*, December 2, 1909; *Evansville Journal*, December 1, 1909; death certificate for Margaret Bacon, Texas Department of Health, Bureau of Vital Statistics. It was learned in the aftermath of Margaret's death that she had previously fainted at dances, but had refused to let anyone tell her family.

44. Bacon, *Beauty for Ashes*, 230–239; *Evansville Journal-News*, January 20, 21, 22, 1910.

45. Bacon, *Beauty for Ashes*, 231–232; *State, ex rel., v. Winterrowd* (174 Ind. 592); meeting of July 7, 1909, Committee Reports, July 1909–January 1913, p. 29, Indianapolis Commercial Club Records.

46. Meeting of June 2, 1910, Committee Reports, July 1909–January 1913, p. 42 and attachments, Indianapolis Commercial Club Records (emphasis in the original).

47. Bacon, *Beauty for Ashes*, 239–240.

48. Ibid., 240. The two books Veiller had just published were *A Model Tenement House Law* (New York, 1910) and *Housing Reform: A Hand-Book for Practical Use in American Cities* (New York, 1910).

49. Meeting of September 12, 1910, Committee Reports, July 1909–January 1913, p. 44, Indianapolis Commercial Club Records.

50. Bacon, *Beauty for Ashes*, 241.

51. Ibid., 241–242; meeting of February 3, 1911, Committee Reports, July 1909–January 1913, p. 51 and attached letter from Cox, Indianapolis Commercial Club Records; Albion Fellows Bacon, "Women, the Legislature and the Homes of Indiana," *Indiana Federation of Clubs Year Book* (1911–1912), 136.

52. Bacon, *Beauty for Ashes*, 243; Bacon, "Autobiography," [31]; *Evansville Journal-News*, January 8, 1911.

53. Bacon, *Beauty for Ashes*, 245. Although Bacon does not name the "parties" who caused the delay, Cox blamed "the committees of the architects' association and . . . the building inspector of Indianapolis." Meeting of February 3, 1911, Committee Reports, July 1909–January 1913, p. 51 and attached letter from Cox, Indianapolis Commercial Club Records.

54. *Evansville Journal-News*, February 23, 1911; Indiana *House Journal* (1911), 1256.

55. *Indianapolis Star*, February 22, 1911.

56. Indiana *House Journal* (1911), 1385–1386; Bacon, *Beauty for Ashes*, 245–246; *Indianapolis News*, February 22, 1911.

57. *Evansville Journal-News*, February 23, 1911; Indiana *Senate Journal* (1911), 1395, 1424, 1468; Bacon, *Beauty for Ashes*, 246–247.

58. *Evansville Journal-News*, March 6, 1911.

59. *Indianapolis News*, March 7, 1911; *Evansville Journal-News*, March 8, 1911.

60. *Indianapolis News*, March 7, 1911. The reporter noted that "this schoolhouse has been pictured to the legislators many times."

61. Bacon, "Women, the Legislature and the Homes of Indiana," 138. See also Bacon, *Beauty for Ashes*, 254–256, and Indiana *Senate Journal* (1911), 1822–24. For a somewhat more detailed discussion of the roll call proceedings, see the *Indianapolis Star* and the *Indianapolis News*, March 7, 1911. Both accounts indicate that the Senate Roll Clerk, one William Steelman, cooperated with Senator Harlan to prevent the original vote from being announced promptly.

62. *Indianapolis Star*, March 7, 1911; *Evansville Journal-News*, March 7, 1911.

63. Bacon, *Beauty for Ashes*, 257–258; Bacon, "Women, the Legislature and the Homes of Indiana," 138.

4. The Homes of Indiana

1. Albion Fellows Bacon, *Beauty for Ashes* (New York, 1914), 300.

2. Mrs. T. J. Bowlker, "Woman's Home-Making Function Applied to the Municipality," *American City*, 6 (June 1912), 863; Helen M. Winslow, "The Modern Club Woman: What Women's Clubs Really Stand For," *Delineator*, 81 (January 1913), 57; Ida Husted Harper, "Woman's Broom in Municipal Housekeeping," ibid., 73 (February 1909), 213. A reporter who attended the annual convention of the New York Federation of Women's Clubs in 1911 subtitled his subsequent article: "Startling Experiences of a Man Who Thought She [the club woman] Devoted Herself to Italian Art and Browning." Arthur Ruhl, "Discovering the Club Woman," *Collier's*, 48 (December 9, 1911), 20–21.

3. Anne Firor Scott, *Natural Allies: Women's Associations in American History* (Urbana and Chicago, 1992), 155, 154, 142; Karen J. Blair, *The Clubwoman as Feminist: True Womanhood Redefined, 1868–1914* (New York, 1980), 3–4.

4. Barbara A. Springer, "Ladylike Reformers: Indiana Women and Progressive Reform, 1900–1920" (Ph.D. diss., Indiana University, 1985), 31–33, 3.

5. Indiana Federation of Clubs, program of the fourth annual convention, October 25–27, 1910, Box 3, Indiana Federation of Clubs Papers, Indiana Division, Indiana State Library, Indianapolis. This talk was printed as a small pamphlet by the Charity Organization Society of Indianapolis; a copy is in the pamphlet collection of the Indiana Division.

6. Bacon, *Beauty for Ashes*, 261–265. "A Tale of the Tenements" was published in 1912 by the Indiana Housing Association; a copy is in the pamphlet collection of the Indiana Division, Indiana State Library.

7. Bacon, *Beauty for Ashes*, 281–285; Albion Fellows Bacon, "Women, the Legislature and the Homes of Indiana," *Indiana Federation of Clubs Year Book* (1911–1912), 133–142.

8. Bacon, *Beauty for Ashes*, 294; "Here's To the Homes of All Hoosierdom," *The Survey*, 27 (November 18, 1911), 1196; Indiana Housing Association, "Constitution and By-Laws," March 1912, copy in pamphlet collection, Indiana Division, Indiana State Library. The officers of the association were Linton Cox (president), Charles S. Grout (treasurer), and Bacon (secretary).

9. *Indiana Federation of Clubs Year Book* (1912–1913), 100; Bacon, *Beauty for Ashes*, 270, 287.

10. Albion Fellows Bacon, "The Housing Problem," *Indiana Federation of Clubs Year Book* (1912–1913), 80–81, 87.

11. Albion Fellows Bacon, "Regulation by Law," *Housing Problems in America*, 2 vols. (Proceedings of the Second National Conference on Housing, Philadelphia, December 1912), II, 47–57 (quotations, 48–49, 52).

12. Bacon, *Beauty for Ashes*, 296–297; *Evansville Journal-News*, January 3, 5, 1913; Bacon "To the Pastors" (draft), Folder 8, Box 1, Albion Fellows Bacon Papers, Willard Library, Evansville, Indiana.

13. Minutes of the Executive Board, Records of the State Board of Health, microfilm, reel 4, pp. 385, 394, Archives Division, Indiana Commission on Public Records, Indianapolis. See also *Thirty-Second Annual Report of the State Board of Health . . . 1913* (Indianapolis, 1914), 42.

14. *Evansville Journal-News*, January 5, 1913; *Indianapolis Star*, January 22, 24, 28, 1913. Organizations instrumental in calling the meeting at the Propylaeum included, besides those mentioned in the text, the Charity Organization Society, the Jewish Council of Women, the Children's Aid Association, the Equal Suffrage Association of Indiana, the YWCA, and the Woman's Christian Temperance Union. Note that the Indianapolis Commercial Club, so heavily involved in the housing reform struggles of 1909 and 1911, is not mentioned here. The Commercial Club transformed itself into the Indianapolis Chamber of Commerce in 1912 and seems to have become somewhat less interested in issues (especially when statewide) of this kind.

15. Bacon, *Beauty for Ashes*, 319–320; column headed "Fairbanks Meets

Y.M.C.A. Workers," *Indianapolis Star,* January 25, 1913. The meeting at which Ralston spoke was held in the home of former United States vice-president Charles Warren Fairbanks.

16. Bacon, *Beauty for Ashes,* 301–302; Richard John Del Vecchio, "Indiana Politics during the Progressive Era" (Ph.D. diss., University of Notre Dame, 1973), 145.

17. Indiana *Senate Journal* (1913), 117, 174. Clarke, a newly elected legislator, had decided to run for the General Assembly after hearing Bacon appeal for support during a lay sermon she delivered in an Indianapolis church. (Bacon, *Beauty for Ashes,* 297–298.) His wife, Grace Julian Clarke, the daughter of Indiana abolitionist George W. Julian, was herself an influential lecturer and writer. Active in the women's suffrage movement, she and Bacon had become acquainted through their involvement with the Indiana Federation of Clubs. Grace Clarke was also active in the Indiana Housing Association.

18. Indiana *Senate Journal* (1913), 117, 174, 483; Bacon, *Beauty for Ashes,* 307–308; *Evansville Journal-News,* February 3, 1913; *Indianapolis Star,* February 4, 1913.

19. Indiana *Senate Journal* (1913), 612–614; *Indianapolis Star,* February 4, 1913; *Indianapolis News,* February 4, 1913. Kistler replied to Clarke by challenging the assertion "that the tenements breed disease and degeneracy. Why, gentlem[e]n[,] it is not true. Every one knows that if the rich were suddenly transported to the tenements and the poor to the mansions of the rich, the mansions of the rich would soon look like tenements and the tenements would soon resemble mansions." *Indianapolis Star,* February 4, 1913.

20. Indiana *Senate Journal* (1913), 615–618; *Indianapolis Star,* February 4, 1913; *Indianapolis News,* February 4, 1913; Bacon, *Beauty for Ashes,* 308. The 36 "aye" votes were cast by 28 Democrats, 7 Republicans, and 1 Progressive; all 9 "no" votes were cast by Democrats.

21. *Indianapolis News,* February 6, 1913 (the *News* identified the *Courier* as a Progressive paper); Bacon, *Beauty for Ashes,* 310–314.

22. *Indianapolis News,* February 14, 1913.

23. Bacon, *Beauty for Ashes,* 319.

24. Indiana *House Journal* (1913), 1268; *Indianapolis Star,* February 22, 1913; *Indianapolis News,* February 22, 1913. The *News* reported that "Thomas Taggart is credited with 'building a fire' under some of the committee members contributing toward getting the bill out." On at least one occasion during the 1913 session Taggart is reported to have "literally appeared on the floor of the House to cajole the more reluctant members into endorsing necessary reform measures." Del Vecchio, "Indiana Politics during the Progressive Era," 145.

25. Indiana *House Journal* (1913), 1400–1402; *Indianapolis Star,* February 27, 1913; Bacon, *Beauty for Ashes,* 322–323; Indiana *Senate Journal* (1913), 1335; *Laws of Indiana* (1913), chapter 149. The overwhelming margin of support on the final House vote is perhaps misleading. As a result of the Republican-Progressive split in 1912, Democrats held a uniquely one-sided plurality in

the 1913 session—95 of the 100 House seats. With both Democratic governor Ralston and Democratic kingpin Taggart supporting the bill, at least some members' votes may have been cast more out of a spirit of party regularity than personal (or constituent) conviction.

26. *Indianapolis News*, March 1, 1913; Del Vecchio, "Indiana Politics during the Progressive Era," 199–202 (quotation, 200); Clifton J. Phillips, *Indiana in Transition: The Emergence of an Industrial Commonwealth, 1880–1920* (Indianapolis, 1968), 110, 118; Jacob Piatt Dunn, *Indiana and Indianans* (5 vols., Chicago and New York, 1919), II, 778–779. As one scholar notes, the 1913 session of the General Assembly had so many female lobbyists in attendance that it became known as "the woman's session." Springer, "Ladylike Reformers," 106.

27. Bacon, *Beauty for Ashes*, 324–325; *Indianapolis News*, March 1, 1913; *Evansville Press*, March 4, 1913.

28. Bacon, *Beauty for Ashes*, 234–235.

29. Evansville city directories; *Evansville Courier* and *Evansville Journal*, February 17, 1936. The business, which Hilary Bacon sold to Southern Department Stores, Inc., of Nashville, Tennessee, continued to operate under the H. E. Bacon Company name for several years after his retirement. In 1937 the property was leased by the F. W. Woolworth chain, which operated one of its variety stores at the location for over fifty years.

30. *Evansville Courier*, February 17, 1936; Witwer interview #1, p. 48; Bacon, *Beauty for Ashes*, 203.

31. Bacon, *Beauty for Ashes*, 181; Witwer interview #1, pp. 37–38.

32. Witwer interview #1, pp. 37, 72.

33. Witwer interview #1, p. 50; Witwer interview #2, pp. 23–24; Margaret McLeish oral history interview, November 16, 1988, pp. 13–14, 30–31.

34. Witwer interview #1, pp. 32, 63, 69.

35. Witwer interview #2, pp. 15–16.

36. Bacon to Grace Julian Clarke, September 28, 30, 1920, Grace Julian Clarke Papers, Indiana State Library; Witwer interview #1, pp. 63–64.

37. Bacon to Samuel M. Ralston, March 15, 1916, Ralston Papers, Lilly Library, Indiana University, Bloomington; *Evansville Courier*, November 4, 1917, November 9, 1921.

38. Witwer interview #1, pp. 80–81, 37; Bacon, *Beauty for Ashes*, 278.

39. Bacon, *Beauty for Ashes*, 53; Darrel E. Bigham, *We Ask Only a Fair Trial: A History of the Black Community of Evansville, Indiana* (Bloomington and Indianapolis, 1987), 111; *Evansville Courier*, June 28, 1930.

Bigham, *We Ask Only a Fair Trial*, 112, also cites Bacon's admission that, initially, she paid little attention to the state of African-American housing in Evansville, and he concludes that this statement "revealed as much about her perspectives on race relations as her knowledge of housing conditions." Perhaps. However, he goes on to say, without documentation, that when Bacon was "introduced to the existence of such conditions, she seemed less interested in the social forces creating them than in their aesthetic quality." I know of no evidence that supports this assertion, and there is much evidence that refutes it. See especially Chapter VI of *Beauty for Ashes*.

40. Witwer interview #1, pp. 48, 71; Witwer interview #2, pp. 20–22.

41. Witwer interview #1, pp. 52–54, 56; Witwer interview #2, pp. 2, 17–18; Bacon to Annie Fellows Johnston, July 17, August 14, 1909, May 26, June 23, 1914, Johnston Collection, Willard Library, Evansville; *Bay View Bulletin* (1914), 21, 25; *Daily Resorter and Petoskey Evening News*, August 5, 8, 1914.

42. Bacon to Grace Julian Clarke, August 14, 1915, Clarke Papers, Indiana State Library.

43. Witwer interview #1, pp. 23–24. Lura's last child was born in 1902 when she was almost 45 years old. She was widowed in 1914 and died in 1942 at age 85.

44. Witwer interview #1, pp. 75–76; *Notable American Women*, II, 279–280; Dunn, *Indiana and Indianans*, V, 2184–2186; Mary Boewe, "Annie & Albion: Reformers of Riverville," *Traces of Indiana and Midwestern History*, 7 (Winter 1995), 4–11. For correspondence from Albion to Annie, see the Johnston Collection, Willard Library. When writing to her sister, Albion always signed her letters with her childhood nickname, Allie.

45. Bacon to Ralston, March 12, 1913, Folder 4, Box 91, Samuel M. Ralston Papers, Governors' Papers, Archives Division, Indiana Commission on Public Records; *Evansville Press*, March 4, 1913.

46. *Laws of Indiana* (1913), chapter 149.

47. Indiana Federation of Clubs, *Official Report of Seventh Annual Convention* (1913), 31. Taking an even longer view, Bacon commented in a letter to the president of Indiana University: "I talked with Dr. [Ulysses Grant] Weatherly [a professor of economics and sociology who became a leader in the field of applied social work] about the possibility of having a few definite and vital principles of housing infused into certain courses in all the colleges and higher institutions in the state. . . . The fact is that, after having educated three legislatures on housing, and being both sadder and wiser thereby, myself, I am realizing more than ever that we ought to catch the members of our legislature before they get there, in fact, while they are in school or in college." Bacon to William Lowe Bryan, October 29, 1913, Presidential Papers (Correspondence), Indiana University Archives, Bloomington.

48. Bacon to Grace Julian Clarke, July 1, 1914, Clarke Papers, Indiana State Library.

49. Bacon to Ralston, December 18, 1914 (with enclosures), Folder 4, Box 91, Ralston Papers, Governors' Papers. The "long bill" was, with a few minor changes, a copy of a model law just published by Lawrence Veiller; the "short bill" was essentially sections 112 and 113 of the model law. Lawrence Veiller, *A Model Housing Law* (New York, 1914).

50. Bacon to Ralston, December 18, 26, 1914, Folder 4, Box 91, Ralston Papers, Governors' Papers.

51. *Indianapolis News*, January 8, 1915; *Indianapolis Star*, January 19, 1915. For the full text of the measure, see the manuscript copy of Senate Bill 61 (1915) in the Archives Division, Indiana Commission on Public Records. Properly speaking, S.B. 61 was more of a public health measure than a true housing law.

52. *Indianapolis News*, February 17, 1915.

53. *Indianapolis Star*, January 22, 1915; *Indianapolis News*, February 17, 1915; Indiana *House Journal* (1915), 157, 627, 783–784 (for H.B. 90), 235, 475, 549, 906, 947–948 (for H.B. 172), 590–591, 940, 1191 (for H.B. 372).

54. Indiana *Senate Journal* (1915), 141, 159, 210; *Indianapolis News*, January 27, 1915. Both the *Senate Journal* and the *News* report that the bill passed by a vote of 39–2; the *Senate Journal*, however, actually lists the names of only 38 senators who voted in the affirmative. The Senate was heavily Democratic that year (41 of 50 seats), and 33 of the "aye" votes were cast by members of the majority party.

55. Albion Fellows Bacon, "There Ain't No Law!" Indianapolis *Indiana Daily Times*, February 13, 1915.

56. *Indianapolis Star*, February 18, 1915; Indiana *House Journal* (1915), 280, 621, 742, 849. Both the *Star* and the *House Journal* report that the bill was defeated by a vote of 44–46. But the *House Journal* lists—apparently erroneously—the names of 46 representatives who supposedly voted in the affirmative. Republican members of the House were somewhat more favorable toward the bill than their Democratic colleagues, but it was by no means a straight party-line vote. Twenty-three of the 39 Republicans (59 percent) voted for the measure, while 22 of 60 Democrats (37 percent) supported it. The lone Progressive voted "aye." In a letter to the governor just days before the final vote, Bacon observed that Charles Bedwell (D–Sullivan County), the speaker of the House, seemed to be opposed to the measure. Bedwell did not vote on the bill's final consideration; what influence he may have exerted behind the scenes is not known. Bacon to Ralston, February 13, 1915, Folder 4, Box 91, Ralston Papers, Governors' Papers.

57. *Evansville Press*, February 18, 1915; Indiana Federation of Clubs, *Official Report of Ninth Annual Convention* (1915), 75.

58. Indiana Federation of Clubs, *Official Report of Ninth Annual Convention* (1915), 75–76; *Indianapolis News*, May 16, 1916; *Indianapolis Star*, May 17, 1916. For examples of Bacon's speeches during this period, see typescripts of her addresses before the Johnstown, Pennsylvania, Chamber of Commerce (February 14, 1916) and two talks to a meeting of Indiana's local health officers (May 2–3, 1916). Folders 6, 42, 53, Box 1, Bacon Collection, Willard Library.

59. Eleanor (Mrs. Robert) Lansing to Julia Lathrop (carbon copy), December 16, 1916 [1915], Papers of Pan-American Congresses (Box 1, Women's Auxiliary Conferences, 1915–1923), Manuscript Division, Library of Congress; Emma (Mrs. Glen Levin) Swiggett, *Report on the Women's Auxiliary Con-*

ference Held . . . in Connection With the Second Pan American Scientific Congress (Washington: Government Printing Office, 1916), 12–15, 18.

60. Swiggett, *Report on the Women's Auxiliary Conference*, 27, 69; *Washington Post*, December 30, 1915. At the opening session of the conference, Bacon made a motion, which was accepted unanimously, to create a permanent Pan American Union of Women. When the Third Pan American Scientific Congress met in Lima, Peru, a decade later, a Second Women's Pan American Conference was indeed part of the event, although there is no evidence that Bacon was involved in that meeting. *Washington Post*, December 29, 1915; *Washington Times*, December 28, 1915; Alice Thatcher Post, "Women of Pan-America in Conference," *The Public*, 19 (January 28, 1916), 87–88; Papers of Pan-American Congresses (Box 6, Minutes).

61. Indiana *House Journal* (1917), 89, 143, 185, 220–221; *Indianapolis News*, January 31, 1917; *Indianapolis Star*, February 1, 1917.

62. Indiana *Senate Journal* (1917), 428, 532, 620, 781; *Indianapolis Star, Indianapolis News*, and *Evansville Press*, February 16, 1917. The *Star* reported that the bill passed by a vote of 40–0, while the *News* said 41–0. The *Senate Journal* records 43 affirmative votes, but actually lists the names of 44 senators who voted "aye." The law was promulgated as chapter 21 of *Laws of Indiana* (1917).

63. Bacon, *Beauty for Ashes*, 163.

64. Daniel T. Rodgers, "In Search of Progressivism," in *The Promise of American History: Progress and Prospects*, ed. Stanley I. Kutler and Stanley N. Katz (Baltimore, 1982), 117, 125; John D. Barnhart and Donald F. Carmony, *Indiana: From Frontier to Industrial Commonwealth* (4 vols., New York, 1954), II, 374. On the background of many Progressive era reformers, see Wayne E. Fuller, "The Rural Roots of the Progressive Leaders," *Agricultural History*, 42 (January, 1968), 1–13.

65. Arthur S. Link and Richard L. McCormick, *Progressivism* (Arlington Heights, Ill., 1983), 68.

66. Lawrence M. Friedman, *Government and Slum Housing: A Century of Frustration* (Chicago, 1968), 44; Link and McCormick, *Progressivism*, 84.

67. This should not be read as a sharply critical evaluation, but merely as a recognition of many reformers' honest beliefs in a somewhat simplistic environmental determinism and "the almost unlimited potentialities of science and administration." As two historians of the Progressive era suggest: "Our late twentieth-century skepticism of these wonders should not blind us to the faith with which the progressives embraced them and imbued them with what now seem magical properties. . . . They missed some of their marks because they sought to do so much . . . [but] despite all their shortcomings, they accomplished an enormous part of what they set out to achieve." Link and McCormick, *Progressivism*, 116–117.

68. Phillips, *Indiana in Transition*, 128.

69. See, for example, Albion Fellows Bacon, *Housing—Its Relation to Social Work*, National Housing Association Publications, No. 48 (New York, 1918).

70. Edith Elmer Wood, *The Housing of the Unskilled Wage Earner: America's Next Problem* (New York, 1919), 287.

5. Child Welfare

1. Albion Fellows Bacon, *Beauty for Ashes* (New York, 1914), 78–79.

2. Annie [*sic*] Fellows Bacon, "The Homes of the Poor," *Indiana Bulletin of Charities and Correction* (June 1908), 50; Albion Fellows Bacon, *A Tale of the Tenements* ([Indianapolis]: Indiana Housing Association, 1912), 4–5; Albion Fellows Bacon, *What Bad Housing Means to the Community* (Boston: American Unitarian Association, ca. 1913), 9 (emphasis in the original).

3. Clarke A. Chambers, *Seedtime of Reform: American Social Service and Social Action, 1918–1933* (Minneapolis, 1963), xi; Richard Hofstadter, *The Age of Reform* (New York: Vintage Books paperback ed., 1955), 275.

4. Arthur S. Link, "What Happened to the Progressive Movement in the 1920's?" *American Historical Review*, 64 (July 1959), 844–845; Melvyn Dubofsky, *Industrialism and the American Worker, 1865–1920* (Arlington Heights, Ill., 1985), 126.

5. Clarke A. Chambers, *Paul U. Kellogg and the* Survey: *Voices for Social Welfare and Social Justice* (Minneapolis, 1971), 64; William L. O'Neill, *Everyone Was Brave: A History of Feminism in America* (Chicago: Quadrangle paperback ed., 1971), 206; William J. Breen, *Uncle Sam at Home: Civilian Mobilization, Wartime Federalism, and the Council of National Defense, 1917–1919* (Westport, Conn., 1984), xvi.

6. Robyn Muncy, *Creating a Female Dominion in American Reform, 1890–1935* (New York, 1991), 96.

7. David M. Kennedy, *Over Here: The First World War and American Society* (New York, 1980), 114–115; Breen, *Uncle Sam at Home*, 13.

8. Breen, *Uncle Sam at Home*, 115, 117, 118–119; Kennedy, *Over Here*, 286. See also Ida M. Tarbell, "Mobilizing the Women," *Harper's Magazine*, 135 (November 1917), 841–847.

9. Clifton J. Phillips, *Indiana in Transition: The Emergence of an Industrial Commonwealth, 1880–1920* (Indianapolis, 1968), 597. Although the members of the State Council of Defense were doubtless chosen because of their statewide reputations and the constituencies they represented, they were more than mere figureheads. Carlisle, for example, was actively engaged in the work of the Woman's Section. Ade, who chaired the Publicity Committee, "threw himself into the task" and prepared a series of pamphlets explaining the war effort. Ibid., 597–598.

10. Ibid., 597–598; *Indiana Year Book* (1918), 591–593, 598.

11. Kennedy, *Over Here*, 117, 286; O'Neill, *Everyone Was Brave*, 191.

12. *Indiana Year Book* (1918), 591.

13. Breen, *Uncle Sam at Home*, xiii, xvi.

14. Anne Studebaker Carlisle to Bacon (AFB), October 3, 1917, AFB to Carlisle, October 5, 1917, Indiana State Council of Defense: Papers and Cor-

respondence, Woman's Section, Child Welfare, Part 1: General Correspondence, Indiana State Archives, Indianapolis (hereafter cited as Child Welfare Correspondence). Bacon's only hesitation in accepting the position, which she obviously overcame, was that she had been ill. She wrote Carlisle that "I have been forced to resign many of my duties, on account of physical weakness, and am struggling to fill the few engagements I had made for this fall, which I had to cut to the minimum." Ibid.

15. Richard A. Meckel, *Save the Babies: American Public Health Reform and the Prevention of Infant Mortality, 1850–1929* (Baltimore, 1990), 200; Breen, *Uncle Sam at Home*, 127; *Seventh Annual Report of the Chief, Children's Bureau* (Washington: Government Printing Office, 1919), 6–7; "Preliminary Report of the Child Welfare Committee . . . January 1, 1919," [3], Indiana State Council of Defense: Papers and Correspondence, Woman's Section, Child Welfare, Part 3: Reprints, Indiana State Archives. Lathrop apparently held the concurrent positions only briefly. By spring 1918 the national Child Welfare Committee was being chaired by Dr. Jessica B. Peixotto, on leave from her position as professor of social economics at the University of California.

16. Muncy, *Creating a Female Dominion in American Reform*, 96–97; Breen, *Uncle Sam at Home*, 127. See also Kriste Lindenmeyer, *"A Right to Childhood": The U.S. Children's Bureau and Child Welfare, 1912–46* (Urbana and Chicago, 1997), 71–74.

17. AFB to Carlisle, November 26, 1917; AFB to Woman Members of the County Council of Defense (mimeographed), November 28, 1917, both in Child Welfare Correspondence.

18. AFB to Carlisle, January 5, 1918, Child Welfare Correspondence. Bacon's commitment to "the great war organization" appears to have gone beyond serving as director of the state's Child Welfare Committee. Limited evidence suggests that she supported the federal government's wartime pleas for consumer restraint, and that she was influenced to some degree by Washington's campaign of anti-German propaganda. For example, she not only pledged to forgo clothing made of wool or kid leather "until the war is over or until the Government demand is supplied," she also wrote a short play in support of such conservation. (Characters included "The American Girl," "Fashion," and "The Sheep.") She observed on one occasion that war work was being carried on in her home county (Vanderburgh) by "a limited number of faithful men and women . . . working themselves to death, in this nest of Germans." Once, when she was particularly frustrated with local child welfare committees that were not being responsive, she wrote to the Woman's Section in Indianapolis that "some [counties] act like Huns." AFB to Carlisle, February 14, January 16, 1918, AFB to Mrs. Kelly, April 19, 1918, all in Child Welfare Correspondence.

19. Council of National Defense, State Councils Section, Bulletin No. 85, February 7, 1918, copy in Child Welfare Correspondence; *Seventh Annual Report of the Chief, Children's Bureau*, 7.

20. Council of National Defense, State Councils Section, Bulletin No. 85; AFB to Carlisle, February 12, 1918, both in Child Welfare Correspondence.

21. *Save 100,000 Babies*, Children's Year Leaflet No. 1, Children's Bureau Publication No. 36 (Washington: Government Printing Office, 1918), 4–5.

22. "First Clinic for Baby Welfare Is Saturday," *Muncie Star*, March 29, 1918, clipping in Child Welfare Correspondence; Meckel, *Save the Babies*, 201; *Save 100,000 Babies*, 3; AFB to Child Welfare Chairmen, Bulletin No. 36 (mimeographed), March 11, 1918, Indiana State Council of Defense: Papers and Correspondence, Woman's Section, Child Welfare, Part 2: Publicity, Indiana State Archives. In her recent study of the Children's Bureau, historian Kriste Lindenmeyer observes that the agency "relied on patriotism in its entire endeavor to save children's lives immediately before and after U.S. entrance into the war." Lindenmeyer, *"A Right to Childhood,"* 73.

23. AFB to M. Foley, April 18, 1918, Woman's Section, Child Welfare, Part 2: Publicity. Michael E. Foley was chairman of the State Council of Defense.

24. Ibid.

25. Indiana State Council of Defense, meeting of March 6, 1918, vol. 5 of "Proceedings," 209–218, Indiana State Archives; AFB to Mrs. Kelly (Woman's Section), March 8, 1918, Child Welfare Correspondence.

26. AFB to "JMK" (Woman's Section), February 27, 1918; to Carlisle, March 2, 1918; to Dr. [Ada] Schweitzer, March 11, 1918; and to Mrs. Kelly, March 12, 1918, all in Child Welfare Correspondence.

27. The cards that were to be completed at the weighing and measuring examination were headed with the question "Does Your Child Pass?" and were divided into two parts. The top half, to be detached and retained by the parents, included spaces for the child's name, address, date of birth, height, and weight. By consulting a table on the reverse side of the card, parents could determine whether their child's height and weight were "above, below, or equal to the average for his [or her] age." Space was also provided to record the results of subsequent exams, presumably to be performed by a family physician or public health nurse—or even the parents themselves. The bottom half of the card, to be returned to the Children's Bureau, asked for the same information as the top half, plus the country of birth and race of the child's parents.

28. AFB to Mrs. Henderson, April 15, 1918; and to Mrs. Kelly, April 19, 1918, both in Child Welfare Correspondence. Bacon's concern when the cards did not arrive on time, aside from her desire that the project be carried out smoothly and as planned, was that many communities would be forced to reschedule their children's examinations for later in the year. As she wrote Lathrop: "I fear the effect of the hot weather on our women, who are exhausted by successive drives—and on our babies, too, for, when the summer sickness begins, we can't get the mothers out." AFB to Lathrop, April 18, 1918, file # 8–3–1–1, Central File 1914–1920 (Box 82), Records of the Children's Bureau (RG 102), National Archives, Washington, D.C. (hereafter cited as Children's Bureau Records).

The initial shortage of cards for the weighing and measuring test was not a problem unique to Indiana. The Children's Bureau apparently underestimated the public's interest in the campaign (which, in the aftermath, it described as "swift and widespread") and initially ordered only 500,000 cards printed. Within three months the number had to be increased to 6 million, and ultimately 7.6 million cards were distributed. *Children's Year: A Brief Summary of Work Done . . . ,* Children's Year Follow-up Series No. 4, Children's Bureau Publication No. 67 (Washington: Government Printing Office, 1920), 7.

29. AFB to Carlisle, May 27, June 19, 1918, Child Welfare Correspondence.

30. AFB to Mrs. Rabb, July 28, 1918, AFB to Mrs. Kelly, April 12, 19, 20, 1918, all in Child Welfare Correspondence; *Indiana Year Book* (1918), 592.

31. AFB to Carlisle, June 13, 11, August 12, 1918, Child Welfare Correspondence; AFB to Lathrop, July 11, 1918, file # 12–8–3–8, Central File 1914–1920 (Box 144), Children's Bureau Records.

32. AFB to Carlisle, June 13, September 10, 1918, Child Welfare Correspondence; AFB to Foley, June 12, 1918, Woman's Section, Child Welfare, Part 2: Publicity; AFB to Lathrop, July 11, 1918, file # 12–8–3–8, Central File 1914–1920 (Box 144), Children's Bureau Records; "Preliminary Report of the Child Welfare Committee . . . January 1, 1919," 12.

33. AFB to Lathrop, August 14, 1918, file # 12–8–3–4, Central File 1914–1920 (Box 144), Children's Bureau Records; AFB to Carlisle, September 10, 1918, Child Welfare Correspondence.

34. "Preliminary Report of the Child Welfare Committee . . . January 1, 1919," [4–6]; AFB to Lathrop, March 18, April 18, May 3, 1918, file # 8–3–1–1, Central File 1914–1920 (Box 82), Children's Bureau Records; *Indianapolis Star,* May 10, 1918 (for Lathrop quotation).

35. AFB to Carlisle, October 19, November 12, 1918; Acting Secretary, Woman's Section to AFB, November 16, 1918, both in Child Welfare Correspondence; AFB to Peixotto, November 20, 1918, file # 12–8–3–0, Central File (Box 142), Children's Bureau Records.

36. AFB to Child Welfare Chairmen, Bulletin No. 112 (mimeographed), November 24, 1918, copy in Child Welfare Correspondence.

37. AFB to Lathrop, April 18, 1919, file # 12–8–4–0, Central File (Box 146), AFB to Peixotto, November 20, 1918, file # 12–8–3–0, Central File (Box 142), Children's Bureau Records; *Laws of Indiana* (1919), chapter 197; Edmondson to State Committee Members, December 11, 1919 (with attachments), copy in file # 12–8–4–0, Central File (Box 145), Children's Bureau Records; Edna Hatfield Edmondson, *The Indiana Child Welfare Association,* Indiana University Extension Division *Bulletin,* 5 (January 1920), esp. 8–13; Muncy, *Creating a Female Dominion in American Reform,* 96.

38. AFB to Lathrop, April 18, 1919, file # 12–8–4–0, Central File 1921–1924 (Box 146), Children's Bureau Records; Bacon, "Autobiography," [33].

39. "Preliminary Report of the Child Welfare Committee . . . January 1,

1919," 7–8, 11. In spite of Bacon's disappointment that there had not been greater participation, Indiana fared quite well in comparison with other states. Wisconsin workers returned cards for about 65 percent of that state's preschool children; besides Indiana, only a few other states reported having measured about half of their children. Alisa Klaus, *Every Child a Lion: The Origins of Maternal and Infant Health Policy in the United States and France, 1890–1920* (Ithaca, N.Y., 1993), 259.

40. Lathrop to AFB, April 26, 1919, file # 12–8–4–0, Central File (Box 145), Children's Bureau Records.

41. Chambers, *Seedtime of Reform*, 3; Allen F. Davis, "Welfare, Reform and World War I," *American Quarterly*, 19 (Fall 1967), 518.

42. AFB to County Chairmen, Child Welfare Committees, Bulletin No. 98 (mimeographed), September 13, 1918, Woman's Section, Child Welfare, Part 2: Publicity (emphasis in the original).

43. *Laws of Indiana* (1919), chapter 197; *Minimum Standards for Child Welfare*, Conference Series No. 2, Children's Bureau Publication No. 62 (Washington, 1919). The creation of Indiana's Commission on Child Welfare and Social Insurance supports the assessment of historian J. Stanley Lemons regarding the importance of the Children's Year: "The effort was significant if measured only by official state action. In 1917 only eight states had child welfare divisions, but by 1920 thirty-five had a child hygiene or child welfare division. . . . By 1921 seventeen states had commissions drafting a children's code, and 1924 found twenty-nine states and the District of Columbia with children's code commissions." Lemons, *The Woman Citizen: Social Feminism in the 1920s* (Urbana, Ill., 1973), 145.

44. AFB to Lathrop, April 22, 1919, file # 12–8–4–0, Central File 1921–1924 (Box 146), Children's Bureau Records; "Report of the Commission on Child Welfare and Social Insurance" (December 1920), copy in Indiana Division, Indiana State Library, Indianapolis. The commission's typewritten report consists of two parts: an 18-page "brief summary" and a 212-page "full report," which are bound together but paginated separately. Citations will specify which part of the report is being referenced, along with appropriate page numbers.

For another, more formal version of most of the material in the commission's report, see Albion Fellows Bacon and Edna Hatfield Edmondson, *Child Welfare Legislation: Work of the Indiana Sub-Commission on Child Welfare of the Commission on Child Welfare and Social Insurance*, Indiana University Extension Division *Bulletin*, 7 (September 1921). Publication of the report in the bulletin of the Extension Division, at a cost of $325, was approved at the highest levels of the university's administration; both the president and the board of trustees signed off on the proposal. Edmondson to William Lowe Bryan, March 25, 1921, Bryan to Edmondson, June 11, 1921, William Lowe Bryan Presidential Papers (Correspondence), Indiana University Archives, Bloomington.

45. AFB to Lathrop, April 18, 1919, file # 12–8–4–0, Central File 1914–1920 (Box 146), AFB to Emma Lundberg, December 30, 1919, file # 10,034.16, Central File 1914–1920 (Box 110), Children's Bureau Records; "Report of the Commission on Child Welfare and Social Insurance," full report, 4–5.

Three members of the commission—Wade (chair), Hays, and Frederick—constituted a Sub-Commission on Social Insurance that was supposed to evaluate the need for state legislation regarding such problems as old-age dependency, unemployment, and disability. They made no investigations or recommendations, however, merely observing in the final report that "at no time has the Commission had a request for a hearing on this subject or any intimation from any part of the state that action at this time is desired." Ibid., full report, 212.

Edmondson was granted two-thirds released time from her position at the Indiana University Extension Division in order to serve as the commission's secretary; the commission paid two-thirds of her $150 monthly salary during the time of her service. Edmondson to U. H. Smith (Indiana University bursar), March 30, 1920, Smith to Edmondson, April 6, 1920, Bryan Presidential Papers (Correspondence).

46. Ibid., full report, 5–6; Edmondson to Caroline Fleming, April 29, 1920, Fleming to Edmondson, May 6, 1920, file # 12–3–2, Central File 1914–1920 (Box 138), Children's Bureau Records.

47. "Report of the Commission on Child Welfare and Social Insurance," brief summary, 3, 16–18.

48. Ibid., brief summary, 3–6.

49. Ibid., brief summary, 8–9.

50. Ibid., brief summary, 6–12 (quotations on 10, 11).

51. Ibid., brief summary, 12–13, full report, 163–169; *Laws of Indiana* (1919), chapter 58, pp. 191–192.

52. "Report of the Commission on Child Welfare and Social Insurance," brief summary, 13–16, full report, 170, 197–198, 204–205.

53. *Laws of Indiana* (1921), chapter 230.

54. *Laws of Indiana* (1921), chapter 27, p. 76; *Indiana Year Book* (1920), 769–797, (1921), 563–580.

55. *Laws of Indiana* (1921), chapter 132.

56. *Laws of Indiana* (1929), chapter 76; Charles E. Gibbons, *School or Work in Indiana?* (New York: National Child Labor Committee, 1927), esp. 5–6, 20–22; James H. Madison, *Indiana Through Tradition and Change: A History of the Hoosier State and Its People, 1920–1945* (Indianapolis, 1982), 276.

57. AFB to Lathrop, July 10, August 12, September 15, September 20, September 27, October 4, 1920, file # 4–2–3–0, Central File 1914–1920 (Box 66), Children's Bureau Records; AFB to Lathrop, January 4, 1921, file # 10–11–1(16), Central File 1921–1924 (Box 239), ibid.

58. Bacon, "Autobiography," [29–30].

59. Information in this and the following two paragraphs is drawn princi-

pally from the annual reports of the State (Juvenile) Probation Officer/State Probation Department contained in the annual *Indiana Year Book* for the years 1921 through 1933. See also *Laws of Indiana* (1921), chapter 230; James A. Collins, "Probation—A Practical Help to the Delinquent," *National Municipal Review*, 4 (April 1915), 217–223; and James A. Collins, "The Juvenile Court Movement in Indiana," *Indiana Magazine of History*, 28 (March 1932), 1–8. For a discussion of the problems faced by the state's first probation officer see Carina C. Warrington, "The Work of the State Probation Officer in Indiana," *The Social Service of the Courts; Proceedings of the National Probation Association, 1922* (New York, 1923), 192–199.

Two contemporary volumes that discuss the evolution of the "probation idea" during the early twentieth century are Lewis E. MacBrayne and James P. Ramsay, *One More Chance: An Experiment in Human Salvage* (Boston, 1916), the final chapter of which is titled "Probation No Longer an Experiment," and Bernard Flexner and Roger N. Baldwin, *Juvenile Courts and Probation* (New York, 1914).

60. Lathrop to AFB, June 9, 1921, AFB to Lathrop, June 11, 1921, file # 7–1–3–1, Central File 1921–1924 (Box 206), Children's Bureau Records.

6. City Plans and National Housing Standards

1. Bacon to Grace Julian Clarke, November 13, 1917, Grace Julian Clarke Papers, Indiana Division, Indiana State Library, Indianapolis; Albion Fellows Bacon, "Autobiography," [29], [32].

2. Bacon's involvement with the Public Health Nursing Association and its predecessor organizations is documented in the records of the Visiting Nurse Association of Southwestern Indiana, Special Collections/University Archives Department, University of Southern Indiana Library, Evansville. See, for example, Daisy Potter Viele et al. to Gentlemen of the [City] Council, October 1, 1926; "Program of the Dedication of the Health Center," November 20, 1927; and clippings dated November 21, 1927 (in Scrapbook #1), October 6, 1928 (in Scrapbook #3), and October 10, 1929, January 30, October 19, 1930 (in Scrapbook #5).

3. Vanderburgh County Tuberculosis Association, program for twenty-fifth anniversary (1932), Scrapbook #7, Visiting Nurse Association of Southwestern Indiana Collection; clipping from *Evansville Courier*, January 10, 1932, Scrapbook #7, ibid.; *Evansville Journal*, December 12, 1933; *Evansville Courier*, December 10, 1933.

4. Raymond W. Blanchard, *Ten Years of City Planning in Evansville* (Evansville, Ind.: Evansville City Plan Commission, [1932]), 3, 15–16. This pamphlet is a reprint of an article by the same title that appeared in the April 1932 issue of *City Planning*. Page citations are to the pamphlet, a copy of which is in the Indiana Division, Indiana State Library.

5. Frank G. Bates, *City Planning* (Indianapolis: Indiana Bureau of Legislative Information, Bulletin No. 8, December 1916), 5.

6. Mel Scott, *American City Planning since 1890* (Berkeley, Calif., 1969), 146–150.

7. *Laws of Indiana* (1921), chapter 209, esp. 561–563; Frank E. Horack, Jr., *The Development of Planning and Zoning in Indiana* (Indianapolis: State Planning Board, January 1939), 4 (copy in the Indiana Division, Indiana State Library).

8. Blanchard, *Ten Years of City Planning*, 4, 6; Evansville City Plan Commission, Minutes, October 17, 1921 (hereafter cited as Plan Commission Minutes with appropriate dates). The ledger book containing the commission's minutes for 1921–1927 is located in the office of the Evansville–Vanderburgh County Area Plan Commission.

9. Plan Commission Minutes, October 17, 1921; *Evansville Courier*, October 18, 1921.

10. Plan Commission Minutes, October 17, 1921; *Evansville Courier*, October 18, 1921. The minutes state that the "committee of three" was comprised of the commission's officers: Bacon (president), Carson (vice-president), and Dickman (secretary). The *Courier* reported that it was made up of Dickman, Hoffman, and Joyce.

11. Plan Commission Minutes, November 18, 23, December 21, 28, 1921, January 16, 1922; Norman J. Johnston, "Harland Bartholomew: Precedent for the Profession," in *The American Planner: Biographies and Recollections*, ed. Donald A. Krueckeberg, 2nd ed. (New York, 1994), 221–222. Bartholomew's initial contract with the City Plan Commission was for $2^1/_2$ years at $4,500 per year. *Evansville Journal*, January 17, 1922.

12. Plan Commission Minutes, December 21, 1921, January 16, February 8, 1922.

13. Ibid., July 5, August 8, September 5, 1923, January 9, 1924.

14. *Evansville Press*, July 17, 22, 1922; Plan Commission Minutes, July 21, 1922.

15. Plan Commission Minutes, July 28, 1922. A report issued by the commission at the end of the decade included several pages that discussed aspects of a river terminal. The final recommendations were that the city should own the waterfront; long-term use of the waterfront by private concerns should be avoided; and the operation of riverfront facilities should be handled by an outside contractor "owing to the specialized knowledge required to manage such equipment." See Evansville City Plan Commission, *A Plan for Railroad and Harbor Development* (Evansville, 1929), 34.

16. Plan Commission Minutes, September 14, October 3, 1923; Johnston, "Harland Bartholomew," 225. The issue of hiring a full-time executive secretary was first broached in March 1923. Dickman, who in his capacity as secretary had been responsible for most of the commission's correspondence since its inception, urged the employment of someone "to do office, publicity and mapwork, stating that from now on there would be sufficient work to keep him busy." Plan Commission Minutes, March 7, 1923.

17. Johnston, "Harland Bartholomew," 231–132. See also E. F. Porter, Jr., *Harland Bartholomew* (St. Louis: Saint Louis Public Library and Landmarks Association of St. Louis, Inc., 1990), and Eldridge Lovelace, *Harland Bartholomew: His Contributions to American Urban Planning* (Urbana: Department of Urban and Regional Planning, University of Illinois, [1993]).

18. Plan Commission Minutes, February 13, April 28, 1922; *Evansville Journal*, April 16, 1922.

19. Johnston, "Harland Bartholomew," 232.

20. Evansville City Plan Commission, *Plans for the Development of a System of Major Streets* (Evansville, 1925); Plan Commission Minutes, November 7, 1923, December 3, 1924. The commission accepted a low bid from a local printer of $637 for 1,500 copies of the Major Street Plan. Copies of all five reports issued by the commission are held by the Willard Library, Evansville.

21. Blanchard, *Ten Years of City Planning*, 7–9; *Plans for the Development of a System of Major Streets*, Appendix B (quotation, 49).

22. *Laws of Indiana* (1921), chapter 225.

23. Plan Commission Minutes, March 7, 1923.

24. Ibid., January 9, 1924.

25. Ibid., August 6, 1924.

26. Ibid., September 3, 1924.

27. Ibid., December 11, 1924; *Evansville Courier*, December 11, 1924.

28. Horack, *Development of Planning and Zoning in Indiana*, 5.

29. *Evansville Courier*, August 4, 18, 1925; *Evansville Press*, August 4, 1925; Evansville Common Council, Ordinance No. 1269, August 17, 1925.

30. Blanchard, *Ten Years of City Planning*, 10–12.

31. Ibid., 3–4.

32. Plan Commission Minutes, May 3, 19, 1922.

33. Ibid., April 9, May 7, 1924; *Lafayette Journal and Courier*, April 24–25, 1924.

34. *Evansville Journal*, April 9–10, 1925.

35. John M. Gries and James Ford, eds., *Housing Objectives and Programs*, vol. XI of *Publications of the President's Conference on Home Building and Home Ownership* (Washington, D.C., 1932), xv–xvi.

36. Ibid., xvi–xvii.

37. *Evansville Journal*, September 21, 1931; *Evansville Courier*, September 22, 1931. See also Lawrence Veiller to James Ford, September 22, 1931, in "Standards and Objectives" folder, Box 31, President's Conference on Home Building and Home Ownership Collection, Hoover Institution Archives, Stanford, California (hereafter cited as President's Conference Collection).

38. Minutes of first meeting, September 25, 1931, President's Conference Collection.

39. Ibid.

40. Minutes of second meeting, October 12–13, 1931, ibid.

41. Minutes of third meeting, October 28–29, 1931, ibid.

42. *Evansville Journal*, November 13, 1931; AFB to Mrs. K. F. Listom [Liston] (telegram), November 30, 1931, President's Conference Collection.

43. "Proceedings [of] Standards and Objectives," 32–36, ibid.

44. Ibid.

45. Ibid.

46. Ibid.

47. Gries and Ford, eds., *Housing Objectives and Programs*, 150–201 (esp. 150–151, 155, 161).

48. The conference serves as an excellent example of Hoover's conception of the role of the federal government and his administration's heavy reliance on private initiative to solve the nation's economic woes. In his keynote address on December 2, the president told the conferees: "This conference has not been called primarily on legislative questions. Its major purpose is to stimulate individual action. . . . The conference . . . is not to set up government in the building of homes, but to stimulate individual endeavor and make community conditions propitious." *Washington Post*, December 3, 1931.

49. Kenneth T. Jackson, *Crabgrass Frontier: The Suburbanization of the United States* (New York, 1985), 193–194, 219–224.

50. Albion Fellows Bacon, *Beauty for Ashes* (New York, 1914), 326.

7. Prose, Poetry, and Pageants

1. Witwer interview #1, pp. 17, 41–42; Witwer interview #2, p. 10; Albion Fellows Bacon (AFB) to Annie Fellows Johnston (AFJ), October 1, 1915, AFJ Collection, Willard Library, Evansville; Bacon, "Autobiography," [26], [21]. Albion's letter to Annie indicates how important the "typery" was to her: "My new room in the third story is nearly complete. I wish you and Mary would help me name it. It is not a study, for I only write up there. It is not a den, for I am not wild or dangerous. It is not a 'tower,' though I wish I might call it that, as I also have a 'bower.' It is a 'Writery,' in fact, but I want a cute name, not sentimental or far-fetched. It is a sky-parlor, in a way. . . . It is really a 'retreat,' but that sounds weak. It is an 'isolation' place, but that savors of germs and disease. It is a haven, too. . . . It won't be a 'just so' room, but just the place where I have only what suits my fancy. I know I shall enjoy it, and do better writing there."

2. Annie [sic] Fellows Bacon, "The Homes of the Poor," *Indiana Bulletin of Charities and Correction* (June 1908), 47–49.

3. Ibid., 49–51.

4. Albion Fellows Bacon, "The Housing Problem in Indiana," *Charities and the Commons* [later *The Survey*], 21 (December 5, 1908), 376–383 (quotation, 380). The first page of this article features a picture of a tenement's front porch that is captioned "Death Keeps Watch Over This House." The magazine's editor added a line drawing of a human skeleton eying the picture, which made for an arresting title page. For basic information regarding *The Survey*,

see Judith Trolander's entry in the *Historical Dictionary of the Progressive Era, 1890–1920*, ed. John D. Buenker and Edward R. Kantowicz (New York, 1988), 467.

5. Albion Fellows Bacon, "The Awakening of a State—Indiana," *The Survey*, 25 (December 17, 1910), 467–473 (quotation, 467).

6. Albion Fellows Bacon, *Beauty for Ashes* (New York, 1914), 264; Albion Fellows Bacon, *A Tale of the Tenements* (n.p.: Indiana Housing Association, 1912), copy in pamphlet collection, Indiana Division, Indiana State Library.

7. Bacon, *A Tale of the Tenements*, 1–2, 28.

8. For a list of Bacon's publications, see Select Bibliography.

9. Bacon, *Beauty for Ashes*, 14; AFB to AFJ, September 10, 1913, AFJ Collection. Paul U. Kellogg edited *The Survey* from 1912 to 1952. An influential figure in social welfare circles, he called for (and practiced, in the famous "Pittsburgh Survey") thorough investigation of social ills, and he championed numerous reform efforts. See Buenker and Kantowicz, *Historical Dictionary of the Progressive Era*, 238.

10. AFB to AFJ, September 10, 11, 28, 1913, AFJ Collection; *The Survey*, 31 (December 6, 1913), 271; Isa. 61:2–4 (King James Version).

11. AFB to AFJ, February 15, 1914. Riis, as noted earlier, was the author of *How the Other Half Lives* and a strong supporter of Bacon's housing reform work. The professor, Edward Steiner, was a minister and sociologist who taught at Iowa (later Grinnell) College and had written several books on American immigration. Addams co-founded and directed Hull-House, the famous settlement house in Chicago. Taylor, a Social Gospel minister and educator, established what became the School of Social Service Administration at the University of Chicago. See Buenker and Kantowicz, *Historical Dictionary of the Progressive Era*, 6–7 (Addams), 402 (Riis), 474 (Taylor); *Who Was Who in America*, III, 816 (Steiner).

12. AFB to AFJ, September 28, December 9, 1913, January 1, 1914, AFJ Collection.

13. AFB to AFJ, January 1, 1914, AFJ Collection.

14. AFB to AFJ, February 22, 15, May 26, June 23, 1914, AFJ Collection.

15. Bacon, *Beauty for Ashes*, 14, 338–339.

16. Witwer interview #1, p. 78.

17. *The Outlook*, 108 (December 30, 1914), 1021; *The Nation*, 100 (January 7, 1915), 27; *Boston Evening Transcript*, December 5, 1914; *Book Review Digest* (1914), 19. John Spargo published *The Bitter Cry of the Children* in 1906, an important contribution to the literature of the child welfare movement. Buenker and Kantowicz, *Historical Dictionary of the Progressive Era*, 453.

18. AFB to AFJ, December 5, 1914, AFJ Collection; Bacon, "Autobiography," [25].

19. *Notable American Women*, I, 77; Roy Lubove, "Albion Fellows Bacon and the Awakening of a State," *Midwest Review* (1962), 72.

20. Bacon, "Autobiography," [1]; Albion Fellows Bacon, "What the Day's Work Means to Me," *The Bookman*, 42 (October 1915), 201; Bacon, *Beauty for Ashes*, 10.

21. Albion Fellows Bacon, "The Divine Call: Follow Me," *The Survey*, 29 (October 5, 1912), 37–38.

22. Ibid., 38–40.

23. Bacon, "Autobiography," [10]; Albion Fellows Bacon, *The Path to God* (New York: Harper & Brothers, 1928), 1, 61.

24. Bacon, *The Path to God*, 4–5.

25. Ibid., 5–6.

26. Ibid., 39–40.

27. Ibid., 41, 63; Witwer interview #1, p. 31.

28. AFB to Editor of the Atlantic Monthly, June 17, 1921, Albion Fellows Bacon file (microfilm), Atlantic Monthly Press, Boston (hereafter cited as Atlantic Monthly file).

29. Sedgwick to AFB, June 30, 1921, Atlantic Monthly file. Sedgwick served as editor of the *Atlantic Monthly* from 1909 to 1924, a period when "the small elite circulation was enlarged as the *Atlantic* addressed more of the social and political issues of the day." Buenker and Kantowicz, *Historical Dictionary of the Progressive Era*, 29–30.

30. AFB to Sedgwick, July 5, 12, August 3, 1921, Sedgwick to AFB, July 20, August 9, 1921, Atlantic Monthly file; Albion Fellows Bacon, "Consolation: A Spiritual Experience," *Atlantic Monthly*, 128 (December, 1921), 732–737.

31. Sedgwick to AFB, December 20, 1921, AFB to Sedgwick, December 26, 1921, Atlantic Monthly file.

32. Sedgwick to AFB, December 29, 1921, January 7, 10, 16, March 7, 1922, AFB to Sedgwick, January 3, 6, 10, 13, March 17, 1922, Atlantic Monthly file; Albion Fellows Bacon, *Consolation: A Spiritual Experience* (Boston: Atlantic Monthly Press, 1922).

33. Unsigned copy of a letter from *Atlantic Monthly* to a James Hoyt, August 24, 1922, Atlantic Monthly file.

34. AFB to DeWolfe Howe, September 12, 1922, March 5, September 6, 1923, March 4, 1924, and to Editor of The Atlantic Monthly Press, September 4, 1924, Atlantic Monthly file.

35. *Book Review Digest* (1922), 19; *Boston Evening Transcript*, May 31, 1922; Bacon, "Autobiography," [11].

36. Albion Fellows Bacon, *The Charm String* (Boston: L. C. Page & Company, 1929), vii–ix.

37. Ibid., [v].

38. Hilary Edwin Bacon and Joy Bacon Witwer, preface to *The Charm String*, reprint ed. (Evansville, Ind.: Unigraphic, 1977), [iv].

39. Bacon, "Autobiography," [21].

40. Bacon's poetry journal is a $7^1/_2$ inch by 12 inch lined notebook. Her handwritten title page reads: "Verses" by Albion M. Fellows. Most of the po-

ems are dated, but they were not copied into the journal in precise chronological order. This suggests that a particular verse was only entered after a period of refinement and revision, not immediately after its creation. Several other poems, handwritten or typed on separate sheets of paper, were placed inside the notebook's front cover. The journal, which will be deposited in the Willard Library, Evansville, Indiana, at the conclusion of this study, was made available to the author by Bacon's youngest daughter, Joy Bacon Witwer. In subsequent references it will be cited as: "Verses" Journal.

41. Bacon, "Autobiography," [22]; Bacon, *Beauty for Ashes,* 201.

42. Bacon, "Autobiography," [22–23].

43. Ibid., [34].

44. Witwer interview #1, pp. 66–67. None of the poems that Bacon indicated should not be published have been included here.

45. "Verses" Journal, 190; "Miscellaneous Poems" file, Box 3, AFB Collection, Willard Library.

46. "Verses" Journal, 173; Johnston and Bacon, *Songs Ysame,* 124. A variation of this poem, with the title "The Wreck," appears on page 127 of *Beauty for Ashes*; a footnote says (correctly) that it had originally been published in *Songs Ysame* and (incorrectly) that that volume of poetry had appeared in 1888.

47. "Unpublished Poems by Albion" file, Box 3, AFB Collection.

48. "Verses" Journal, 208; "Unpublished Poems by Albion" file, AFB Collection.

49. "The Family Tree" was typed on a separate sheet of paper located inside the front cover of the "Verses" Journal.

50. "Go, bury thy sorrow" was handwritten on a separate sheet of paper located inside the front cover of the "Verses" Journal.

51. "Verses" Journal, 193; "Unpublished Poems by Albion" file, AFB Collection.

52. "Verses" Journal, 209.

53. Ibid., 210.

54. Ibid., 207.

55. "Unpublished Poems by Albion" file, AFB Collection.

56. "Verses" Journal, 208.

57. Ibid.

58. "Unpublished Poems by Albion" file, AFB Collection.

59. Bacon, "Autobiography," [34–35].

60. David Glassberg, *American Historical Pageantry: The Uses of Tradition in the Early Twentieth Century* (Chapel Hill and London, 1990), 1, 4, 75; Naima Prevots, *American Pageantry: A Movement for Art & Democracy* (Ann Arbor, Mich.: UMI Research Press, 1990), ix.

61. Harlow Lindley, ed., *The Indiana Centennial* (Indianapolis, 1919), 71–75, 260–261; Prevots, *American Pageantry,* 6.

62. Lindley, ed., *Indiana Centennial,* 260–261; *Evansville Courier,* May 11,

12, 1916. In a letter encouraging an Indianapolis friend to visit Evansville during the event, Bacon observed, "Having had an inspiration about the pageant, I couldn't let it bubble out and go to froth, and, having set it down, and it having been approved, I am in for it, as its parent." Several weeks later she wrote to the same friend: "My pageant is working me day and night. Why will one be so forgetful as to have inspirations?" AFB to Grace Julian Clarke, March 4, April 11, 1916, Grace Julian Clarke Papers, Indiana State Library.

63. *Official Program and Souvenir of the Thirty-seventh Annual Encampment of the Department of Indiana, Grand Army of the Republic and Evansville State Centennial Celebration Parade and Historical Pageant* (Evansville, Ind., 1916), 25, 27, 29. A copy of this program is in the collection of the Evansville Public Library.

64. AFB to Anne Studebaker Carlisle, September 10, 1918, Child Welfare Correspondence.

65. Albion Fellows Bacon, *A Pageant of War and Peace* (typescript), Box 2, Bacon Collection, Willard Library; Bacon entry in *Who's Who in America* (1934–35), 217; *Evansville Courier*, November 12, 1921.

66. Bacon, *Pageant of War and Peace*, passim; *Indiana Magazine of History*, 18 (March 1922), 122–123. Bacon wrote Grace Julian Clarke that the production of her "Disarmament Pageant" was "really beautiful, and most impressive, with the costumed figures, the changing lights, the wailing choruses, etc. . . . I am really quite proud of it. . . . I think it is my best effort to date." AFB to Grace Julian Clarke, November 22, 1921, Clarke Papers, Indiana State Library.

67. Robert H. Ferrell, *American Diplomacy*, revised ed. (New York, 1969), 562–573; *Evansville Courier*, November 12, 1921.

68. Albion Fellows Bacon, *Citizenship Day Program: July 4, 1923* (Washington: General Federation of Women's Clubs, 1923); Albion Fellows Bacon, *Supplement of Songs to the Citizenship Day Program: July 4, 1923* (Washington: General Federation of Women's Clubs, 1923). Copies of both are in the pamphlet collection, Indiana Division, Indiana State Library. See also *Who's Who in America* (1934–35), 217; *The Chautauquan Daily* (Chautauqua, N.Y.), July 20–21, 1923.

69. Bacon, *Citizenship Day Program*, 14–16.

70. Arthur W. Shumaker, *A History of Indiana Literature* (Indianapolis, 1962), 221–223, 260.

71. Bacon, "Autobiography," [29].

8. Municipal Housekeeper and Inadvertent Feminist

1. AFB to Grace Julian Clarke, May 10, 1923, May 26, 1924, Grace Julian Clarke Papers, Indiana Division, Indiana State Library; death certificate for AFB, Evansville–Vanderburgh County Department of Health; Witwer interview #1, pp. 38–40.

2. *Evansville Courier*, December 10, 11, 1933.

3. Albion Fellows Bacon, *Beauty for Ashes* (New York, 1914), 233.

4. Bacon, "Autobiography," [32].

5. Bacon, *Beauty for Ashes*, 201.

6. Witwer interview #1, pp. 62, 60; Bacon, *Beauty for Ashes*, 326.

7. *Evansville Press*, February 18, 1915 (emphasis added); AFB to Grace Julian Clarke, January 31, 1915, Clarke Papers; Witwer interview #1, pp. 61–62. Historian Nancy Cott, quoting a *Harper's Weekly* article from 1913, usefully reminds us that "all feminists are suffragists, but not all suffragists are feminists." See Nancy F. Cott, "Across the Great Divide: Women in Politics Before and After 1920," in *Women, Politics, and Change*, ed. Louise A. Tilly and Patricia Gurin (New York, 1990), 153 (n. 2).

8. William L. O'Neill, *Everyone Was Brave: A History of Feminism in America* (1969; paperback rpt., Chicago, 1971), x; Nancy F. Cott, "What's in a Name? The Limits of 'Social Feminism'; or, Expanding the Vocabulary of Women's History," *Journal of American History*, 76 (December 1989), 810; J. Stanley Lemons, *The Woman Citizen: Social Feminism in the 1920s* (1973; paperback rpt., Charlottesville, Va., 1990), ix.

9. Cott, "What's in a Name?" 809, 815, 818–819, 820–821.

10. Lemons, *The Woman Citizen* (1990 ed.), viii–ix, vii.

11. Cott, "What's in a Name?" 821, 828–829, 809.

12. Ibid., 826.

13. Nancy Cott cites a study of the Bryn Mawr Summer School for Women Workers (1921–1938) that found that former teachers there rejected (social) feminism as an accurate description of themselves or the school's purpose. One respondent, however, "conceded that an '*implicit* feminism—not formulated, and unconscious' might have been involved." Ibid., 822n (emphasis added).

14. Witwer interview #1, p. 61; Barbara A. Springer, "Ladylike Reformers: Indiana Women and Progressive Reform, 1900–1920" (Ph.D. diss., Indiana University, 1985), 250, 54n; *Indianapolis News*, January 8, 1915. Springer (p. 5) uses the term "domestic feminists" to characterize those women who "expanded their spheres outside the home, but claimed their primary responsibility to be wives and mothers." Historian Suzanne Lebsock suggests that even after ratification of the Nineteenth Amendment "it seems probable that domesticity remained at the center of adult female identity." See Lebsock, "Women and American Politics, 1880–1920," in Tilly and Gurin, *Women, Politics, and Change*, 58.

15. Springer, "Ladylike Reformers," 250–252. The quotation from Bacon comes from one of her "Beauty for Ashes" installments in *The Survey*, 32 (May 2, 1914), 168.

16. Roy Lubove, "Albion Fellows Bacon and the Awakening of a State," *Midwest Review* (1962), 72.

17. Albion Fellows Bacon, "What the Day's Work Means to Me," *The Bookman*, 42 (October 1915), 201.

18. Donald K. Gorrell, *The Age of Social Responsibility: The Social Gospel in*

the Progressive Era, 1900–1920 (Macon, Ga., 1988), 93. The quotation is from Gorrell's Chapter 6, "Methodism to Serve the Present Age."

19. Kevin J. Corn, "'Forward Be Our Watchword': Indiana Methodism and the Modern Middle Class" (M.A. thesis, Indiana University at Indianapolis, 1996), 36.

20. Robert M. Crunden, *Ministers of Reform: The Progressives' Achievement in American Civilization, 1889–1920* (New York, 1982), 15; Corn, "'Forward Be Our Watchword,'" 36.

21. *Evansville Courier*, December 10–13, 1933; *Evansville Journal*, December 11–12, 1933; *Evansville Press*, December 11–12, 1933.

22. Grace Julian Clarke, "Influence of Albion Fellows Bacon to Go On through Years as Benefit," *Indianapolis Star*, December 12, 1933.

23. "Proceedings [of] the Indiana State Conference on Social Work . . . 1934," *Indiana Bulletin of Charities and Correction*, no. 217 (March, 1935), 398–399.

24. *Housing*, 22 (June, 1934), 224.

SELECT BIBLIOGRAPHY

Primary Sources

Manuscript Materials Relating to Albion Fellows Bacon

The largest body of relevant manuscript material is the Albion Fellows Bacon Collection at the Willard Library in Evansville, Indiana. (See also the Annie Fellows Johnston Collection at the same institution.) Much of the material in these two collections was donated by Albion's youngest daughter (and Annie's niece), Joy Bacon Witwer. The Bacon Collection includes: copies of many of Bacon's speeches regarding housing reform; one of Bacon's grade school copybooks; files labeled "Miscellaneous Poems" and "Unpublished Poems by Albion"; and photographs. The Johnston Collection, which also contains some photographs, includes letters written by Albion to her sister.

Joy Witwer retained some of her mother's manuscript materials, and kindly granted the author of this study access to them. In addition to family photographs (some of which are reproduced in this volume), two items are of particular relevance: a journal Albion kept while she and Annie toured Europe in 1888 (referred to in the notes as the "Grand Tour Diary"); and a ledger containing poetry written by Albion over the course of many years. The latter item, which will be deposited in the Willard Library at the conclusion of this study, is cited as Bacon's "Verses" Journal.

In late 1926 and early 1927 Bacon prepared a 36-page reminiscence for her children. Her granddaughter, Albion Bacon Dunagan, discovered this manuscript among her late father's possessions in 1989 and readily made it available for use by the author and other researchers. It is cited as Bacon's "Autobiography" in the notes, and a copy is in the Willard Library's Bacon Collection.

Biographical information regarding Reverend Albion Fellows and his wife, Mary, was gleaned from the archives of Indiana Methodism at DePauw University. The well-organized archives of Trinity United Methodist Church in Evansville (for which recognition is due Bill Bartelt) permit a glimpse of Albion Bacon's virtually lifelong involvement with her father's church.

Bacon's association with and support from the Indianapolis Commercial Club during the first several years of her housing reform efforts can be traced through the club's records in the Indiana Historical Society Library (Collection M422).

There are several collections of note in the Archives Division, Indiana Commission on Public Records (better known as the Indiana State Archives). Copies of letters from Dr. John Hurty (secretary of the State Board of Health) to Bacon, as well as other letters by Hurty on behalf of Bacon's housing reform proposals, are in the John Hurty Letter Books, Records of the State Board of Health. Letters from Bacon to Governor Samuel Ralston are in the Ralston Papers, a part of the Governors Papers collections. And Bacon's role in child welfare work during World War I is well documented in the records of the Indiana State Council of Defense (as well as in the Records of the Children's Bureau [Record Group 102], National Archives, Washington, D.C.).

A small but useful collection of letters from Bacon to her friend Grace Julian Clarke, a well-known Indiana clubwoman, suffragist, author, and journalist, is in the Grace Julian Clarke Papers, Indiana Division, Indiana State Library.

Bacon's involvement with the Public Health Nursing Association and its predecessor organizations in her hometown is reflected in the records of the Visiting Nurse Association of Southwestern Indiana, Special Collections/University Archives Department, University of Southern Indiana Library, Evansville. Her work on the Evansville City Plan Commission is documented (at least for the years 1921 to 1927) in a ledger containing the commission's minutes. This volume is in the office of the Evansville–Vanderburgh County Area Plan Commission.

Published materials written by Albion Fellows Bacon

All items listed were authored solely by Bacon and published under her name unless otherwise indicated.

"The After-Care of a Housing Law." *Housing Problems in America* (Proceedings of the National Housing Association, Vol. 6, 1917), 200–213.

"Alleys." *Housing Problems in America*, 2 vols. (Proceedings of the First National Conference on Housing, New York, June 1911), I, 39–46.

"The Awakening of a State—Indiana." *The Survey*, 25 (December 17, 1910), 467–473.

Beauty for Ashes. New York: Dodd, Mead and Company, 1914.

The Charm String. Boston: L. C. Page & Company, 1929; reprint, Evansville, Ind.: Unigraphic, 1976.

——— and Edna Hatfield Edmondson. *Child Welfare Legislation: Work of the Indiana Sub-Commission on Child Welfare of the Commission on Child Welfare and Social Insurance*. Indiana University Extension Division *Bulletin*, 7 (September 1921).

Citizenship Day Program: July 4, 1923 and *Supplement of Songs to the Citizenship*

Day Program: July 4, 1923. Washington, D.C.: General Federation of Women's Clubs, 1923.

"Consolation: A Spiritual Experience." *Atlantic Monthly*, 128 (December 1921), 732–737.

Consolation: A Spiritual Experience. Boston: Atlantic Monthly Press, 1922.

"The Divine Call: Follow Me." *The Survey*, 29 (October 5, 1912), 37–40.

"Facts Which Commercial Bodies Must Face." *The American City*, 10 (June 1914), 555.

"Heading Off the Slum—Why Housing Laws Are Necessary." *Housing Problems in America* (Proceedings of the National Housing Association, Vol. 7, 1918), 251–265.

Bacon, Annie [sic] Fellows. "The Homes of the Poor." *Indiana Bulletin of Charities and Correction* (June 1908), 47–52.

"Housing—Its Relation to Social Work." *Proceedings of the National Conference of Social Work* (1918), 194–200.

Housing—Its Relation to Social Work. National Housing Association Publications, No. 48 (New York, 1918).

[Bacon, Albion Fellows]. "The Housing Problem." *Indiana Bulletin of Charities and Correction* (June 1909), 212–219.

"The Housing Problem." *Indiana Federation of Clubs Year Book* (1912–1913), 80–89.

"The Housing Problem in Indiana." *Charities and the Commons* [later *The Survey*], 21 (December 5, 1908), 376–383.

The Housing Problem of Indiana. Indianapolis: Charity Organization Society, n.d. [ca. 1911].

"How to Get Housing Reform." *Proceedings of the National Conference of Charities and Correction* (1911), 319–326.

"The Illinois Housing Bill." *Illinois Health News*, 5 (March 1919), 99–100.

The Path to God. New York: Harper & Brothers, 1928.

"Philadelphia's Housing Problems." *Housing Problems in America* (Proceedings of the National Housing Association, Vol. 9, 1923), 175–180.

"A Problem of the Growing City." *Municipal Engineering*, 43 (September 1912), 212–216.

"Regulation by Law." *The American City*, 8 (January 1913), 27–29.

"Regulation by Law." *Housing Problems in America*, 2 vols. (Proceedings of the Second National Conference on Housing, Philadelphia, December 1912), II, 47–57.

——— and Annie Fellows Johnston. *Songs Ysame*. Boston: L. C. Page and Company, 1897.

A Tale of the Tenements. N.p.: Indiana Housing Association, 1912.

"There Ain't No Law." Indianapolis *Indiana Daily Times*, February 13, 1915.

[Untitled address]. *Report of the Fifteenth Annual Meeting of the State Bar Association of Indiana* (1911), 181–187.

"What Bad Housing Means to the Community." In *Homes for Workmen: A*

Presentation of Leading Examples of Industrial Community Development, 245–249. New Orleans: Southern Pine Association, 1919.

What Bad Housing Means to the Community. American Unitarian Association, Department of Social and Public Service, Social Service Series, Bulletin No. 13. Boston, n.d.

"What the Day's Work Means to Me." *The Bookman*, 42 (October 1915), 201–206.

"Woman's Interest in a State Housing Law." *Iowa Health Bulletin*, 4 (January–June 1919), 11–14.

"Women, the Legislature and the Homes of Indiana." *Indiana Federation of Clubs Year Book* (1911–1912), 133–142.

Oral History Interviews

(Tapes and transcripts are in the possession of the author)

Margaret McLeish interview with author, November 16, 1988.

Joy Bacon Witwer interview with author, August 13, 1988 (cited in the notes as Witwer interview #1).

Joy Bacon Witwer interview with author, September 23, 1988 (cited in the notes as Witwer interview #2).

Secondary Sources

Barnhart, John D. and Donald F. Carmony. *Indiana: From Frontier to Industrial Commonwealth*. 4 vols. New York, 1954.

Barrows, Robert G. "'Building Up the State': Women Reformers and Child Welfare Work in Indiana during World War I." *Mid-America*, 77 (Fall 1995), 267–283.

Barrows, Robert G. "'The Homes of Indiana': Albion Fellows Bacon and Housing Reform Legislation, 1907–1917." *Indiana Magazine of History*, 81 (December 1985), 309–350.

Bennett, Helen Christine. "Albion Fellows Bacon." In *American Women in Civic Work*, 117–137. New York, 1915.

Bigham, Darrel E. *An Evansville Album: Perspectives on a River City, 1812–1988*. Bloomington and Indianapolis, 1988.

Bigham, Darrel E. *We Ask Only a Fair Trial: A History of the Black Community of Evansville, Indiana*. Bloomington and Indianapolis, 1987.

Blair, Karen J. *The Clubwoman as Feminist: True Womanhood Redefined, 1868–1914*. New York, 1980.

Blanchard, Raymond W. *Ten Years of City Planning in Evansville*. Evansville, Ind., [1932].

Boewe, Mary. "Annie & Albion: Reformers of Riverville." *Traces of Indiana and Midwestern History*, 7 (Winter 1995), 4–11.

Breen, William J. *Uncle Sam at Home: Civilian Mobilization, Wartime Federalism, and the Council of National Defense, 1917–1919*. Westport, Conn., 1984.

Buenker, John D. and Edward R. Kantowicz, eds. *Historical Dictionary of the Progressive Era, 1890–1920*. New York, 1988.

Chambers, Clarke A. *Paul U. Kellogg and the Survey: Voices for Social Welfare and Social Justice*. Minneapolis, 1971.

Chambers, Clarke A. *Seedtime of Reform: American Social Service and Social Action, 1918–1933*. Minneapolis, 1963.

Corn, Kevin J. "'Forward Be Our Watchword': Indiana Methodism and the Modern Middle Class." M.A. thesis, Indiana University at Indianapolis, 1996.

Cott, Nancy F. "Across the Great Divide: Women in Politics Before and After 1920." In *Women, Politics, and Change*, ed. Louise A. Tilly and Patricia Gurin, 153–176. New York, 1990.

Cott, Nancy F. "What's in a Name? The Limits of 'Social Feminism'; or, Expanding the Vocabulary of Women's History." *Journal of American History*, 76 (December 1989), 809–829.

Crunden, Robert M. *Ministers of Reform: The Progressives' Achievement in American Civilization, 1889–1920*. New York, 1982.

Davis, Allen F. *American Heroine: The Life and Legend of Jane Addams*. New York, 1973.

Davis, Allen F. "Welfare, Reform and World War I." *American Quarterly*, 19 (Fall 1967), 516–533.

Del Vecchio, Richard John. "Indiana Politics during the Progressive Era." Ph.D. diss., University of Notre Dame, 1973.

Dye, Charity. "Mrs. Albion Fellows Bacon: Torch Bearer in Housing Reform." In *Some Torch Bearers in Indiana*, 200–207. Indianapolis, 1917.

Edmondson, Edna Hatfield. *The Indiana Child Welfare Association*. Indiana University Extension Division *Bulletin*, 5 (January 1920).

Fuller, Wayne E. "The Rural Roots of the Progressive Leaders." *Agricultural History*, 42 (January 1968), 1–13.

Glassberg, David. *American Historical Pageantry: The Uses of Tradition in the Early Twentieth Century*. Chapel Hill and London, 1990.

Gorrell, Donald K. *The Age of Social Responsibility: The Social Gospel in the Progressive Era, 1900–1920*. Macon, Ga., 1988.

Gosling, F. G. *Before Freud: Neurasthenia and the American Medical Community, 1870–1910*. Urbana and Chicago, 1987.

Gries, John M. and James Ford, eds. *Housing Objectives and Programs*. Publications of the President's Conference on Home Building and Home Ownership, vol. XI. Washington, D.C., 1932.

Haller, John S., Jr. "Neurasthenia: The Medical Profession and the 'New Woman' of [the] Late Nineteenth Century." *New York State Journal of Medicine*, 71 (February 15, 1971), 473–482.

Horack, Frank E., Jr. *The Development of Planning and Zoning in Indiana*. Indianapolis, 1939.

Iglehart, John E., ed. *An Account of Vanderburgh County from Its Organization*. Dayton, Ohio, 1923.

Johnston, Annie Fellows. *The Land of the Little Colonel: Reminiscence and Auto-biography*. Boston, 1929.

Kennedy, David M. *Over Here: The First World War and American Society*. New York, 1980.

Klaus, Alisa. *Every Child a Lion: The Origins of Maternal and Infant Health Policy in the United States and France, 1890–1920*. Ithaca, N.Y., 1993.

Lebsock, Suzanne. "Women and American Politics, 1880–1920." In *Women, Politics, and Change*, ed. Louise A. Tilly and Patricia Gurin, 35–62. New York, 1990.

Lemons, J. Stanley. *The Woman Citizen: Social Feminism in the 1920s*. 1973. Reprint. Charlottesville, Va., 1990.

Lindenmeyer, Kriste. *"A Right to Childhood": The U.S. Children's Bureau and Child Welfare, 1912–46*. Urbana and Chicago, 1997.

Lindley, Harlow, ed. *The Indiana Centennial*. Indianapolis, 1919.

Link, Arthur S. and Richard L. McCormick. *Progressivism*. Arlington Heights, Ill., 1983.

Lipin, Lawrence M. *Producers, Proletarians, and Politicians: Workers and Party Politics in Evansville and New Albany, Indiana, 1850–87*. Urbana, Ill., 1994.

Lubove, Roy. "Albion Fellows Bacon." In *Notable American Women, 1607–1950*, ed. Edward T. James et al. Cambridge, Mass., 1971.

Lubove, Roy. "Albion Fellows Bacon and the Awakening of a State." *Midwest Review* (1962), 63–72.

Lubove, Roy. *The Progressives and the Slums: Tenement House Reform in New York City, 1890–1917*. Pittsburgh, 1962.

Lutz, Tom. *American Nervousness, 1903: An Anecdotal History*. Ithaca, N.Y., 1991.

McCutchan, Kenneth P. *From Then Til Now: History of McCutchanville*. Indianapolis, 1969.

Madison, James H. *Indiana Through Tradition and Change: A History of the Hoosier State and Its People, 1920–1945*. Indianapolis, 1982.

Madison, James H. *The Indiana Way: A State History*. Bloomington and Indianapolis, 1986.

Meckel, Richard A. *Save the Babies: American Public Health Reform and the Prevention of Infant Mortality, 1850–1929*. Baltimore, 1990.

Morlock, James E. *The Evansville Story: A Cultural Interpretation*. [Evansville, Ind.], 1956.

Muncy, Robyn. *Creating a Female Dominion in American Reform, 1890–1935*. New York, 1991.

Murolo, Priscilla. *The Common Ground of Womanhood: Class, Gender, and Working Girls' Clubs, 1884–1928*. Urbana and Chicago, 1997.

O'Neill, William L. *Everyone Was Brave: A History of Feminism in America*. 1969. Reprint. Chicago, 1971.

Phillips, Clifton J. *Indiana in Transition: The Emergence of an Industrial Commonwealth, 1880–1920*. Indianapolis, 1968.

Prevots, Naima. *American Pageantry: A Movement for Art & Democracy*. Ann Arbor, Mich., 1990.

Scott, Anne Firor. *Natural Allies: Women's Associations in American History*. Urbana and Chicago, 1992.

Shumaker, Arthur W. *A History of Indiana Literature*. Indianapolis, 1962.

Springer, Barbara A. "Ladylike Reformers: Indiana Women and Progressive Reform, 1900–1920." Ph.D. diss., Indiana University, 1985.

Tiffin, Susan. *In Whose Best Interest?: Child Welfare Reform in the Progressive Era*. Westport, Conn., 1982.

Trattner, Walter I. *From Poor Law to Welfare State: A History of Social Welfare in America*. 4th ed. New York, 1989.

Warrington, Carina C. "The Work of the State Probation Officer in Indiana." In *The Social Service of the Courts; Proceedings of the National Probation Association, 1922*, 192–199. New York, 1923.

Wood, Edith Elmer. *The Housing of the Unskilled Wage Earner: America's Next Problem*. New York, 1919.

Index

Note: AFB refers to Albion Fellows Bacon. Page numbers for illustrations are in italics.

Index

Bacon, Hilary, Jr. (son), 39, 79, 80, 83, 185n40; birth of, xvi, 38; death of, 176

Bacon, John (brother-in-law), 83

Bacon, Margaret Gibson (daughter), *ii*, 60; birth of, xvi, 24–25; scarlet fever, 32; Flower Mission, 38–39; high school graduation, 78; illness, 189n43; death of, 59–61, 149–151; obituary, 60; burial, 176; effect on AFB's poetry, 154

Bacon, Margaret Gibson (mother-in-law), 16

Bacon, Tom (brother-in-law), 83

Bacons' home: first home, 22–23; Jacob Riis, 61; meetings in, 37, 45; move to second home, 30

Baptisttown, 82–83, 120

Bartholomew, Harland, 124, 127, 131, 132; contracts for city plan, 121; employees, 123

Bates, Frank G., 119

Beard, George M., 26

Beauty for Ashes, 34, 42, 55, 75, 89, 142–146, 166; as autobiography, 145; contract, 149–150; excerpt, 95; on General Assembly, 145; on poetry, 154, 170; referred to in obituary, 177; reviews, 146; spirituality, 147

Bedwell, Charles, 195n56

Better Homes in America, 132

Blair, Karen, 68

Blanchard, Raymond W., 118–119, 126, 127, 129; executive secretary, 123, 204n16

Board of Children's Guardians, 40

Board of State Charities, 177

Boehne Camp, 118

Boehne, John, 47

Bosse, Benjamin, xix, 82, 120, 121

Bosse Field, 162

Bowlker, Mrs. T. J., 67

Breen, William, 97, 99

Bryan, William Jennings, 57

Bryn Mawr Summer School for Women Workers, 211n13

Buehler, Eugene, 53

Bull Moose party, 175

Bureau of Legislative Information, 119

Butler, Amos, 177

Carlisle, Anne Studebaker, 98, 99, 101,

102–103, 197n9; letter to, 197n14; "Organization of Women for War Service," 105

Carson, William A., 120, 126, 128

Chambers, Clarke, 96, 108

Charities and the Commons, 140

Charity Organization Society (COS), 50, 184n26, 185n32, 191n14

Charm String, The, 152, 152–153, 166

Chautauqua House, 84

Chautauqua Institution (N.Y.), 83, 165

Cheese Hill tenement, 55

child labor laws, xviii, 100–101, 111–113, 175; inspectors, 114

Child Labor Tax Board, 111

child welfare, xviii, 95–116, 163; associations, xviii–xix, 99–100, 107, 168, 198nn15,18; Conference on Child Welfare Standards, 108–109; county chairwomen, 104; state conference, 105; wartime agenda, 97, 102

Child Welfare Bureau at Indiana University, 107

Child Welfare Committee, 99–100, 198nn15,18

children, weighing and measuring. See baby drive

Children's Aid Association, 191n14

Children's Bureau, xviii, 199n22; Children's Year, 104; Conference on Child Welfare Standards, 108–109; Council of National Defense, 101; model for juvenile commission, 110; State Councils of Defense, 99; World War I, 97

Children's Year, 101–102, 104, 201n43

Church Federation of Indianapolis, 91–92

Citizenship Day, 165

City Plan, 119–120, 129, 131

City Plan Commission (Evansville), xix, 94, 118–119, 124, *125,* 126, 132, 168, 172; AFB president, 130; budget, 129; creation, 120; memorial for AFB, 175; relationship with other political bodies, 121–123; zoning committee, 126; zoning ordinance, 127

city planning, xix, 118–131, *125*

city planning engineer, 121

Civic Improvement Association, 32

Civic Improvement Commission, 61–63

Index

Robert G. Barrows is Associate Professor of History at Indiana University at Indianapolis. He previously worked as an editor at the Indiana Historical Bureau. He has published several journal articles and book chapters dealing with Indiana history and American urban history, and he co-edited the *Encyclopedia of Indianapolis* (Indiana University Press, 1994).